BERT SUGAR
ON BOXING

The Best of the Sport's Most Notable Writer

Bert Randolph Sugar

THE LYONS PRESS

Guilford, Connecticut

An imprint of The Globe Pequot Press

Dedication

*To those thousands of fans who follow the most ancient of sports,
boxing—as well as this most ancient of sports—and have, over the
four-plus decades I've covered the sport of boxing, filled my pages
with copy and my hours with conversation and camaraderie.*

The Lyons Press is an imprint of The Globe Pequot Press

10 9 8 7 6 5 4 3 2 1

Printed in the United States of America

Library of Congress Cataloging-in-Publication Data

Sugar, Bert Randolph.
    Bert Sugar on boxing : the best of the sport's most notable writer /
Bert Randolph Sugar.
        p. cm.
    ISBN 1-59228-048-X (hard : alk. paper)
    1. Boxing—United States—History.   I. Title.
    GV1125.S93 2003
    796.83—dc22   2003017227

Contents

Contents

II

The Fighters

III

The Fights

IV

History

Bert Sugar on Boxing
(or "The Best of Bert Sugar, The Worst of Bert Sugar, What the Hell's the Difference?")

Chuck Wepner, dubbed the "Bayonne Bleeder" because of his propensity to bleed—usually somewheres between "Oh, Say . . ." and "Can You See . . ."—stood at the rostrum at a Friar's Club jolly-hop smelling blood. Only this time it wasn't his; it was mine. Extending his massive arm, which had the effect of making him look like a railroad crossing, he pointed in my direction and, in a voice sounding like he had just gargled with ground glass, said: "Some people say Bert Sugar is disgusting, obnoxious and revolting. I say they're wrong. Bert Sugar is revolting, obnoxious and disgusting."

It has always been thus, people viewing me as a lineal descendant of Jack the Ripper. Take Chris Jones' description of me in his book, *Falling Hard*: "The veteran writer and boxing historian has one of the sport's most recognizable mugs. He's somewhere between sixty and one hundred years old. He's as bald as a coot and wears a fedora to cover his dome. His eyes are sunken behind a bulbous nose, and a cigar is forever stuffed into his black, wet mouth. Sugar wears clothes that match his outdated personality. Doesn't talk so much as bark . . ."

Nik Cohn, in his book, *Heart of the World*, not only seconds the emotion but raises it several levels, describing me as "A large, wet man, his face all mouth and bloodshot eyes, he was possessed of great hungers, even greater thirsts, and his acts are scaled to match. When he sang, he caterwauled; when he danced, he dervished; and when he laughed, which was virtually nonstop, he would unleash a Godzilla roar, a widemouth juddering blast that ripped through brick walls and plate-glass windows, drowned all that stood in its path. At its coming, strong men dove for cover, else they were mowed down in a machine-gun hail of spittle, cigar ash and used whiskey."

And Frank Prial of *The New York Times* added, for good or bad measure: "(Sugar is) an old time, hard drinking, wisecracking newsman . . . Sugar's signature fedora, with a wide 1920s brim, framed a high forehead and long animated face and a mouth that, it soon became evident, rarely closed."

If there were footnotes, you could write *ibid* as writer-after-writer weighed in with their gleefully abusive and bristly comments on yours truly, all sounding like the annual parade in vilification of the ex-snakes of Ireland.

Oh, sure, there are a few kind words written about me—Ira Berkow of *The New York Times* calling me "Boxing's Thucydides," Al Silverman of *Sport* magazine, "the longtime Pericles of boxing," and Rob Ryan of *The Boston Globe*, "one of sport's greatest living historians"—but so-called rave reviews could easily fit on a post-card crowded with a description of the view on the obverse side and with more than enough room left for an address and an over-sized postage stamp. Granted, I was never in the running for "Prom King," but how did I wind up being subject to soaking up so many stones thrown in my direction? What was it that made me more Prince Harming than Charming?

Introduction

Maybe the answer lies somewhere back in time, back when, as the aforementioned Nik Cohn wrote, "Sugar was not designed to walk straight, he'd always known that. The only questions was where and when he would go askew."

Tracing the breadcrumbs all the way back, the moment when I first showed signs of going "askew" came when, as a young paper-boy in Washington, D.C., I chanced to find myself knocking on the door of one of the subscribers on my route, someone identified in my collection book only as a "Mr. McAuliffe." But when the door was opened, what to my wondering eyes should appear but a man bedecked in enough medals to start a scrap metal drive. Stuttering sounds that made an attempt at words, I spat forth something that sounded like, "Are you the General McAuliffe who said 'Nuts!' at the Battle of the Bulge?" Or somesuch. To which he merely said, "No . . . I said 'Fuck 'em! . . .'" And with that, he slammed the door.

That was when I first realized that not only was truth the first casualty of war, but that what I read came as close to the truth as calling a myth a female moth.

The scales fell from my eyes and I suddenly became aware of writers like H.L. Mencken who saw things as they were, not as they ought to be. Then it was on to Ambrose Bierce, Oscar Wilde, Ring Lardner, Damon Runyon and others who, almost as if smelling flowers began to look around for the coffin, trafficked in the same unpleasant way of telling the truth, their writings crackling with wit and barbed-wire irony—called "cynicism" by those who didn't understand truth when they saw it.

I found many such fugitives from the law of averages, all co-holders of the original copyright on unapologetic, unsympathetic and unmitigated acid observations. Take Ring Lardner's line: "The America's Cup is as exciting as watching grass grow." Or Red Smith's on Primo Carnera: "the world's most beautiful, most ferocious and most talented heavyweight champion in the era between Jack Sharkey and Max Baer." Or Jim Murray's on the Indy 500:

"Gentlemen, start your hearses." Et cetera, etc., etc., the et ceteras going on for about five pages or more.

As a young cynic-in-training, these writers, and their lines, became my guiding star. I now determined to be another Ring Lardner, Red Smith or Jim Murray—although by the time I found I never would be, it was too late.

Having graduated law school—if finishing 313th in a class of 313 can be called "graduating"—and passing the bar, which was the only bar I ever passed, I came to New York, ambition in mind and résumé in hand.

Now there are many places provided in this world where those in need may repair for purposes of extricating themselves from sundry and diverse difficulties called "Watering Holes." But on the island of Manhattan, there was only one, called "The Mother Lode" by none other than Red Smith: Toots Shor's.

Shor's was the saloon where the New York sporting crowd hung out for the meat of the last century, a bar for guys' guys, as much an altar as a bar, catering to those who wished to be seen and obscene, the writers, the athletes and anyone who was anyone, or wished they were. It was always crowded to the gunwales, as it had been the night Charlie Chaplin, nervously waiting for a table, complained to Toots about the need to stand on line. To which Toots, paying him no-never-mind, merely shouted over his shoulder, "Just stand there and be funny, Charlie," leaving the world's funniest man—who was not in a funny mood at the moment—still waiting on line, although not very still.

Another time, Toots, who was partial to athletes, especially those from New York, found himself talking to Sir Alexander Fleming, the inventor of penicillin. Not exactly sure who he was talking to or why and trying to make polite conversation—which didn't come easily to Toots, an old-time salooniere whose dialogue was peppered with a cheerful contempt for the English language and salted with more than a few words like "Crumbbum." Toots was overjoyed to be interrupted by one of his retainers informing him that Mel Ott, the then-manager of the New York baseball Giants, had just arrived. Glad to be rescued from his uncomfortable situation, Toots merely gave a Toots-a-loo and an "Excuse me, someone important just came in," and left Sir Alexander there to molder.

Just as every musician who comes to New York heads directly to Carnegie Hall without passing "Go" and collecting $200, so, too, did I now head off in my own direction, to Toots Shor's.

On the afternoon as a youngster, my face only recently introduced to the razor, I first wandered into Shor's and belly'd up to the bar in search of liquid and other nourishment, I found a group of happy mummers, most of whom would be first-ballot selections to the Sports Writers Hall of Fame, if there were one, bivouacked at the bar with oceans of time seemingly on their hands—and plenty of water with rye or scotch in front of them.

I had heard it told that the bar was an important part of every writer's road map, even Red Smith, who always ordered his drinks, "No fruit, please." Making a note of it in one of his columns on Joe Louis: "Joe Louis was a newspaperman's champion. He always finished in time for the first edition so us guys could get our stories done and make it to the bar with hours to go before closing time." Which meant that Red had plenty of time to excuse the fruit and the stories.

With a tentativeness born of youth, I took my place at the bar, feeling less like a patron than a fly in coffee, attracting attention and comment but hardly enjoying it. Soon, however, it became draw-up-a-chair-and-I'll-tell-you-a-story time as the newcomer was included in the storytelling, which by this time in the shank of the afternoon had gone far beyond the three-mile limit and was traveling far out to sea as each and every told their Rubyiats of the scotch-and-sodas.

As those in concert assembled began to pick up their pace, going through more stories than Hans Christian Andersen and more glassware than Moe Greene in *The Godfather*, I remembered an old truism that any story worthy of telling had to have some form of spirits attached. And that most good sportswriting came with some marination. For, as Ring Lardner, Jr. once said of his old man, "He never wrote a line drunk he could write better sober."

The drinking went on and on and on . . . almost as if those at the bar had found drinks so ill they had to stay up half the night to tend to them. And with the drinks went the stories.

One I remember, as if you could remember anything while flying on four or five wings, had to do with a newspaperman named Bugs Baer, who had written for the old *Journal-American* back in the '20s and '30s. Baer had penned such memorable lines as the one about a hat batter he described as having "the greatest day since Lizzie Borden went 2-for-2 in Fall River, Massachusetts." Or another, this one on Fred Fulton, who had been KO'd by Jack Dempsey in seconds: "He could sell advertising space on the soles of his shoes."

Anyway, the story went that one day Baer was sitting at his desk writing his column when a fight manager chanced to come in with his fighter in tow. Trying to sell Bugs a column, he said, "Bugs, meet the heavyweight champion of South Africa." "Who let you in?" demanded Bugs. "Sorry, can't talk to you now, I'm busy . . . some other time, maybe . . ." But the manager was persistent. "Bugs, really, this is the champion of South Africa . . . Would make a good story . . ." Baer again dismissed him, "Sorry, too busy . . ." Still the manager went on his merry, "Bugs, you ought to meet this kid . . . he's the champion of South Africa . . ." With that Bugs looked up from his typewriter for the first time and, getting up, threw one of the most pluperfect right hands even seen, in or out of the ring, nailing the so-called "Champion of South Africa" square on the puss, knocking him down in a heap. "Now *I'm* the champion of South Africa," said Baer, who sat down and went back to typing his column.

There were more, many more, but all I came away with before the bewitching hour, like Thurber's bat, and getting the hell out, were a few lines, like Jimmy Cannon's upon the sudden dimming of the lights during a Baseball Writers' dinner when he said, "Thank God! They've electrocuted the chef." And Tom Meany's putdown to an unpopular sports writer: "Here's a dime, call all your friends." And Kenny Smith's on the constant playing of the National Anthem before every baseball game: "For Christ sakes, we're running a business here. Does Macy's play the Star-Spangled Banner before opening its doors every day?"

I also came away with a tremendous headache. As well as the belief that writers subscribe to the theorem that being a good liver is better than having one.

Oh, and another thing I learned in my introductory course at Toots U. was that hats were more than merely an article worn to conceal the shape of a newspaperman's head. As some of the older writers would have it, hats were part and parcel of every newspaperman's protective gear, sitting as they did on the floor below the early linotype machines which rained a steady stream of hot type down on their heads from above through ill-fitting floor boards. The practice of protecting their heads was so prevalent that when Ben Hecht and Charles MacArthur wrote their popular play "Front Page," they made sure every newspaperman in their script came adorned with a hat, worn inside and out.

And the cigar? How did that become part and parcel of a young writer? Trying to sort through the dual manipulations of time and memory as best I can, maybe I took up cigars because of a talk given by Walt Kelly, the creator of that wonderful comic strip *Pogo*, who said that "the ability to twirl a cigar as a youngster gave the young manipulator a sense of freedom and courage." Or maybe it was because Knobby Walsh, the manager of the comic-strip character Joe Palooka, always had a cigar as a go-with his hat and I thought it was part of the boxing scene. But whatever it was, I adopted the cigar and the lifestyle that supposedly went with it—although by the time I reached a certain age the cigar gave me something to hold on to in case I was falling down.

Both hat and cigar became so much of my persona that CNN's Aaron Brown thought they gave me the look of someone who "came right out of Central Casting." Hell, without the two I could go into the Witness Protection Program and nobody would recognize me.

With a leave-taking so tardy it rivaled times theretofore accounted for only in train timetables by an asterisk, I wandered home with thoughts of a sportswriting career dancing in my had, along with other things. And when, the next morn, the brew of the night met the cold of the day, I was more determined then ever to become part of the scene I had experienced the night before, to, as Nik Cohn called it, "go askew."

But even with the blueprint for a dream, I had no idea which sport I wanted to write about. Here, like Roy Campenalla, who, when asked by his high school coach to take the position he wanted to play along with other hopefuls, ran to the outfield and found seventy other kids in left, eighty in center and ninety in right and nobody behind home place and decided at that moment to become a catcher, I found seventy writers in left covering basketball, eighty in center football, ninety in right baseball, and nobody behind home plate covering boxing. So, like Campanella, as fast as I could get there, I became a boxing writer, buying a publication called *Boxing Illustrated*.

That was more than four decades and four boxing magazines ago (here insert *The Ring, Boxing Illustrated* (again) and *Fight Game*), back when Muhammad Ali was champion. Through the intervening years I have witnessed more champions than Wheaties ever fed and many more has-beens, never-wases and household names who weren't even household names in their own households strut and fet upon boxing's stage and then exit, heard of no more. Put in more than enough time at press conferences where near-perjury was committed in the name of selling fights. Watched as those clowns in clowns' clothing, the ones I named the "Alphabet Soups," who couldn't find their backsides with both hands on a windy day, act as somebody had died and named them kings of boxing. And observed do-gooder groups like the AMA in their fancied piety call for the abolition of the sport.

Believing all along that the faint of heart never won so much as a scrap of paper, I have picked scraps with almost all of the above—sometimes taking on both sides. Or, as Allen Barra of *The Wall Street Journal* once wrote, "Bert Randolph Sugar will argue about anything at the drop of a hat and have a contrary opinion before the hat hits the floor."

And what have my efforts begotten me? Along the way I've been sued, screwed and tattoo'd—the latter by two thugs who obviously didn't much care for what I had written and broke into my office to render their complaint with their fists, although I would much preferred that they had communicated their dissatisfaction via Western Union. I also have been the recipient of death threats, serial phone harrassment and more than enough "loving" reviews of my character by those who have reacted as if I had just pointed out a case of hoof and mouth disease in a personal favorite of theirs in the herd to fill an oversized scrapbook.

Ah, but boxing has many, many redeeming factors. I mean, where else would I have had an opportunity to watch as many of those on the lowest rung of society find hope for a way out by using boxing as their step-ladder? Or had the chance to meet some of the most interesting people in the world of sports, if not the world, period—writers like Eddie Schuyler, Bob Waters, Pat Putnam, Phil Berger, Jon Saraceno, Budd Schulberg, Jim Murray, Thom Loverro, Sam Skinner, Barney Nagler, Mike Katz, John Phillips, Wally Matthews and many more; or managers and trainers like Ray Arcel, Angelo Dundee, Manny Steward, Lou Duva, Teddy Atlas and so many others; or the reason for the sport, the fighters themselves, like Muhammed Ali, Larry Holmes, Tommy Hearns, Joe Frazier, Marvelous Marvin Hagler, Archie Moore, Roberto Duran, Ray Leonard, Sugar Ray Robinson (there being only one Sugar Ray!), Willie Pep, Jose Torres, Gerry Cooney and too many more to acknowledge in this small space. Or appear in "cameos" in four movies, all of which won for me Worst Supporting Actor awards.

No, it's been one helluva ride and I wouldn't trade it for anything, the most fun I've ever had with my clothes on. So when Tom McCarthy of Lyons Press called and told me he wanted to include an anthology of my boxing writing in the publisher's "On" series—as in "Lardner on Baseball" and "Hemingway on Fishing"—I was not only flattered but jumped at the chance. Hell, it would give me a chance to recycle some of my works over and beyond their having been part of the read-and-throw magazine world and give them some sort of permanency as well as airing them to an all-new group of readers. (Also, tongue not far removed from cheek, it would make me not only the series' *only* living author, but therefore its greatest living author.)

But here I have one small quibble on the title: Why, oh why, couldn't we have titled this volume "The Best of Bert Sugar, The Worst of Bert Sugar, What the Hell's the Difference?"? Over the years I know that while I haven't won any Pulitzer Prizes, I have won several P.U.-litzer Prizes, and I'd like the reader to decide which are my so-called "Best" and "Worst" pieces, not some editor.

However, if you believe this is my swan song, please take down the effigies hung in my honor and sheath your knives. For you will continue to find me at every big fight, seated there at ringside. You'll recognize me, just look for the snap-brimmed hat, the cigar and "the clothes that match his outdated personality" and "the Godzilla roar . . ." Oh, never mind!

Bert Randolph Sugar
Chappaqua, New York
June 3, 2003

I

Rants and Raves

Statement of Bert Randolph Sugar before the Senate Committee on Commerce, Science and Transportation

Senator McCain and members of the Senate Committee on Commerce, Science and Transportation, thank you for inviting me back again to testify . . .

Since the last time we foregathered to discuss the state of the union of boxing it has continued to be one of disunion, continuing on its merry, committing mistakes and misdeeds. For although boxing is a sport in its own right, it is also a sport in its own wrong.

And the primary culprits are those clowns in clowns' clothing, those sanctioning bodies called "The Alphabets"—shorthand for "The Alphabet Soups," a term I coined as editor of *Ring* Magazine back in the early '80s to describe organizations like the WBC, the WBA and the IBF, all dedicated to the belief that you can fool too many people too much of the time.

For references, I give you the WBC (without the Henny Youngman punchline: Take them, please!). When Roy Jones Jr. announced he would leave the light heavyweight division vacating his title to campaign as a heavyweight for the first time, the WBC declared its light heavyweight title vacant and matched the two contenders for what they called a "championship fight"—collecting the necessary sanctioning fees, thank you! And although the fight was won by Graciano Rocchigiani and he was awarded a championship belt—which looked like it was made out of the broken Budweiser bottles found on the San Diego Freeway—and was listed in the WBC ratings sheets for several months as their "champion," when Jones returned to the light heavyweight division, the WBC changed their minds and their designation, taking away Rocchigiani's title, claiming it was all, and I quote, a "typographical error."

Then there is the WBA, which issued ratings which belonged in a Lewis Carroll fictional work with fighters leap-frogging over other fighters after they had signed with a certain promoter. When they were met with howls of indignation by other promoters and scathing criticism from the press, they *mea culpa*'d and changed them, claiming they had been, in their words, the result of "a computer error."

And, finally, there is that third wonderful "Alphabet," the IBF, which, after their head was convicted on several charges, up to and including arrogance, was placed under a government monitor by the court. But that hasn't stopped them. Only recently Tim Smith of the New York *Daily News* brought to light a "mux-ip" which occurred when a fighter, Sharmba Mitchell, won an "eliminator" bout, having paid the appropriate sanctioning fees for the 12-round championship-length fight, was passed over in their ratings by another fighter, Arturo Gatti, who, not incidentally, had won a 10-round fight without paying sanctioning fees. The reason given by the IBF was—get this!—that the head of the IBF ratings committee and the head of the IBF championship committee had not communicated with one another. And this is an organization under a governmental monitor!

Gentlepersons (and I say that because Senators Barbara Boxer and Olympia Snowe are members of this august body), enough is enough is enough! Enough with "typographical errors." Enough with "computer errors." Enough with "non-communication."

I remember, lo those many years ago, when my then-young daughter came down the stairs holding a newborn kitten in her hands after the cat had gone into her closet and given birth, saying, "The cat has just fallen apart." Well, today boxing has fallen apart. And this Committee must act, like all those king's men tried with Humpty Dumpty, to put it back together again.

And if, as has been said, a journey of a thousand miles begins with a single step, we still need a road map. Here, I hope, is one . . .

First, as an oversight Committee, you shouldn't lose sight of the fact that the IBF is currently being run by a government monitor. Here you must become guardians of not only law and order, but order itself by monitoring the government monitor to insure that the IBF becomes a model organization. Only in that way can you inspire the necessary confidence in the boxing community that the government's Muhammad Ali Reform Act will be more effective than the government-run IBF is, and that what the Muhammad Ali Bill proposes to do, it will do.

And, secondly, if those two other "Alphabets," headquartered in Mexico City and Caracas—probably located somewhere above charm and beauty schools—the WBC and the WBA, don't conform to your reforms, then initiate sanctions on these sanctioning bodies. For they come to the U. S. for the same reason Willie Sutton robbed banks, "cause that's where the money is." And when they do, if they don't conform, impound the sanctioning fees they collect from fighters fighting here. Then they, too, will pay more than attention.

To do otherwise and not give the Muhammad Ali Bill teeth means burying your head in the sand. And that can invite a very inviting target for critics.

February 5, 2003
Russell Senate Office Building

5

After One Hundred Years, Boxing's Critics Continue to Sharpen Old Saws

Boxing turns one hundred years of age September 7th—one hundred years to the day when John L. Sullivan and James J. Corbett met in the first major gloved fight in boxing history—and instead of flowers, cards and even a mention from Willard Scott on the "Today Show," boxing will receive several calls from members of the Flat Earth Society demanding its reform and/or abolition.

But this should come as no surprise to anyone who follows boxing. Over the past century boxing has been the favorite whipping boy of those so-called reformers who continue to stick their No's in other people's business. Back at the turn of the century, the sport was practiced in only three states, outlawed in others for various reasons—up to and including not allowing blacks to appear in the same ring with whites—and has faced cries to abolish it over almost each and every one of the intervening ninety-nine.

Now come two groups who believe they beat Ivory Soap by 56/100 percent and want, once again, to make boxing the sandbox of sports. One of those, a Senate Investigating Committee chaired

7

by Senator William Roth of Delaware, got into the boxing investigatory business because one of Senator Roth's constituents, Dave Tiberi, lost a split decision to James Toney in an IBF middleweight title bout earlier this year. According to the bill introduced by Senator Roth, the legislation was based on the fact that it "appeared to many, including the announcers of this nationally televised bout," that Tiberi had "pulled off a dramatic upset." This is the basis for legislation? Is it now the function of the Congress of the United States to play bingo with billions, wasting the taxpayers' money investigating subjective decisions on the field of play not to the liking of their members? Is Senator Roth now going to open up his inquiry to investigate the blown call made by umpire Don Denkinger in Game Six of the 1985 World Series which allowed the Kansas City Royals to beat the St. Louis Cardinals? Or any one of hundreds of thousands of questionable calls throughout sports history? Of course not. He selected boxing. And why? Because, one of his constituents was involved. If you don't believe me, just look at who the co-sponsor of this boondoggle legislation was: Senator Joseph Biden, who, not coincidentally, just happens to be the *other* Senator from the State of Delaware.

This entire bill is, to do a turn on one of John Steinbeck's titles, nothing more than "The Gripes of Roth." And it is a perfect example of minority rule. No matter what he does to justify his public whining, Senator Roth stands accused of using his powers in the name of doing justice for one of his constituents and doing an injustice to the whole of boxing and all of sports.

The other group to come forward—and against boxing at the same time—is some group of do-gooders called "The National Coalition on Television Violence." Their ranks include several activists from previous wars, including the heads of such organizations as "Bothered about Dungeons & Dragons," "Women Against Pornography," and other such pressing issues of the day who have now dragged their soap boxes over to boxing's corner of the street. In a press release they "reveal" their findings that "New Research Confirms Boxing Promotes Aggression" and "protest the presence of boxing at the Olympic Games." Great! These idiots in idiots' clothing would have you believe, as it says in their press release, that because "brawls broke out in the boxing arena at both the 1987 Pan-American Games and at the 1988 Olympic Games," the sport should be banned. Have they ever looked at the rioting at soccer games in Europe? Do they advocate banning soccer? No, just boxing.

With just a little more research this group of Tree-huggers raised to the 10th power could probably find that a myth is a female moth. And that's exactly what they're perpetuating: a myth.

But, then again, why shouldn't every group practicing freedom of screech single out boxing. Hell, they've been doing it for one hundred years and promise to keep it up for the next one hundred. And it will take everything we have to keep boxing up and going so that it can reach its second one hundreth birthday in spite of these smothers of inventions.

Ring Magazine, November 1992

I'd Rather Poke My Eye Out
With A Sharp Stick Than Watch
Women's Boxing!

Laila Ali versus Jacqui Frazier in Ali-Frazier IV? What in the name of the Marquess of Queensberry is going on?

While the ink-stained wretches of the press corps, with all the ardor of astronomers discovering a new star in the chorus of galaxies, are wearing their pencils down to stubs chronicling women's boxing, I, for one, am having great difficulty accepting it as a sport.

Trying to explain my position expansively, if not plausibly—possibly because little about it is plausible—I believe it must have something to do with the feminist movement; somewhat along the lines of the song *Anything You Can Do, I Can Do Better.* But, then again, I've always thought that women who wanted to be the equal of men have no ambition.

On sure, women have the right to fight, just as men have the right to do "The Full Monty." But I also retain some rights, such as the right not to watch. As far as I'm concerned, the best fight between women I ever saw was the one between Marlene Dietrich and Una Merkle in the movie *Destry Rides Again*, with a lot of hair-pulling and rolling around in the dust.

Now, before you call the Politically Correct police, please let me explain. You see, I was raised in a society, many moons ago, which held to two general axioms: That men were stronger; and women, smarter. And if women are so damned smart, why are they interested in having their features rearranged and acquiring cauliflower ears so pronounced they can be covered with hollandaise sauce? In fact, if they're so smart, why do they, in a turn on an old Ginger Rogers' line, spend their lives dancing backwards?

I have no intention of following the mincing footsteps of those in the "PC" world who insist that society fall in line and homogenize everything down to their faddish terms-like calling manhole covers "personhole" covers or airplane cockpits "flight decks." (Hell, I can hardly wait till they start calling menus "person-u's.")

Recently I appeared as a guest on a BBC program called Sport International where I was asked about Laila Ali's upcoming pro debut and a just-conducted male-female match in Washington State. During the course of my reply, I referred to the mixed male-female bouts as "a circus and a freak show." (Remember, this is the same state that brought you Tonya Harding!) And, having nothing to go on concerning Laila, other than her background, I went on to describe her physical attributes (height, weight, etc.) and her then-occupation as that of a manicurist.

Well, that brought out the PC Gestapo in full force. One member, writing from New Zealand, weighed in with: "How dare you, Sports International? In one fell swoop, you not only insulted women listeners (as well as those keen on sports), but failed in your job. You interviewed Bert something-or-other about the male-female boxing bout in Seattle, and he said it was a circus, a freak show. Okay, so he's entitled to his puerile opinion. But then you asked him about Laila Ali's (daughter of the great Muhammad) bout, and the most informative thing he could say was that she was a 'very pretty lady.' ARGH!"

Well, considering the fact that Laila Ali had not yet fought her first fight, what the hell was there to say? That if she entered the world of boxing, heretofore a man's world, she would have to be measured by their standards—not by the standards set by some blithering PC idiot down in New Zealand.

Back in the golden days of Samuel Goldwyn's Hollywood, when two young boys squared off, instead of saying, "My father can beat your father," they'd say instead, "My father might *be* your father." Today, in women's boxing, the theme has changed, along with the times. Now it's gotten to the point—with the daughters of George Foreman, Joe Frazier, Archie Moore, Roberto Duran, and Ingemar Johannson all entering the ring—where they say: "My daughter can beat your daughter."

Maybe they're fighting because they love the accessories. After all, they're wearing gloves, fighting for a purse and a belt, and wearing satin shorts. Or maybe it's because they're getting in touch with their masculine side. But whatever it is—and show me a man who understands women and I'll show you a man who's in for a big surprise—it would help if they could fight. To many, this unhumble correspondent included, most of them look like women going down in quicksand for the last time, wielding frying pans.

Is it asking too much that, if they wish to be boxers, at least they could look like boxers? And that their fights be somewhat competitive? Isn't competition the very nature of sports?

As George Diaz of the Orlando *Sentinel* wrote: "We have every right to applaud Elizabeth Dole as a presidential candidate, or Demi Moore as a down-and-dirty GI Jane. Even equal opportunity has reasonable limits, and there is nothing in Helen Reddy's 'I Am Woman' empowering anthem about signing promotional contracts with Don King."

As for me, I view women's boxing with the same cynicism George Carlin applies to another sport when he says: "Swimming is not a sport, it's just a way to keep from drowning."

Smoke Magazine, Summer 2001

I Didn't Know Writing
Was a Contact Sport

Last May 15th, the following story appeared in the New York *Daily News* under the headline, "Toughs Leave Bert Sugar Feeling Beat":

"Two thugs entered the West 43rd St. offices of *Boxing Illustrated* yesterday and punched the magazine's illustrious publisher and editor, Bert Sugar, who seemed more perplexed than hurt. 'I've been hit harder,' said Sugar, 'but I'm justifiably peeved. If this was a message, who was it from? The detectives asked me if anybody had a grudge against me. I said, "How long do you have?" All I know, these two guys, about 25, came in, one cut my telephone lines and the other hit me twice and missed a third punch.' The worst thing, Sugar said, was the hoods knocked off his ubiquitous hat. Anyone with information as to the assailants will probably be given a medal."

It was almost as unbelievable as a down-on-her-luck palmist trying to get business by tucking her calling card in a passing coffin. Understanding fully that boxing is a damnably serious business and that those in the writing dodge constantly risk irritating somebody or other in fulfilling their First Amendment role, there is absolutely no reason why writers have to answer for their opinions by posing as heavy bags.

The attack by those two thugs will have about as much effect on my mindset and style of writing as a deck chair blowing off the Queen Mary. I will not be dissuaded from attacking those with souls like the undersides of flat rocks anymore than ice can be welded or iron melted. There is no shaking knee factor here.

Who could it have been? Irate subscribers? Somebody who took issue with something I said? As Larry Holmes said, "Who'd want to bother you? You never bothered no one . . . unless it was in the no-smoking section with that smelly cigar of yours . . ."

As for wasting time trying to figure out who sent these two messengers of hate, it's a train of thought that never quite reaches its final destination. To even bother to conjure up names of possible perpetrators would probably result in some of the strangest cases of free association since Professor Rorschach toppled over his inkstand.

But, regardless of who it was, the next time they have a message to send, let them use Western Union. Don't bother me with visitations. If these faceless—and gutless—crumbbums want me, let them challenge me, like real men, to a fight in the ring with gloves.

One hopes this is the end of the story. But it probably isn't. However, let it be known that if someone took offense at something I've written, just wait. By the time I'm through they'll wish the wolves had stolen them from their cradles.

Boxing Illustrated, 1992

Boxers Need a Defense Against the A.M.A.'s Blows

Away back in 1916, Jess Willard fought Frank Moran in the old-old Madison Square Garden for what was billed as "The Heavyweight Championship of the World." This, despite the fact that in those days the bout would go to a "no decision" if one of the two participants had not scored a knockout within the prescribed ten rounds.

However, there was no fear that the bout would run its full course, the two participants being who they were: Jess Willard conqueror of the invincible Jack Johnson and a man who looked as if he could be found at the top of the beanstalk, and Frank Moran, he of the famed "Mary Ann" haymaker, with eighteen knockouts to his credit. But despite the buildup attendant to New York's first heavyweight championship fight since the Jeffries-Fitzsimmons bout some seventeen years before, only one punch of any consequence landed over the ten-round distance, that a desultory right uppercut by Willard.

The next morning the two correspondents for the Hearst papers, The New York *Journal* and The New York *American*, filed stories describing the fight as "boring" and "devoid of action." Ironically, the same two papers carried a front-page editorial by the owner of both, William Randolph Hearst, calling for the abolition of the sport, a sport he found "barbaric" and "brutal," not to mention "uncivilized"—all of which was based on the Willard-Moran fight, a fight he hadn't seen, only imagined.

Today, some 63 years later, boxing is still under attack, still the whipping boy. The modern muckraker is the American Medical Association. Down through the ages, this group has lobbied against Medicare—at least until it was assured that all doctor bills would be paid, in cash. In concert assembled, they have come out with a resolution calling for "the elimination" of boxing approved by a voice vote from the hotbed of boxing: Waikiki, Hawaii.

Where is the A.M.A. on the pressing medical issues of the second half of the twentieth century: Rising medical costs? Care for the aged? The dispensing of generic drugs to save money for those who cannot afford brand names? If we were dealing in the stock market of the soul here, we could sell short, for the A.M.A. to avoid discussing so many of those important issues has used misdirection the same way a magician does. In the classic words of Claude Rains, it has sought to misdirect attention by "round(ing) up the usual suspects"—in this case, boxing. Traditionally, boxing has been the sport of the dispossessed, their social staircase for entering the mainstream of society. Before the turn of the century, when signs in Boston's windows read, "NINA," for "No Irish Need Apply," a young man named John L. Sullivan turned to boxing and became America's first great sports hero. When, in the 1910s and 1920s, Jews and Italians from New York's teeming ghettos on the Lower East Side had nowhere else to turn, they turned to the ring and gave Americans without hope heroes like Benny Leonard and Tony Canzoneri. And in the '30s, when blacks were invisible, they gained instant visibility and respectability with Joe Louis. That's what boxing has meant down through the ages, a sport that has given many of us heart, hope and heroes. And that's what the A.M.A. now seeks to eliminate.

It is the hope Bishop Desmond Tutu, the Nobel Peace Prize winner, once uttered after a recent meeting of the World Council of Churches. Someone asked him whether Martin Luther King had been an inspiration. The diminutive Bishop Tutu pulled himself up to his full five feet-plus and said: "Yes, of course. But, more importantly, when I was a boy, what really inspired me was reading of the Brown Bomber and Sugar Ray Robinson. And reading about them and what they did made me feel inches taller."

How can so many of these doctors know what it is like to have nowhere else to turn? How can they know that kids with no fathers turn to boxing and find in the trainers surrogate fathers, and in boxing itself the first rules of discipline for living their lives within the context of society, rather than outside? And how do they have the right, singularly or collectively, to attempt to take the civil rights of people away from them, denying them the right both to make a living and to rise above their station, something that democracy guarantees them?

This spokesman for the chapter of the Flat-Earth Society, known as the A.M.A., is Dr. Joseph Boyle, who, in his infinite non-wisdom, said: "The body of evidence on the long-term effects of boxing has accumulated to the point where we know that people who engage in it sustain acute brain injury and are left with evidence of brain misfunction."

But when Dr. Boyle was asked to identify the types of testing that had led to his conclusions, he was hard pressed to cite any, saying only that the tests were somewhere in the files of the Journal of the American Medical Association in Chicago. Wonderful! Before Dr. Boyle sticks his *No's* into other people's business, he should know that the doctor who conducted the research that started this entire brouhaha (in the Journal's issue of last Jan. 14) is Dr. Ronald J. Ross. Dr. Ross told me afterward: "I'm not against boxing. I'm against war and I'm against poverty, but I'm not against boxing."

Floyd Patterson once asked why "you never see a black or Hispanic doctor speak out against boxing, only the older, white doctors?" Because, Floyd, those doctors do not understand that boxing transcends medical considerations, that it is the catalyst for attempting to become part of the mainstream of society. And it is something that those Dr. Grinches who are attempting to steal our sport cannot understand.

Also, and not unimportantly, boxing is a highly individualistic sport, one that does not require ten or eight or even four others as do football, baseball and basketball. It is something that takes only one. And in a day and age when the tendency is to homogenize society by making us all part of some huge, monolithic something-or-other, private enterprise is no more understood in sports than it is in the rest of society. Do the doctors with their tax shelters, medical corporations and lobbying groups understand individuality, especially the individual who is, not incidentally, a professional?

There is some medical evidence that shows boxing is like cigarettes, dangerous to the health. But even the A.M.A. ranks boxing seventh in terms of deaths per thousand participants, behind such establishment sports as football and auto racing. But the A.M.A., like any other lobbying group, knows better than to take on another well-entrenched lobbying group.

What will happen if the A.M.A. is successful in its plans to persuade state legislatures to draw up laws abolishing boxing? Will they help take the kids off the mean streets of inner cities? Will they donate five percent of their purses to underwrite social programs that are already in place and that include boxing as an integral part? Will they be able to offer the hope and the heroes the sport does now? Or will they press that out of millions who follow the sport, as they have done through the ages, all in the name of societal consciousness, as defined by the A.M.A.?

For it must now be understood that the A.M.A. has stepped out of its element, offering itself up as a group that makes moral rather than medical judgments.

It could be argued, hopefully, that the A.M.A. was just confused by the proliferation of Alphabet-Soup organizations in boxing—such as the W.B.A., the W.B.C., and the I.B.F.—and thought that it, too, as a three-letter group, should become part of boxing. But, like the rest, they should have stopped at recognizing a heavyweight champion and let well enough alone.

For them to attempt to deny the civil rights to millions of others, who are, not incidentally, mostly minority groups, constitutes turning their collective backs on an important part of the democratic system, the right of all persons to select their way of earning a living. And if the A.M.A. is successful, it will merely force the sport underground, much as Prohibition did drinking a half-century ago.

The A.M.A. has once again proved it can make headlines—too many papers using their space to holler "gesundheit" every time they sneeze—has political muscle and can misdirect our attention away from the many problems that beset the medical fraternity. But until the A.M.A. meets in Watts or Harlem, or finds a cure for the common cold, it cannot presume to speak with a social awareness or pass moral judgments. Until then, it should simply take two aspirins and call us in the morning.

The New York Times, December 9, 1984

On Howard Cosell

It has always been one of the principia worthy of this corner to
bring comfort to boxing's afflicted and afflict boxing's comfortable.
At one and the same time, if that were possible. And, this month,
instead of selecting one subject and devoting our entire harrangue
on something-or-other, we have decided to select two subjects and
give them one more embalming, hoping that there might be something here which catches the eye. And the conscience.

Our first subject is television announcers, those electronic
know-nothings behind the mikes who adopt sonorous platitudes
recently borrowed from Hallmark cards to describe a fight. Most of
them are as standardized as a row of filling-station pumps, full of
transparent absurdities in English that would disgrace a fight manager. But for every one that throws light on the matter at hand,
such as a Gil Clancy, there are two or three who give off verbal
sleights-of-hand, mindless palaver which show a relentless incapac-
ity for distinguishing clearly between appearance and substance.

One of those whose name readily comes to mind is Howard
Cosell—although, if the truth be known, the sound of Chris

Schenkel's voice is enough to launch a "Bring Back Howard" campaign. Cosell, who once said, "I MADE Muhammad Ali," and meant it, applied the same garnishment of humility to his place in sports history as he had his place in "making" Ali: "I didn't ask to be a sports journalist, that was just fate. I never planned to be a superstar. I'd rather be a private person. People are always after me because I tell the truth." Humble Howard then went on to underscore his truthfulness by adding, "Nobody cares about sportswriters. Who are they? They aren't important. Papers are dying all over the country!"

Howard, who belongs to that long line of sportscasters who have tried to write—and who, according to his editor, the late Ed Kuhn, had difficulty putting two words together—should remember what his function in his life has been: A purveyor of amusement for people who do not have sufficient wit to amuse themselves. To call himself a "Journalist," or anything else for that matter, is intellectually dishonest. But what else can you expect from a man who continues to say he "Tells it LIKE it is," when good English and William Shakespeare would suggest that the line should be "Tells it AS it is."

Perhaps now we understand why former New York Jets coach Weeb Ewbank used to refer to Cosell as "Our father who art in Heaven, HOWARD be thy name . . ." How else can you describe this man with delusions of grandeur as wide as the Grand Canyon?

Next we have another so-called journalist of the airwaves, Barry Farber, who wallows in trivialities and manhandles important events. Farber is a New York talk show host who just went national recently with his pilot show devoted to the question, "Should We Abolish Boxing?" And guess who the protagonist for the above mentioned question-subject was? If you said "Barry Farber" hold up your hand. But this man for all reasons knew nothing about either the sport nor the argument he put forward, citing wrong facts and even admitting, as Big Daddy called it in "Cat on a Hot Tin

Roof," to smelling of "mendacity" and hypocrisy, admitting he went to fights. Here, however, the glib-tongued Mr. Farber said, "It is for the spectacle, not the sport of it." Now that's a difference without a distinction. Add him to your list of montebanks garbed in grotesque blathering for the purpose of making themselves seen. And obscene as well.

Ring Magazine, November 1982

Boxing: Where Something's Going on All the Time . . . Most of It Unsolved

It was almost as much a thrill to read about the federal indictment of the International Boxing Federation as it was to read *Fortune* magazine and find out that the heads of the IBF are among the dozen richest men in the country.

Bribery going on in boxing? I almost felt like Claude Rains in *Casablanca* when Humphrey Bogart handed him his gambling winnings and he said, tongue firmly wedged in cheek, "I'm shocked . . . Shocked! to know that gambling goes on here, Rick."

I, too, was "Shocked!" (*wink-wink, nudge-nudge*) to know that the government had indicted the four heads of the IBF for taking bribes that amounted to more than $300,000. $300,000? That's chump change compared to what's being going on in boxing since sometime right after the Great Flood.

The government's indictment was a statement that would rank right up with Jack the Ripper's Mum asking him, "Why don't you ever go out with the same girl twice?" It was *that* self-evident.

For years the Alphabet-Soup groups have been operating under one rule, and one rule only: I got mine, now you get yours. But there's no truth to the rumor they take money under the table. Hell, they've taken it over the table, around the table and sometimes even taken the table itself!

And what has boxing gotten out of it for the moneys passed to these Alphabet "bandits," as Pat Putnam calls them? Well, for one thing, they've gotten *chintzy* championship belts that look like they were made out of the broken beer bottles found on the San Diego Freeway. And, for another . . . let me think . . . oh yes, bogus ratings.

Now, under the RICO Act, the government wants to run the IBF. Why? As Michael Katz sez, we thought the whole idea was to get rid of them. After all, the man selected to run the IBF for the government has never, ever, been to a boxing bout. That's supposed to help boxing? And who will give out their *chintzy* belts? Janet Reno, mid-ring? If the government can't get a postcard across the street in two weeks, how can they run a boxing organization?

Why not go after the WBC and the WBA, who have their offices above charm and beauty schools somewhere in downtown Mexico City and Caracas, and whose actions make the IBF look like pikers? Is it because the IBF is located in the U.S. and the others are not within federal jurisdiction? Until all three groups of bandits are brought under some sort of control, indicting one is not enough.

Should the three bandit organizations go "bye-bye," or the TV networks no longer accept their ratings, who then would take their place?

One idea, espoused in a *New York Times* Op-Ed piece by Allen Barra, goes something like this, and I quote: "*Fight Game* magazine uses a panel of experts, all veteran boxing writers from around the world, for rating fighters. Why not make membership in a voting organization open to, say, one hundred boxing beat writers around the world, and let them choose trainers and managers who can also vote? A hundred journalists would be much tougher to bribe than two or three self-appointed boxing officials, and there are always journalists to blow the whistle on the corrupt."

We thank Mr. Barra and *The New York Times* for their kind words about *Fight Game* and their ratings. But that's only a starter kit. Until something is done about these three groups, one of boxing's time-dishonored traditions will continue: that of the Alphabet-Soup groups taking money to rank fighters and telling the managers and promoters who cross their palms, "Thank you!" To which the promoters and managers reply, "Don't mention it!" Which they never do.

But we will . . . until this mess is cleared up and boxing can once again take its place in the community of sports with a clean reputation and a clear conscience.

Fight Game, March 2000

Lewis-Tyson: Hell No, I Won't Go!

Although it's been rumored I've covered every major fight since Cain rendered Abel *hors de combat*, when it comes to the Lennox Lewis-Mike Tyson fight on June 8 in Memphis, in the immortal words of film mogul Samuel Goldwyn, "Include me out."

This is not to be taken as an anti-boxing stance, merely an anti-Tyson one. No, I'm not turning my back on the sport, as announcer Howard Cosell did after the Larry Holmes-Tex Cobb mismatch back in 1982, a fight so one-sided that Cobb, who couldn't have caught Holmes with the aid of a taxi cab, at one point threw up his hands and, turning to referee Steve Crossen, hollered, "You're white, help me!"

Instead, I'm boycotting the fight because of my love for the sport and what Mike Tyson has done to demean it. For, in the strangest association since Professor Rorschach toppled over his inkwell, Mike Tyson has become, in the public's mind, the poster boy for boxing, even though he is less representative of the sport than Dracula is for the Red Cross's annual blood drive.

His association hurts the whole sport, as witnessed by a recent Internet poll where the question, "Is it time to ban boxing as a pro sport?" placed under a picture of Tyson biting Evander Holyfield's ear generated 2,272 responses, with almost forty percent of those responding answering "Yes."

Nor is this my being a moral guardian for the sport. My stance has nothing to do with Tyson's out-of-the-ring behavior. Hell, boxing has never recruited its participants from the debutante line at the local country club and few of those who box could be described as altar boys in search of a service.

But almost all of those who turned to boxing turned their lives around, as middleweight champion Rocky Graziano, of *Somebody Up There Likes Me* fame, did. Speaking in New Yorkese, peppered with more than a few "deses" and "doses," Graziano would say of his less-than-exemplary behavior: "I never stole nuthin' unless it began with an 'A' . . . 'A truck' . . . 'A car' . . . 'A payroll' . . ." Then, in a telling indication of just what the sport meant to him, would add: "If it wasn't for boxing, I woulda wounded up electrocuted at Sing Sing prison."

However, Mike Tyson has not been one of those who has redeemed himself through boxing, but instead has brought the sport down to his level. And it's not a level I wish to be associated with, nor have associated with the sport I love. And therein lies the reason I will not cover Mike Tyson: his behavior within the four squares of the ring.

For, bottom-line, boxing is little more than legalized assault. What distinguishes it from something that would get its two participants arrested were it a garden-variety back-alley brawl and elevates it to the level of a sport are its rules and regulations, much as auto racing, without rules and sanctions, would be plain ol' illegal speeding.

It is these rules and regulations that Mike Tyson has habitually declined to uphold, neither adhering to them nor having any use for them. His violations are like an in-the-ring rap sheet and include such crimes against the senses as biting Evander Holyfield, hitting

Buster Mathis Jr. after he was down, hitting the referee during the Lou Savarese debacle, striking Bruce Seldon with an elbow, head-butting Holyfield, attempting to break Frans Botha's arm, and hitting Orlin Norris, among others, after the bell, et cetera, et ceteras. The et ceteras go on for about five pages or so.

Now some indulgences are accorded in the name of human nature. But Mike Tyson has exceeded any and all excuses for behavior in the ring, boxing's rules and regulations having about as much effect on him as a fig leaf at a nudists' convention. And where once, in his early career, he was a human trash compactor, now he has become a trasher of the sport and all it's supposed to stand for.

After his equally reprehensible behavior at the press conference to announce the Lennox Lewis fight—where he charged across the stage to get at Lewis, then bit him in the leg and, finally, in response to one of the members of the assembled press screaming out "Get him a straitjacket," spewed out a string of hate-filled four-letter words, accompanied by constant crotch-cradling—he was denied a license by the Nevada State Athletic Commission and was forced to find another site for the Lewis fight.

Finally, after hustling the bout around like a $25 hooker on Main Street, Team Tyson's travels took them to Memphis, Tennessee, that capital of boxing on the Mississippi River. And despite the fact that Memphis's community leaders believe, in much the same optimistic manner as a man who believes his wife has stopped smoking cigarettes because he found cigar butts in the ashtray, that they will be able to host a fight that will go off without incident, one cannot help but wonder if they are ready for the circus that seems to follow Tyson everywhere.

I'm thinking about the one at the MGM Grand, for example, after the second Holyfield fight that closed the casino for hours, or the one after the Seldon fight in which rapper Tupac Shakur was shot to death in front of Caesars Palace.

As for me, when the pay-per-chew starts and the ring announcer intones: "Let's get ready to nibble," I'll be as far away from Memphis as I can get, up in Canastota, New York, at the International Boxing Hall of Fame induction ceremonies, where I'll be surrounded by some real monuments to boxing—the likes of which will include Marvelous Marvin Hagler, Alexis Arguello, Kid Gavilan, Emile Griffith, Aaron Pryor, Ken Norton and Earnie Shavers amongst many—rather than be at Memphis to watch that monumental boor, Mike Tyson.

If I feel an urgent desire on that weekend of June 8th to visit the home of Elvis, I'll immediately decamp to Liverpool to visit the home of Elvis Costello rather than to Memphis to see Elvis Presley's Graceland.

At least that way I won't have to put up with the antics of Tyson and his flying circus. Memphis can have 'em.

SportsBusiness Journal, May 2002

Put Boxing's So-Called "Officials" in Charge of the Sahara, and It Would Soon Run Out of Sand

Over the past few months we've been "treated," if that's the correct word, to so many stupid person tricks by those in control of our sport that you begin to wonder if those in and around boxing are geniuses—'cause only intelligent people could fake such stupidity.

Take the recent IBF trial, for example. Its head, Bob Lee, was found "not guilty" of bribery, yet convicted for money laundering, tax evasion and racketeering. Prior to that verdict, the Nevada State Athletic Commission suspended promoter Bob Arum for admitting he had bribed Lee. Did I miss something here? How is someone guilty of bribing someone who is innocent of taking the bribe? Did Arum force Lee to take money for rating fighters by sticking a gun down his wallet?

It's nice to know the O.J. jury found more work in the Lee trial—finding a technicality to get him off the hook. But the Nevada Commission's decision is more puzzling than even that of the Lee jury. They not only jumped the proverbial gun, but sent out mixed signals—that while the Alphabet Soups demand money for ratings, only those forced to do business with them are guilty of wrong-doing. Talk about putting the *à la carte* before the horse! These people get things so screwed up I bet they think "Dr. Livingston, I Presume" was the full name of Dr. Presume.

The mixed signals they sent out are the same mixed signals I get when my TV set picks up both Home Box Office and Home Shopping on the same channel and I find I can buy an Alphabet official and his ratings.

Nevertheless, and despite the jury's findings, I still believe that when I look at a group picture of IBF officials I should call "Unsolved Mysteries" immediately and tell them, "Yeah, I found everybody!"

And just in case you missed it, there was the recent fight between Stevie Johnston and the man who won his WBC lightweight title, José Luis Castillo from Mexico. The first post-fight announcement had Johnston the winner. But then the cards were retabulated and the decision changed to a draw. The more charitable explanation for the post-announcement change would be that the WBC officials are arithmetically-challenged and would have trouble counting to twenty-one even if they were naked. But a more cynical one might be that Castillo is from the same country as José Sulaiman, that wonderful person who continues to push Mexican fighters down our throats (for particulars, see Julio Cesar Chavez versus Kostya Tszyu), and was protecting Castillo.

Then there was the Vivian Harris-Ivan Robinson fight, held in Atlantic City, and scored by something called the "Majority Scoring System." As long-time boxing observer Chris Thorne wrote: "For those who have forgotten or never even knew about the system, it uses the points accumulated on the three judges' scorecards with a master scorecard tallying up the points for each round and awarding each round to those fighters." Understand? It's sorta like reducing scoring to something only a Dr. Irwin Corey could explain—a science unknown to mankind, boxingkind and kind-kind.

In the fight itself, had the normal system of three judges scoring been used, Harris would have won by scores of 94–93, 95–93 and 94–94. However, according to the majority scoring system—the only one read—the fight was announced as 94–94, a draw. This is boxing's version of "the dog ate the scorecards," where the traditional manner of judging has been replaced by somebody or other's idea of improvement. And it proves that old adage: "Never underestimate the ingenuity of complete fools."

Put them all together and you get the impression that the future of boxing is so dim you'd have to squint to see it. And while you might try to change the current system on the theory that the existing cocoon can turn into a beautiful butterfly, that cocoon-to-butterfly stuff only works on cocoons and butterflys.

We've got to do something to save boxing from itself. And to stop those people in boxing who are so dumb that if they saw a sign reading, "Wet Floor," would. Right now, all they're doing is wetting *our* sport.

Fight Game, January 2001

When You're at an Age Where You Go to a Topless Bar and Look at the Menu, then Big George's Win was More than Food for Thought

There is no truth to the rumor that I covered Cain vs. Abel. I mean, I was there, but I just couldn't get credentials. At my age, old age is defined as being fifteen years older than whatever I am. And that's why George Foreman's win over Michael Moorer held special meaning for me—and for anyone 40-something or older.

It was a fairy tale come true: A Father Time figure, 45-going-on-Social Security, winning one for the old geezers' fraternity. It happened with all the suddenness of Bobby Thomson's home run in the 1951 playoffs, giving the Giants the National League pennant over the Dodgers after being 13½ games back. But instead of hollering, "The Giants Win the Pennant! The Giants Win the Pennant!" we began chanting, "The Geezer Won the Moment! The Geezer Won the Moment!"

Foreman found a fountain of age and rejuvenated not only the sport, but all of us. But still there were those cynics—almost like Dr. Seuss' "Grinch Who Stole Christmas"—out there saying it was bad for boxing, bad that someone that old had won the heavyweight championship, had excelled in a young man's sport.

Is it bad that suddenly we know the name of the heavyweight champion after four years of looking at fighters named Lennox, Riddick, Oliver et. al? Is it bad that someone broke the myth that older people should just throw up their hands and quit; that the young rule the world? And why is George Foreman winning the heavyweight championship at the age of 45 years and 11 months any worse than, say, ice hockey's Gordie Howe scoring 100 points at the age of 45 and playing 'til 52? Or golf's Jack Nicklaus winning the Masters at the age of 46? Or baseball's Nolan Ryan pitching a no-hitter at the age of 44? Or Satchell Paige pitching at the age of 59? Or, and here the list goes on and on, Lester Piggott riding horses past his 59th birthday, Jean Borotra playing at Wimbledon past his 65th birthday, Emerson Fittipaldi racing cars past his 48th birthday, Kareem Abdul-Jabbar racing down a basketball court past his 40th birthday or George Blanda playing football past his 48th B-day? (In fact, it was Blanda who said: "I have to keep playing so people over 40 will have somebody to root for on Sunday afternoon.")

No, it's the studied opinion in this corner that youth is, as Frank Sinatra once said, wasted on the young. And today, with "youth creep," meaning the tendency toward keeping physiologically younger than people did a generation ago, extraordinary people do extraordinary things all the time.

By winning, Big George has once again put boxing back in the limelight, made it popular. Advertisers, who in the past shunned the sport because of its unsavory connotations, are flocking to fill George's plate to overflowing with offers making the sport savory and popular again. And George himself is now the most recognizable face of all active sports figures, what with Michael Jordan gone from the basketball courts.

When You're at an Age Where You Go to a Topless Bar

It's a great era for the aging and ageless. It's almost like a sign in my favorite watering hole, Runyon's on New York's East Side: "Old age and guile will always beat youth and strength." So, the next time you look wishfully or wistfully at an aging Lauren Hutton or Angie Dickerson or Sophia Loren (or, in a politically-correct mode, Paul Newman or Robert Redford), just remember what Big George did for all of us. And for boxing.

Boxing Illustrated, December 1994

What Gives with All These Comebacks? Enough, Already.

Look up the word "comeback" in Noah Webster's olde tome and you'll find the definition: "A return to former prosperity or status." Look up the fighters trying same—be they Foreman, Holmes, Duran, Hearns, etc., etc.,—and you'll find none of them returning to their "former prosperity or status." Just a lot of hardened arteries.

Why are so many once-great stars still attempting to ply their trade? Could it be they've got nowhere else to go. Or just that they've missed the adulation of the crowds. Or perhaps it's just that time-honored answer: money. Whatever it is, boxing has taken on a new glow, and it ain't a healthy one as more and more of the once-great climb through the ropes to let us watch the gilt of their once-greatness peel off before our very eyes.

Throughout history there have been countless tales of once-greats attempting "comebacks." Benny Leonard, arguably the greatest lightweight in the world, out of money and out of sorts, came back after five years, won eighteen of nineteen fights and then was laid endwise by Jimmy McLarnin, a sad sight of what once was. Ditto Joe Louis, who, after a year-and-a-half, in hock up to his proverbial eyeballs to Uncle Sam, climbed through the ropes to show but little of his former self before Rocky Marciano put him through the ropes to end his career on a tragic note. Sugar Ray Robinson, Henry Armstrong, Sugar Ray Leonard, Carlos Ortiz, Carlos Zarate, Willie Pep, few have escaped the siren call of the comeback. Is it because so many athletic commissions will pander to their every wish, allowing them to come back? Or because Alphabet Organizations, like the WBC, almost encourage comebacks, having by-laws that allow "former champions," without any comeback fights or being rated, to fight immediately for a championship.

For boxing, unlike any other sport, encourages the "comeback": Unlike football, baseball or basketball or any team sport, where once the team "cuts" an aging athlete loose he has little chance of coming back, in boxing he does. What the hell was George Blanda going to do? Start a whole league just so he could play?

Should we have two standards: one for the up-and-coming and one for the down-and-going? Or should we simply ignore them before they start walking on the backs of their heels and talking to themselves?

It's a shame to watch some of them exhibiting very little of their former wares. And yet some networks will showcase the Larry Holmeses and Roberto Durans even when it's all-to-obvious they have nothing left. Are they encouraged by the fact that they're now three—make that four, if you're counting the WBO, and nobody is—championships in each division and more divisions?

And then there's the George Foreman factor. The if-George-can-do-I-can-do-it thesis. But George Foreman was a Harvard Business School MBA study, packaging himself beautifully and marketing himself like an all-new product to the point where he not only came back but recycled himself as an "all-new" George Foreman.

What Gives with All These Comebacks? Enough Already

We ain't going to see many more George Foremans. And therein is the shame of it all, with every Tom, Dick and Alexis thinking he can pull off the same sleight-of-fist that Foreman did.

Stop them before it's too late! Turn off the damned bubble machine.

Boxing Illustrated, June 1994

II

The Fighters

America Finds a Hero: John L. Sullivan

John Lawrence Sullivan. The very name brings back memories to that rapidly dwindling number of fight fans whose fathers saw this bull-like man club opponents into the earth with an awesome right and told them about his exploits. To the average adult, he is a storied figure in boxing history who gave color to his age, somewhat in the fashion Babe Ruth and P. T. Barnum gave color to theirs. To the younger generation, he is merely a name, spoken in reverential terms by elders and used as a benchmark for modern boxers like Joe Louis and Muhammad Ali.

In a time when national heroes have passed from the American landscape, it is difficult to fathom Sullivan's full impact. People who couldn't care less about boxing knew his name. But John L. Sullivan was more than a name—he was an institution, a deity. He was called "the Boston Strongboy," "Spartacus Sullivan," "Knight of the Fives," "Sullivan the Great," "His Fistic Highness," "Prizefighting Caesar," "the Hercules of the Ring," "the Youthful Prince of Pugilists," "America's Invincible Champion," and hundreds of other names meant to convey just one thing: that he was the idol of American youth and the symbol of boxing the world over.

As each day brought new accolades and exaggerated stories about the man who had become a legend in his own time, Sullivan contributed to the lore by writing and then rewriting the record books with every swing of his mighty fists. "My name is John L. Sullivan and I can lick any sonofabitch in the house," he would roar with a swaggering virility that mirrored the times, times when America was confident and cocksure, already convinced of its place in history but still casting about for its true identity. And John L. Sullivan gave it both history and identity.

His popularity transcended pugilism, transporting every red-blooded American into a hero worship not seen before or since. It gave rise to the pet slogan of the 1890s, "Let me shake the hand that shook the hand of The Great John L.," a line strong enough to open the popular Broadway play *A Rag Baby*, and a line strong enough to carry the feelings of a country imbued with its own strength—and the strength of a man who epitomized America the world over.

Born in Boston of Irish immigrant parents on October 15, 1858, the baby christened John Lawrence was a sturdy and feisty babe at birth, inheriting his size from his mother—a big-boned woman who weighed almost 180 pounds—and his fighting temperament from his father, a five-foot-three street scrapper.

Apparently feeling that one fighter in a family was more than the neighborhood quota, Mrs. Sullivan directed her son toward the priesthood. But young John L. was, at best, whelmed with the idea, and after what he claimed later to be sixteen months of study at an institution that has since become Boston College, left and apprenticed himself first to a plumber and then to a tinsmith. He was dismissed from both jobs for fighting.

Sullivan, in his autobiography, was to admit to being capable of handling his dukes. "I had many a fracas with the other fellows," he was to write, adding, as if there was any doubt, "And I always came out on top."

This young giant, who was well on his way to the top, took a minor detour to indulge himself in yet another American passion—

baseball. By 1886 *Harper's Weekly* heralded the coming of baseball, even then being called "the Nation's Pastime" by saying, "The fascination of the game has seized upon the American people, irrespective of age, sex or other condition." And one man who was in condition, young John L., seized upon the game to exhibit his athletic abilities, which were so great that not only was he paid $25 a game by the semipro team with which he played, but he boasted he had earned an offer from the manager of the Cincinnati Reds for $1,300 a season.

But John L. turned down the offer in order to concentrate on his growing passion, pugilism. It had all begun one night when a touring tough at a boxing exhibition announced he would take on any man in the house and offered any and all comers the then unheard-of amount of $50 if they could but stay three rounds. Almost immediately the chant of "Sull-i-van, Sull-i-van" permeated the theater as they called upon their local hero to take on the stage fighter and make him eat his words.

John L. removed his coat and strode mightily onto the stage, there to put on boxing gloves for the first time in his life. As he reached out to shake hands, he received a punch in the nose for his efforts. Angered by the affront, Sullivan roared into the perpetrator of this foul act and knocked him senseless, head-over-challenge into the orchestra pit.

Soon John L. was fighting professionally, beating the local scrappers, including the man known as the heavyweight champion of Massachusetts. After going on an exhibition tour himself, offering each and every comer $50 if they stayed four rounds—few of whom dared and none of whom did—he got the opportunity to fight Professor Mike Donovan, then-world middleweight champion, in a three-round exhibition. As Sullivan would later relate the tale of his fight with one of the first great scientific boxers in America, "it was my first chance to become famous." And it was a chance he wasn't about to let slip by. "All Boston assembled to witness my slaughter, but I surprised them and my opponent, too, by standing him off." The reputation of the Boston Strongboy grew more than a little bit as he battered the Professor and all but knocked him out.

"After our bout, when we had reached our dressing rooms upstairs, we had a long talk. 'John,' Donovan said, 'I really believe you tried hard to knock me out.' 'Oh no,'" Sullivan claims he replied, and winked at one of his seconds, "I didn't try very hard to finish you." Donovan, according to Sullivan, replied, "Well, I'm going to be honest with you, John, and tell you that I tried my best to knock you out, and I was surprised when I failed."

Sullivan, perhaps embellishing the story but making a good tale in the telling, replied in kind to Donovan, or so he claimed, "Well, I'll also be honest, and tell you that I came within an inch of putting the knockout wallop over. If you hadn't dodged that last one that was aimed at your jaw, you wouldn't have come to yet."

Of such stuff are legends made. And if the fight itself wasn't enough, when Donovan returned to New York he told everyone and anyone who would listen that he had found a comer up in Boston who would soon take the measure of anyone he fought. Among the interested parties listening to Professor Donovan's stories were Joe Goss, the American champion, and George Rooke, claimant to the middleweight champion.

Rooke's comments are unrecorded, but Goss is reputed to have said something like, "Oh, tell that to the sailors," or whatever passed for "applesauce" in those days, and implored Donovan to set something up so, "I can get a peep at him."

William Muldoon and Billy Madden, Sullivan's manager, arranged for Goss to take such a "peep" at Sully at a Boston testimonial for Goss on April 6, 1880. It was an opportunity for Sullivan, one that he later claimed, "Gave me my first chance to demonstrate to the wise ones that I was going to become one of the world's greatest exponents of the manly art of fighting," or so one of his ghostwriters, acting as a dishonest ventriloquist, would put in his memoirs.

The three-round sparring exhibition had hardly started when Goss got his first "peep," a hard right to the chin. In the second the two were slugging toe-to-toe when suddenly Sully, in his own words, "Let loose a right-handed swing and knocked him flat." Goss was dragged to his corner and revived by his seconds. As the two men advanced for the beginning of the third, two of Sullivan's friends advised him to carry the old champ. He did, sparring through the last round and not trying for a knockout. Even so, Goss had become a believer, turning to the referee as he left the ring and confiding, "That fellow's blows feel like the kick of a mule."

The next day the local papers, which barely carried two inches on an important fight or fighter, dedicated an article to Sullivan and his punching power, proclaiming "Sullivan's terrific hitting on this occasion proved quite a sensation." It was the start of the legend of John L.

But the legend of John L. extended only so far—Boston and environs. In order to further his fame and fortune, Sullivan went on a road trip, doing the vaudeville circuit, again taking on all comers.

Sullivan's notoriety would rest on three fights he would have the year after reaching his majority. The first of these was against veteran George Rooke, the self-proclaimed middleweight champion, whom he took out in two rounds. Next stop, Cincinnati, where his manager, Billy Madden, challenged "the Champion of the West," Professor John Donaldson. Madden was famous for advertising his charge by challenging every heavyweight in sight. If the man challenged failed to respond, and quickly, Madden usually laid claim to the delinquent pugilist's title, if he were champion, and promptly announced that his man was ready to defend the newly acquired honor against all comers.

Donaldson chose not to duck the challenge. Instead he saved his ducking, sidestepping, and sprinting for the fight itself, a fight that could have been refereed by Lon Myers, an early-day Jesse Owens, who had just won the national 100-, 220-, 440-, and 880-

yard titles. Donaldson clinched and frequently dropped to the ground without taking a punch, thus ending a round under the old London Prize Fight Rules. The frustrated Sullivan finally caught up with his unworthy adversary in the tenth, laying him endwise.

Notwithstanding the fact that the so-called "fight" was one in name only, the local constabulary arrested Sullivan and charged him with participating in an "illegal" prizefight. Brought before a judge on the charge, Sullivan was vindicated when one witness described the so-called match as a "foot race," and went on to say, "Donaldson is a fine sprinter. He was mostly in the lead by a quarter of a mile, but Sullivan was hot on his trail. . . . Then he barely touched him, just to let him know he had caught up. . . . That was the finish. Donaldson was tripped up and couldn't continue."

The charges were dismissed. But what couldn't be dismissed was Sullivan's reputation. And ambition. The next day he issued an any-man-in-the-house challenge to a match, publishing an ad in the Cincinnati *Enquirer* that read:

> I am prepared to make a match to fight any man breathing, for any sum from one-thousand dollars to ten-thousand dollars at match weights. This challenge is especially directed to Paddy Ryan and will remain open for a month if he should see fit to accept it.
>
> Respectfully yours,
> John L. Sullivan

But heavyweight champ Paddy Ryan would have none of John L., or his braggadocio, and hid behind a public dismissal of the challenge which read, "Go and get a reputation," but which might have sounded more like "Go fly a kite." Sullivan was not deterred, and he went out in search of that reputation, heading toward the city where reputations are often built taller than buildings: New York.

The man Sullivan and Madden selected already had a mighty reputation of his own. Around and about New York, the name John

Flood was bigger than that of John L. Sullivan. A well-connected man with Tammany Hall and a well-proportioned pugilist, the man known as the "Bull's Head Terror" had won considerable fame bowling over anyone put in front of him. Possessing a powerful physique built on a six-foot-two-inch frame, Flood had never failed to "get his man" and was considered, at least by New Yorkers, more than a match for Sullivan, and his superior in every way.

At the time of the Sullivan-Flood fight there were stringent laws in New York—as there were throughout the country—against both boxing and prizefighting. The managers of Sullivan and Flood finally decided to hold the fight aboard a barge to circumvent any possible interference by the local upholders of law and order.

And so it was on the night of Monday, May 16, 1881, that the heroes of the two great Eastern metropolises fought for personal pride, reputation, and $1,000 on a barge moored off Yonkers, New York, with kid gloves and under London Prize Ring Rules. Within 16 minutes Sullivan had battered Flood to the wooden floor three times. Suddenly a shout rose above the crowd. "There's a police boat coming."

Sullivan redoubled his efforts and Flood's seconds mercifully threw in the towel indicating their charge's surrender. "We met as friends and we part as friends," Sullivan was heard to say to his opponent as he went over to shake the fallen hulk's hand. Then, espying Paddy Ryan in the crowd, he shouted, "You'll be the next one." Ryan yelled back, "You'll get your chance yet."

Sullivan would, but it would take the intercession of one of the most powerful men in the United States, Richard K. Fox, publisher of the *Police Gazette*, to get the two parties together—and then, only under the banner of his publication for promotional purposes and personal prestige.

When Richard Kyle Fox, a penniless 29-year-old immigrant, came to the United States in 1874, he found work on a New York newspaper. The bounds of his ambition had hardly been tapped, though. With the few hundred dollars he had saved and a few more that he borrowed, Fox bought the *National Police Gazette*.

Infusing it with a dose of promotional savvy, he was able to revive the moribund publication. Part of the rebirth experience included the addition of a new masthead that read "Richard K. Fox, Editor and Proprietor," and the creation of a sports section, bringing accounts of prizefights and races to the general public. The sports page was a novelty and the ten-cent weekly soon earned Fox a considerable reputation among Americans who were eager for such coverage.

Prizefighting was illegal in every one of the thirty states in 1880, but Fox followed his intuition, assigning a group of artists and reporters to cover the championship match between England's Joe Goss and Paddy Ryan, an American, at Collier Station on the Virginia-Pennsylvania border.

The battle over, a special edition of the *Gazette* was issued. Complete with artist's renderings of the fight and a detailed description of the match, the presses rolled on relentlessly until the magazine answered the sport-thirsty public's demand. As the *Police Gazette* poured into every barbershop, pool hall, saloon, police station, fire hall, and major male gathering-place in the country, Fox knew he had created a journalistic sensation.

His fame, however, issued from yet another occurrence. Due to a slight suffered at the hands of John L. Sullivan, Fox would soon set the course for boxing in America. Spurred by his enormous ego, Fox would become our first boxing promoter. Unofficially, of course.

Harry Hill's Dance Hall and Boxing Emporium, a group of two-story buildings on Houston Street in New York, offered wrestling and boxing exhibitions as a *divertissement* for the stage and sports personalities of the time who made it their second home: P. T. Barnum, Diamond Jim Brady, Lillian Russell, James Gordon Bennett, and also

Richard K. Fox, the most influential sports figure in America. It was to Harry Hill's that Sully went during a brief visit to New York.

A foolhardy challenger from the audience had just added his name to Sullivan's injured warrior list. The $50 won by Sullivan remained liquid as he reinvested it in drinks for his admirers, his friends and various hangers-on.

Suddenly, a waiter appeared next to Sullivan with the message, "Mr. Fox would like a word with you."

The answer, bellowed to the waiter, was heard by everyone in the establishment.

"You tell Fox that if he's got anything to say to me he can Gah-damn well come over to my table and say it!"

Fox, never having been addressed in such a manner, was loathe to forget the affront. He certainly never forgave it.

Soon Fox began an intense search for a boxer who could "get" Sullivan. In Paddy Ryan he found his man.

Ryan, the holder of the belt, had kept it and the title for a little over a year, but showed no proclivity for risking it in the ring, especially against so formidable an opponent as the Boston Strongboy. Finally, with Fox as his backer and operating as the de facto promoter, Ryan agreed to the bout, $5,000 a side. But here a hitch developed. After $500 of the stake money was deposited with Harry Hill in New York, Sullivan's backers had difficulty coming up with the remainder of the $5,000. It was Ryan who saved the bout by appealing to Fox to reduce the stakes by half because of Sullivan's inability to obtain sufficient funds.

The reluctance of Sullivan money was rooted in the unsettled state of boxing at that time in the United States. While most fights were then fought under the old London Prize Ring Rules—bare knuckles and rounds ending when a man was knocked, tripped, or thrown to the ground and having thirty seconds to come "to scratch"—Sullivan was an ardent advocate of the new Marquess of Queensberry Rules.

In fact, Sully had begun a crusade against the use of bare fists in his travels around the country and had started to popularize the use of gloves, called "pillows" by their detractors. While Ryan had established himself as a bareknuckle fighter, Sullivan's ability as one was practically unknown. Stimulated by the relative merits of both fighters, talk of the match filled the land—and, not incidentally, the *Police Gazette.*

Sullivan was then a 24-year-old Adonis, a perfect athlete who, up until this point in his career, had abstained from all forms of tobacco and strong drink, in radical contrast to his later habits. And so, with workouts more of a nicety than a necessity, each person in Sullivan's Mississippi training camp became dedicated to this man and his winning of the crown, but not overly concerned with their warrior's condition or chances.

His camp's somewhat relaxed atmosphere produced one of those little sidebars that illumines boxing's history—one that has totally escaped notice. During a break in the regimen, Madden, trainer Pete McCoy, and second Mike Gillespie were out in the fields kicking a football—or more accurately, a soccer ball—around when the idea suddenly occurred to McCoy that a football hung from the ceiling would improve his charge's proficiency at hitting a moving target. And, from that day on, the punching bag became an important adjunct to every fighter's training program.

The Sullivan-Ryan fight itself was anticlimactic. On the morning of February 7, 1882, Sullivan and Ryan met in a ring pitched in front of the veranda of the Barnes Hotel in the Gulf resort town of Mississippi City, Mississippi. The two men approached the ring and threw their hats into it, indicating they were ready for combat.

Almost immediately the Troy Giant rushed Sullivan with the intention of battering down the defenses of the 100–80 favorite. But Sullivan held his ground and gave back everything with interest, ending the first round by smashing Ryan to the ground with one of his thunderous rights—a right Ryan would later recall as feeling like "a telephone pole had been shoved against me endways." Round 2 saw Ryan come back and throw Sully heavily to the ground, ending the round. That was Ryan's last hurrah. As Sullivan took charge in the third round, throwing fearful punches with either hand, a frustrated Fox screamed vainly to Ryan to inflict damage on his sworn enemy. Finally, after nine rounds, taking ten minutes and thirty seconds, Sullivan caught Ryan with a fearful right and knocked him senseless. Fox was incensed.

Taking one look at his fallen opponent, the new American heavyweight champion vaulted the ropes and sprinted to his quarters, all the quicker to start the postprandial party scheduled for the train trip back to New Orleans.

After some prodigious partying in the Crescent City, the once-abstemious champion went home to a rousing reception. Back in Back Bay the new champion reportedly put on a drinking exhibition seldom seen before, even in Boston. High living and heavy drinking soon became Sullivan trademarks, adding a new dimension to the character of America's new hero, that of the arrogant swashbuckler who could fight or drink two-handed. Both very well, thank you!

The newly crowned American champion immediately set out to merchandise himself, barnstorming across the country on a knockout trip that made boxing popular and John L. well-to-do. The going price was now $1,000 for anyone who could last four rounds with the heavyweight champion under Queensberry Rules. Boasting, "I can beat any sonofabitch in the house," he would totter out nightly to center stage so drunk that his handlers had to help him into his tights and push him in the direction of the curtain. But he was able to back-up his defiance by meeting and beating a collection of local barkeeps, bullyboys, and blacksmiths, with an occasional "professional" fighter thrown in for good measure.

The only one of the hundreds of challengers who stayed the course was an experienced British heavyweight, Joe Wilson. Fighting under the name "Tug" Collins, he was backed by none other than Sullivan's adversary, Richard K. Fox. Persuading Sullivan to agree to the old London Prize Ring Rules, Wilson fought Sullivan at Madison Square Garden on the night of July 17, 1882, in a four-round exhibition hypocritically allowed by the mayor, even though prizefighting was still "illegal." According to *The Ring Record Book*, "Tug Collins (Joe Wilson) stayed by hugging and falling to the floor," thus providing Fox with some small satisfaction and Wilson with $1,000 in prize money.

Fox was now aligned with Sullivan's former manager, Billy Madden, who had had a falling out with Sully. Knowing of his pride in everything American, Madden sought to humiliate John L. by bringing over an Englishman to beat him. Madden advertised in the London *Sporting Life* for warm bodies to fight in a heavyweight elimination contest. In Charley Mitchell, a sturdy 158-pounder, Madden found himself a live one. He had beaten the same Tug Wilson that Sullivan had had problems with. Proclaiming Mitchell champion of England, Madden matched him with Sullivan.

The international fight brought a crowd of more than ten thousand to Madison Square Garden. They weren't disappointed. Fighting with gloves under the Queensberry Rules, the lighter Mitchell took the fight to Sullivan and in the very first round, to everyone's surprise, delivered a short right that knocked Sullivan down for the first time in his career. In the third round—after Sullivan had knocked the Englishman through the ropes in the second and out of the ring in the third—the police jumped into the ring. The master of ceremonies—there being no referee—gave Sullivan the decision, although it was a "no decision" bout. Fox had won part of his pound of flesh.

While Sullivan, the invincible, was making short order of any and all that was put in front of him—be they fighters, women, or drinks—Fox continued his search for the elusive golden fleece, a fighter he could fasten his belt and the title "champion" to by besting the Great John L. He imported Herbert A. Slade, a giant Maori, supposedly the best fighter in the Antilles. He lasted three rounds.

Next he brought over Al Greenfield, one of England's finest. He went in two.

But Fox was far from through. There now hove onto the horizon a native of Long Island christened John J. Killion, who fought under the name Jake Kilrain. During the early 1880s, Kilrain fought, and beat, some of the best of the heavies, including Jack Burke, Jack Ashton, Frank Herald, and Joe Godfrey among others, and fought a four-round draw with Charley Mitchell. Fox challenged Sullivan to battle and when the champion failed to respond, Fox designated his man, Kilrain, as the recipient of the *Police Gazette* belt, a bauble adorned with diamonds, rubies, and, of course, a picture of Richard Kyle Fox.

Sullivan's legion of fans, angered by Fox's gesture, immediately initiated a drive to raise money to buy *their* champion a bigger and better belt, in recognition of his claim to the championship being bigger and better. At least, in their eyes. Finally, after raising more than $10,000 they presented their hero with a goldplated belt studded with 350 diamonds, inscribed with the legend "Presented to the champion of champions by the people of the United States." The name John L. Sullivan, properly enough, was outlined in diamonds, with the biggest diamond of all donated by the smallest idolator, Tom Thumb, P. T. Barnum's mighty midget.

Taking the belt, Sullivan wrapped it around his somewhat expanding midriff and bellowed, "Fox's is like a dog collar compared to mine."

But even as he took possession of the magnificent belt presented to him by his followers, the legend of Sully was beginning to become more than a little sullied. First, to support his prodigious appetite for high living, he took to selling off the diamonds, one by one, replacing them with paste. Then, in the same year as the belt presentation, 1887, he met one Patsy Cardiff, the "Peoria Giant." Cardiff was almost an exact replica of another early-day brawler, Tom Sharkey, and a worthy opponent for Sullivan. But worthy or no, Sullivan trained more in the bars of Boston than in the gyms he was less comfortable with. From the very commencement of hostilities Cardiff held his own. Sullivan, unleashing one of his patented left-hand smashes, hit Cardiff atop the head, breaking the champion's arm at the wrist and rendering him *hors de combat.* Or so the story went when friends of Sullivan's called a halt to the bout after the sixth round. Others, less charitably, ascribed Sullivan's abrupt withdrawal to his lack of condition coupled with the unexpected strength of his opponent.

Meanwhile, Fox had a legitimate claimant to the title. Challenging any living fighter for $5,000 against his $10,000 and finding that Sullivan showed no inclination for such a match, Fox sent Kilrain off to England under the management of Charley Mitchell. There he made a match for Kilrain with the champion of England, Jem Smith. At stake in the first great international battle since Sayers-Heenan was Fox's diamond championship belt. And the reputation of his warrior.

The bout, held on December 19, 1887, at the Isle des Souveraines, River Seine, France, produced few surprises and no winner. Kilrain showed his superiority throughout, but his ignorance of London Prize Fight Rules worked to his disadvantage as his opponent, time and again, took quick falls, ending some rounds in as little as seven to fifteen seconds. Finally after 106 rounds, with both men having sustained much damage—their faces resembling Quasimoto beaten out of all semblance of recognition—the bout was called a "draw" owing to darkness.

Now Fox's campaign against Sullivan picked up momentum. And viciousness. Sullivan, too, picked up, heading for Europe to exploit his popularity, leaving Fox's vituperativeness behind. But first John L. leveled one departing blast: "I've been abused in the papers. I've been lied about and condemned by men who, for commercial reasons, wanted to see some true American, a son of the stars and stripes, whipped by a foreigner. So now I'm intending to get even by unfurling Uncle Sam's victorious flag in the land from which my enemies brought men they hoped would conquer me."

Sullivan's first stop was England. There he met with the warmest welcome ever given an American. Crowds followed him everywhere. And the king of boxing was invited to give an exhibition for the future King of England, the prince of Wales, whom he addressed as "His Princelets." When one of the prince's friends objected to the designation, Sullivan explained he was only doing so because "I heard someone once call the Duke of Argyle 'His Dukelets,' and I thought it would be alright to call the prince 'His Princelets.'" He was admonished by one of his friends not to do it again, "because they're liable to give you a life sentence."

It would be his only social faux pas while in Europe. But not his only problem.

Sullivan's biggest problem was more psychological than physical. He constantly brooded about his antagonist, Richard K. Fox, who had taken a fiendish delight in pelting him with platitudes and bothering him with blatherings. Sullivan, his psyche tortured with tantrums, tried to drown his anguish in drink, if that were possible. He also brooded about the shame of his knockdown at the hands of Mitchell, a mere middleweight.

Finally, a chance came to even the score. He was to get another shot at Mitchell, the man who had humiliated him. And, through Mitchell, at Fox.

Because prizefighting was no longer legal in England, the cradle of boxing, secret arrangements were made to hold the bout in France, a scant three months after the Kilrain-Smith fight on French soil. Scouting around for a site upon which to pitch the ring, the two fighters' parties boarded a train from Paris, and twenty-five miles later hopped off the train in the suburb known as Chantilly. There, on the estate of Baron von Rothschild, on a clean sweep of heather situated between two clumps of trees, they pitched the twenty-four-foot ring on an incline. This latter small detail was the idea of none other than Jake Kilrain, who was seconding Mitchell. He planned to place Mitchell in the corner at the top of the crest of the land if he won the toss, hoping to compensate for Sullivan's advantage in height and reach.

But the loss of the coin toss—and a steady March rain that turned the turf into a quagmire—negated Kilrain's best-laid plans. It didn't matter, however, as Mitchell treated the match less like a fight and more like a footrace, beginning almost immediately after "Time" was called to run Sullivan a merry chase. As their spiked shoes ploughed up the rain-soaked ground, the turf soon began to take on the appearance of a pig's wallow. But neither this nor the torrents of rain slowed up Mitchell, who was out to make the bout a cakewalk, sans music. Every now and then Sullivan would stop in his tracks and snarl, "You bloody stiff, why don't you stand up and fight like a man?" But Mitchell would have none of that. After two early knockdowns by Sullivan and "first blood" by Mitchell, the bout became a farce, the only action being that of Sullivan shouting at Mitchell, "Come on and get at me and I'll knock your English block off." But Mitchell was equal to the task, at least of chiding, if not of fighting, and fired back, "Confound it, John, if you don't want to fight we can make it a draw."

Three hours and ten minutes later, with thirty-five seconds thrown in for good measure, the bout was called a draw by mutual agreement. Sullivan was later to say of the 39-round draw, "I might have licked him if I had had a shotgun."

Even with the draw, Sullivan returned home in April of 1888 to a hero's welcome. Immediately, he sought refuge in the only other world he knew, the bottle. After several bouts with a more formidable opponent than he had ever met in the ring, Sullivan collapsed, stricken with a combination of cirrhosis of the liver and typhoid fever. Certainly, the time was right for Fox to once again challenge this physical wreck of a man, the only man who stood between his man, Kilrain, and universal recognition as "heavyweight champion."

With Fox's pink tabloid banging out a constant harangue against the sick champion, who was, according to *The Police Gazette*, "hovering between death's doorstep and taking the back door out of meeting the real champion," Sullivan finally rose to the bait and accepted Fox's challenge to fight Kilrain for the championship and a side bet of $10,000.

But accepting the challenge was only the proverbial ticket to the ball. Now came the most important element of all, getting in shape. It would take a miracle to turn this physical wreck into the fighting machine he had once been, the man once considered invincible before he succumbed to the wages of sin and gin.

Enter William Muldoon, leading physical culturalist of the time, known as "the noblest Roman of them all." An awesome physical presence himself, Muldoon immediately tracked down Sullivan in one of his favorite watering holes where he was in the process of drowning his misery in another stein of straight alcohol. Confronting the bloated 237-pound shell of a champion, Muldoon dashed the stein to the floor and physically dragged Sullivan to his health farm at Belfast, New York. There Muldoon performed miracles to rival those of Lourdes, transforming the tottering hulk he found at the bar into a toddling 197-pound bear of a man. All in just six months—in time for Fox and his handpicked gladiator, Jake Kilrain.

With Sullivan ready again to "lick any sonofabitch in the house," especially the one named Kilrain, his devoted followers flocked to New Orleans to see if their man was the Great John L. of old, or whether, as Richard K. Fox continually hinted in unsubtle sallies, an overblown and used-up old man, incapable of defending himself or beating the *Police Gazette*'s "world" champion, Jake Kilrain.

With live wires and deadbeats alike all cramming aboard a train destined for place or places unknown, the special fight trains pulled out of the Queen and Crescent Yards at midnight on July 8, 1889. Riding on the cowcatcher in front of the engine or any place they could cling to under the train, thousands of deadheads forced the train to move at a snail's pace toward its ultimate destination, some one hundred miles away.

Finally, after eight hours and what seemed to be an eternity, the trains lumbered into Richburg, Mississippi, a lumber camp 104 miles north of New Orleans, the final destination and the site of the fight. There, right at the siding, was a twenty-four-foot ring set up in full view on the estate owned by Colonel Charles W. Rich.

Except for a small protuberance in his lower belly, Sullivan hardly looked like the dissipated has-been Fox had painted him to be. His followers installed him as the favorite, though there were those with lingering doubts, like the writer for the New York *World* who mused in print, "According to all such drunkards as he, his legs ought to fail him after twenty minutes of fighting."

At exactly ten minutes after ten o'clock, referee John Fitz-patrick called out "Time!" and the two men advanced to the mark. Rushing out, Kilrain grabbed John L. in a toehold and after much pushing and pulling, hurled him to the ground, falling heavily atop him. The first round had taken all of five seconds. But instead of a look of exultation, there was a look of despair on Jake's face when he returned to his corner. His effort had tired him.

By the fourth round, more frustrated than tired, Sullivan shouted at Kilrain: "Why don't you fight, you sonofabitch? You're the champion, huh? Champion of what?" But Kilrain only laughed and continued, in the best manner of Charley Mitchell, to move away from Sully. It was hauntingly familiar, so much so in fact, that during one clinch Sullivan turned to Mitchell, in Kilrain's corner, and jeered, "Oh, Charley Mitchell, you rat. How I wish I had you in this ring instead of this fellow."

In the seventh a Kilrain roundhouse right landed on Sullivan's ear and as first claret was seen, referee Fitzgerald hollered out "First blood!" and an exchange of bills took place. But it seemed, as round followed round, that Kilrain's strategy was not so much tiring Sullivan as himself. Sullivan even eschewed the time-honored custom of sitting on his second's knee, bellowing, "Why should I? I only have to stand back up again." And when Muldoon asked after the twelfth round how much longer Sullivan could "stay," the indominable Sullivan answered, "Till tomorrow morning, if necessary."

Soon the battle and the heat began to wear down both battlers. A blazing sun and a temperature of 104 degrees made it one of the hottest July days in memory. And were one to ask, "How hot was it?" one only would have had look at Chief Hughes, who was Sullivan's bottlewasher. "Maje," as he was called, stood bareheaded in Sully's corner. As the fight progressed his bald head began to blister and his scalp started to balloon up. By the twenty-seventh round, the balloon burst, and there on Maje's head could be seen, in Sully's words, "the nicest crop of hair you ever saw."

Sullivan decked Kilrain in the twenty-seventh round. But then the fight reverted to form—Kilrain's form—and the slow pace resumed. After the forty-third round, Muldoon slipped Sullivan some tea laced with whiskey; Sullivan almost immediately took ill and vomited, ridding himself of the tea, the whiskey, and, apparently, all other vestigal remainders of his fatigue. When Kilrain asked him, "You wanta go quit?" Sullivan bellowed "No!" and punctuated his answer with a straight right. It knocked Kilrain to the turf.

Now it was only a matter of time, and, as the fight continued, the result was becoming more and more apparent. As the exhausted Kilrain was dragged to his corner at the end of the seventy-fifth round, his head rolling loosely as if it were broken, a physician, after examining the broken and beaten warrior, informed Donovan, "If you keep sending that man of yours in he will surely drop dead of exhaustion."

After two hours and sixteen minutes, give or take a few, Donovan threw in the sponge as a symbol of his defeat. John L. Sullivan had again emerged triumphant.

The last great bareknuckle fight was now history. And an age that had started 170 years before on a wooden stage at James Figg's Amphitheatre ended on a clearing in Richburg, Mississippi. The first great act in the continuing drama known as boxing was over. And with it, although it was not known at the time, was the age of one of the greatest men ever to touch the sport: The age of John L. Sullivan.

Hit the Sign and Win a Free Suit of Clothes from Harry Finklestein, 1978

Jack Johnson: Black Champion and White Hopes

In the world of the early 1900s, still awash with Victorian gentility and doily-type embroidery on everything from manners and modes to conversation and conventional heroes, the heavyweight champion's name stood out in stark relief, a man of swaggering virility who epitomized the turbulent, yet proud, surety of the populace of a nation destined for greatness.

However, with Jim Jeffries's retirement, no longer was there one man who could lay claim to the title of "the strongest man in the world"; no longer one man at the top of boxing's mountain. In more ways than one, boxing had plunged into a period of darkness.

Jeffries had tried, in his own naive way, to perpetuate the heavyweight title, by personally handing over his title to the winner of a fight between Marvin Hart and light heavyweight champion Jack Root. But heavyweight championships are not looked upon as a matter of birthright, to be passed on, like the British crown. They are to be won in the ring, and Hart's ascension to the throne was received with one giant yawn.

Meanwhile, in the words of one of those Sweet Caporal cigarette buttons then being worn by some of the so-called gay blades, the year 1906 "just had to get better, 'cause it can't get worse." An economic downturn lay on the land. The United States was suffering through its second depression in ten years—this time complete with millions out of work and the first bread lines in American history.

It was just such a rare combination of occurrences—Jeffries's abdication coupled with the economic muting of vox populi—that gave form and flight to those divisions, which had been relegated to the back of boxing's bus, and now came forward to take their places in the limelight, led by the lightweight division.

The one man who would make the lightweights a major attraction, and make a lasting contribution to boxing, was a sourdough named George L. ("Tex") Rickard. Rickard had gone to Alaska in search of gold, glory, and God-blessed fun, and found a little of all three as he alternated between bust and boom, opening and closing saloons with the same frequency as gold veins were found. Rickard found that the Klondike was a man's world, not because of chauvinism, necessarily, but because there literally were no women to be found. Men were reduced to making their own entertainment, whether it was bellying up to the bar night after night, dancing with the house girls at saloons, or merely seeking out stage shows and other amusements. One such amusement was boxing, a discovery made by Rickard, as valuable as any by a sourdough.

In 1902, after seven long years in Alaska, Rickard decided it was time to cash in his chips and move along. He took $65,000 with him and looked for something else. That something else included a side trip to San Francisco in an attempt to catch a glimpse of the man Rickard called "my idol, 'Gentleman Jim' Corbett." In 1904 Rickard left for Nevada, having heard of a new gold strike in a town aptly named Goldfield.

Everyone seemed drawn to Goldfield. To a nation suffering through a major depression, the news that one mine produced more than $5 million of gold-bearing ore in three months brought thousands to the tent city pretentiously called "the greatest mining camp ever known."

Seeking more lucrative ways to attract the world's attention to their dusty little *El Dorado*, the town fathers, including Rickard, met to consider such ideas as a man-made lake filled with beer; a hot-air balloon with a basket filled with ten-dollar gold pieces that would be thrown down onto Goldfield's streets; a racetrack stocked with camels imported from the Sahara, and so on. Rickard suggested a prizefight.

The men formed the Goldfield Athletic Club the same day and raised $50,000 to back a fight. Their work done, Rickard was appointed to the joint positions of treasurer and promoter. He would be responsible for finding the fighters, negotiating the contracts, and erecting the arena.

Rickard had his work cut out for him. First he wired the managers of Jimmy Britt, claimant to the lightweight crown, and "Terrible" Terry McGovern, former bantamweight and featherweight champion, offering, "fifteen thousand dollars for a fight to the finish." In those days of fighting for a percentage of the gate, such an offer was unheard of. So too was Tex Rickard. No one responded. Thinking he had to increase the ante, Rickard wired Battling Nelson, who had just beaten Britt for something called "the white lightweight championship of the world," an offer of $20,000 for a "finish fight" against the recognized titleholder, Joe Gans. Still, no answer. But Rickard wouldn't take "no answer" for an answer; he just went straight to the champion, Gans. Gans, having just knocked out Mike "Twin" Sullivan, was badly in need of money, having been left high and dry by his less-than-savory manager. Now acting as his own manager, Gans immediately wired back his acceptance, agreeing to any terms Nelson demanded.

With Gans in the fold, Rickard left for Reno to begin construction of an arena. While there he heard that although his offer of $20,000 to Nelson was the largest guarantee ever offered, the number-one fight promoter in the country, Sunny Jim Coffroth, was heading east to meet Gans and offer him more. Realizing he was fast becoming an almost-promoter, Rickard increased his offer to the unheard-of-sum of $30,000. When he returned to Goldfield he found a telegram from Nelson's manager, accepting the bid for the fight, the only stipulation being that Nelson get two-thirds of the total guarantee.

Oscar Battling Matthew Nelson was more simply known as "Bat" or "the Durable Dane." His head was said to be invulnerable to punishment due to the triple-thick Neanderthal construction of his cranium. Typically he took about three punches to every one he landed. His favorite punch—to the kidneys—probably helped earn him a reputation for being less than a gentleman. He liked to use every trick in the book and some that weren't, including gouging, butting, and dirty in-fighting.

Joe Gans, on the other glove, was one of the classic boxers of all time, called—even today—one of the greatest boxer pound-for-pound and punch-for-punch of all time. In his 144 fights before Goldfield, Gans had scored forty-nine knockouts—including a one-round knockout of Frank Erne to win the lightweight title four years earlier—against just five losses. And three of those losses were tainted to satisfy the betting whims of his manager, Al Herford. Now impoverished and unable to get fights, the "Old Master" agreed to each new division of the guarantee Nelson's manager demanded, finally settling for $10,000 to Nelson's $23,000, an amount Rickard stacked up in newly minted, double-eagle gold pieces in the local bank's window.

The day of the fight almost eight thousand fans—among them three hundred women, the first time they had shown up in any number at an exhibition of the "gentlemanly" art of self-defense—made their way into the newly-constructed arena.

Gans, seriously weakened by having to make the weight just minutes before fight time (something insisted upon by Nelson's manager), was the first to enter the eighteen-foot ring (another concession to Nelson). He was still clutching a poignant telegram he had received from his mother in Baltimore: "Joe, the eyes of the world are on you. Everybody says you ought to win. Peter Jackson will tell me the news. You bring back the bacon." Battling Nelson, confident as always, entered next.

For the first ten rounds, his lithe black body glistening under the boiling Nevada sun, Gans exhibited a masterful display of boxing skills. In the eleventh Bat gained control with his stylized roughhousing.

By the forty-first round, it was obvious even to Nelson that his "dirty" techniques were not enough. In the forty-second, while Gans attempted to smother Nelson's cuffing and gouging, the challenger began raining blows somewhere south of Gans's beltline. As referee George Siler was in the process of issuing a stern warning to Nelson, Nelson drove his right hand into Gans's groin. Siler pushed Nelson to his corner, returned to the stricken champion, and raised his arm. In the longest championship fight in Marquess of Queensberry history, Gans was the winner and still lightweight champion. On a foul.

And, just as importantly, he was able to wire his mother after the fight: "Mammy, your boy is bringing home the bacon with lots of gravy on it."

Boxing was to have several other bouts that begot gravy as well, but, unfortunately, none in the heavyweight division. While the lightweight division sported such great names as Nelson, Gans, and Al Wolgast, the Michigan Wildcat, the featherweight division possessed the likes of Abe Attell and Young Corbett; the welterweight division numbered among its top names Honey Mellody and the Dixie Kid; and the middleweight division had such luminaries as Stanley Ketchel and Billy Papke. The heavyweight crown, such as it was, was worn by five-foot, seven-inch, 179-pound Noah Brusso, who fought under the *nom de guerre* of Tommy Burns. It was his misfortune to be a mere bridge to history, a waystation between greats.

The heavyweight "crown," personally presented to Marvin Hart on the occasion of his upset win over Jack Root by none other than the retiring champion, Jim Jeffries, passed on to Tommy Burns in Hart's first defense. Most fight fans still did not accept Burns, feeling that Jeff was still the real champion and that Hart, and now Burns, were merely custodians of the crown until his return.

Nothing Burns did could change their opinion of him. He fought and beat the best American heavyweights around, such as they were, in Fireman Jim Flynn and Philadelphia Jack O'Brien, the light heavyweight champion. Still, his dubious claim to the championship was greeted by an overwhelming apathy that rivaled the sound of one hand applauding.

And so, in keeping with the Biblical passage that holds that a prophet is not without honor except in his own country, Burns took the road several entertainers had at the turn of the century—he traveled abroad. Thus, while ranked as a minor talent at home, Burns was praised and applauded abroad. He met, and in quick succession knocked out, Gunner Moir, Jack Palmer, and Jem Roche in Great Britain, then traveled to France where he faced the likes of Jewey Smith and Bill Squires, adding them to his growing list of KO victims, and then, finally, traveled to Australia, where he knocked out Bill Squires for the third time, and Bill Lang, making it eight straight knockouts in defense of his slightly tainted crown.

But it wasn't so much that Tommy Burns had won the heavyweight championship and wanted to see the world that had transported him to faraway places; it was the presence of a dark shadow in the United States—the shadow of one John Arthur Johnson, better known as Jack Johnson, "the Galveston Giant."

Jack Johnson: Black Champion and White Hopes

To assess Jack Johnson's place in boxing history is as difficult as attempting to categorize Shakespeare's Othello merely as a Moor. And as misleading. The rise and fall of Jack Johnson was as shaped by his blackness as by America's reaction to his blackness; and, in many ways, it was as much a preordained tragedy as that of Othello.

Ever since John L. Sullivan had invoked the color line—challenging "any and all bluffers" to meet him, then adding the caveat, "I will not fight a Negro. I never have and I never will"—blacks had been denied the right to fight for the heavyweight title. They were boxing's, if not society's, invisible people. Assuredly, there had been black champions—Barbados Joe Walcott, Joe Gans, and Dixie Kid—but no heavyweight champion, the supposed symbol of the strongest man in the world and ruler of all he surveyed. Fighting a black man was perfectly acceptable for those trying to make a name for themselves, as when Corbett met Peter Jackson. But the heavyweight champion was not to fight a black man; it was the unwritten law. There was everything to lose and nothing to gain.

Jack Johnson would change all that, just as he would many of America's perceptions of the black man, savaging their sons and ravaging their daughters as he flaunted every convention set out to intercept just such an interloper.

Denied his chance to find his roots in big-time boxing, Johnson blossomed in bootleg fights, Battle Royals—a barbaric pastime indulged in by many communities which saw between six and eight fighters, all blindfolded and almost all black, fight until the last man left standing was adjudged the winner—on the Chitlin' Circuit against other blacks, where his life was an endless chain of rundown rooming houses, broken-down buses, and foul-smelling beaneries.

Relegated into their own isolated world, some black heavyweights had gained a measure of celebrity: Peter Jackson, Sam Langford, Sam McVey, and Joe Jeanette, to name a few. But few got further than that. Now Johnson sought to defy one of boxing's ineluctable verities—that no black man could become heavyweight champion of the world.

Beginning his career in 1897, the year Fitzsimmons dethroned Corbett, Johnson had a measure of success at first, fighting in and around Galveston, Texas. But the real beginning came when two of boxing's all-time greats—Barbados Joe Walcott and Joe Choynski—took a personal interest in the Galveston Giant or, as he had taken to calling himself, "'Lil Arthur."

Johnson had trained with Walcott, the great master, when Walcott was in training for a title fight; Choynski, on the other hand, had an adversarial relationship with Johnson—at least for three rounds, that is. For that was the amount of time the old war horse needed to catch the youngster on the temple and knock him to the ground. Almost before Johnson's face had settled in the dirt, Texas Rangers had overrun the ring, arresting all within sight for participating in an illegal prizefight. The two most notable of the arrestees were Choynski and Johnson, both of whom were sentenced to jail for breaking the law. It was there, in the exercise yard of the local hoosegow, that Choynski imparted some valuable tips to his willing student.

Johnson was to meld together everything Walcott and Choynski had "larned" him, translating their styles into his own, one characterized by the ability to counterpunch brilliantly with a defense that was well-nigh impregnable. Coupled with his enormous strength, which some critics said gave him the ability to name the punch that would take a man out, and catlike moves, Johnson was almost unbeatable and well on his way to becoming one of boxing's all-time greats.

After being released, Johnson stayed in Galveston only long enough to pack, taking the next train to Chicago, where he hoped to get some fights with top-ranking boxers. Instead, too black and too dangerous for Chicago promoters, Johnson nearly froze to death in squatter's shacks before giving up and heading west in quest of fights. There his luck improved—he started getting decent matches and winning them, beating the likes of George Gardner, who had defeated Joe Walcott; Sam McVey; and Denver Ed Martin, for what was called "The Negro Heavyweight Championship."

But it was the *world's* heavyweight championship he coveted, not just the Negro heavyweight championship. And the only way to win it was to meet and beat the champion, James J. Jeffries. So Johnson, as he was always to do, did the unthinkable: he walked into Jeff's San Francisco saloon to challenge him.

Entering Jeffries's saloon, he found the great man at the bar and, as the story goes, walked up to him and demanded a shot at the title then held by Jeff. Jeff, who told the story in later years, remembered that all he knew of the big man facing him was that he had lost to Choynski. He stared at the audacious apparition in front of him for a moment and then said, "I won't meet you in the ring 'cause you've got no name and we wouldn't draw flies. But," the champion remembered saying, "I'll tell you what I'll do . . . I'll go downstairs to the cellar with you and lock the door from the inside. And the one who comes out with the key will be the champ." Johnson couldn't believe the champ was serious. "Oh I am, I am," said Jeff. "And I'll do it right now!" With that, Johnson turned and walked away, his bluff called, and his first challenge for a shot at the championship denied. But he would try and try again.

Jack now wanted three things: revenge for Jeff's slight, a reputation, and, most importantly, the world's heavyweight title. The first he got in his very next fight, against Jeffries's younger brother, Jack, whom he knocked out in five; the reputation continued to come as he won bout after bout on his way through the heavyweight division; but the heavyweight title shot he coveted so dearly was no closer.

His chances seemed to recede, if anything, when he met Marvin Hart in early 1905, the same year Hart would be dubbed by Jeffries as his successor. The 26-year-old, six-foot-one, one-quarter-inches, 210-pound, finely-tuned Johnson manhandled his lighter and smaller opponent and yet lost a decision to a bloodied and battered Hart when the referee mysteriously awarded the fight to a man who resembled a loser in every way but in the final decision. Bitter, but unable to do anything to reverse a miscarriage of justice, Johnson vowed never to let a close bout go to decision again.

By the time Hart relinquished his crown to Burns, Johnson had beaten everyone who would get in the ring with him, including the great Boston Tar Baby, Sam Langford. Yet his goal continued to elude him. Burns did everything within his power to forestall meeting this man who was menacing the heavyweight division like Tamerlane the Tartar and his yellow hordes had menaced the populace in the fourteenth century, including taking his "championship" on a worldwide tour, far from the threat of Johnson. Johnson took off in pursuit of the crown he knew he was always meant to wear.

While Burns was fattening his record on a long list of mediocrities, Johnson was beating the likes of Bob Fitzsimmons, Sam Langford, Joe Jeanette, and Jim Flynn, all victims of what the papers called "the playful Ethiopian." One English paper, the prestigious *Mirror of Life and Boxing World,* said that the man who had issued public challenges to no less than three reigning heavyweight champions would, if he ever met Burns, be "his master."

Finally, halfway around the world, in the unlikely spot of Sydney, Australia, Johnson got his long-awaited shot. But it was not so much the challenger who forced the issue, as Burns, who succumbed to the dual blandishments of public opinion and the monetary rewards offered by Australian promoter H. D. ("Huge Deal") McIntosh. McIntosh made the largest guarantee ever made to a heavyweight champion—the unheard-of amount of $35,000—leaving only the crumbs, some $6,000 worth, for Johnson.

Burns, firing off virulent salvos of racial slurs, as was the custom of the day, made outrageous demands on McIntosh and Johnson, all of which were accepted: he dictated the choice of ring size, the date of the fight—Boxing Day, the day after Christmas, 1908—

and the naming of the referee, the very same H. D. McIntosh, considered by all to be Burns's "friend." Moreover, he insisted that the fight go to a decision, no matter what. If all these demands were meant as bluffs, Johnson called them all. He wanted the fight in the worst way. Some thought that's how he got it, including the gamblers, who installed the champion as the 7-4 favorite, with very little Johnson money to be found anywhere.

On Boxing Day, at approximately one minute of eleven under a hot Australian summer sun, the six-foot-one-and-one-half inches, 195-pound challenger entered the ring first, as was his wont, preceded through the ropes by his manager, Sam Fitzpatrick, and succeeded by overwhelming silence from the crowd of forty thousand. Burns, the five-foot-seven-and-one-half inches, 180-pound champion, defending his title for the twelfth time, climbed into the ring three minutes later to resounding cheers emanating from the forest of white faces in the specially constructed arena at Rushcutter's Bay.

The fight was, in the words of novelist Jack London, covering the match for the New York *Herald*, "No fight." Instead, this boxing match-hyphen-sociological struggle was one of the cruelest scenes ever played out within the confines of a ring, a play that would have made the Marquis de Sade proud.

From the very first punch, a long left by Johnson, to the end of the fight some fourteen rounds later, the Galveston Giant played out his one-and-a-half years of frustration in a manner never before seen, taunting his smaller opponent, who was outweighed and outgunned in every department, except, ironically, in reach; Burns's 74½-inch reach was almost two inches longer than his six-inch taller opponent's. Johnson leered at him, the hot sun reflecting off his bared gold teeth, and jeered at him with remarks that amounted to verbal winks—"Come on leedle Tahmmy, come right here where I want you"—all the while pushing Burns around at will. During the brief interludes when he tied up the advancing champion, he would talk to the press and once even expectorated over the heads of the all-white press corps. Occasionally he would indulge in a semi-obligatory pugilistic interlude, lacing Burns unmercifully with combinations.

The worst fears of white men everywhere were confirmed as Burns tried time and again to penetrate the impenetrable defenses of the big black man and was rebuffed by masterful counter-punches or tied up, helpless as a small white mouse in the hands of a large black cat. Burns never could get to his challenger-cum-tormentor, who spent much of the afternoon ridiculing the champion, his pitiable efforts, and his followers.

For thirteen rounds Johnson was insufferable. And unbeatable. As "time" for the fourteenth round was called, an exhausted Burns had barely gotten off his stool when he was met by Johnson. Burns warily moved away as Johnson stalked his opponent, sure of himself and his ultimate victory. He threw a straight right to the head, dropping Burns heavily. As McIntosh counted, Burns raised himself to his haunches and slowly regained his feet at "eight," arising only to find Johnson, who had been standing over him, on him at once like a panther, battering the soon-to-be-ex-champ at will.

With Burns tottering helplessly, unable to defend himself and leaning against the ropes in an attempt to avert Johnson's heavy blows, the Sydney police took matters into their own hands, rushing into the ring, shutting off the movie cameras and mercifully stopping the fight. It having been previously decided that if the police intervened a decision would be rendered on points, referee McIntosh walked over and held the hand of Johnson aloft, signifying his victory—and his becoming the new heavyweight champion of the world.

The stoppage of the fight unleashed a tide of hatred. It was unthinkable that the white man's burden had become his master; that the so-called inferior race was superior to the white man in this, the most supreme of all contests between two men. Suddenly, the man who represented the strongest, most powerful, and most visible figure in the world was black.

Disbelief refused to suspend itself. With sanctimonious smugness, white men everywhere demanded that other white men, called, for lack of a better name, "White Hopes," rescue back *their* title, their heritage, to take it away from this defiler of all that was sacred.

Jack London sounded the first call to arms in his closing paragraph from Sydney, demanding that Jim Jeffries "must emerge from his alfalfa farm and remove that smile from Johnson's face." His call was like a pebble thrown into a pond, as the ripples reached every corner of the world and a grizzled collection of ranch hands, gandy dancers, rodeo riders, carpenters, plowboys, and all manner of men joined in the crusade to avenge what they considered to be an historical inaccuracy. All hardy, if not foolhardy, they became part of one of boxing's longest-running spectacles—the finding of a "White Hope," a title given to any fighter of more than 175 pounds and the right complexion, all the better to throw the rascal out.

And Johnson just might have been that rascal. At least, according to most observers. A subtle spirit defiant, he lived the life of fast women, fast cars, and sloe gin, flaunting every excess to excess and living life to the fullest. But his high style of living, his marriages to three white women, and his opening of a nightclub in Chicago—the freewheeling Café de Champion, which served all comers and none of society's mores—brought, like decaying fish, the redolent stench of scandal to the nostrils of the moralists. He was a national hero unworthy of his position and one who had to be disposed of.

But who could beat this man whose fighting style was unbeatable, whose defense made him unhittable, and whose catlike movements and counterpunching abilities made any opponent's chances against him unthinkable? Especially when the "White

Hopes" merely proved out Gresham's law of bad heavyweights, the bad ones forcing out the good ones.

And so it was, with the heavyweight division devoid of hope or hopes, that the first man to challenge Johnson was the middleweight champion of the world, Stanley Ketchel, in an attempt to duplicate Bob Fitzsimmons's feat of leapfrogging from the middleweight to the heavyweight title just twelve years before.

Stanley Ketchel was the stuff dreams—and legends—are made of. Born Stanislaus Kiecal on a Michigan farm of a Russian father and a 14-year-old Polish mother, he ran away at 14, rode the rails, and lived the life of a hobo, picking up fighting as a saloon bouncer in Butte, Montana, where he fought any and all for pocket money. Or fun. He claimed 250 fights before the first official one showed up in *The Ring Record Book*. But in all of his matches, recorded or no, his blond hair and handsome face radiated a ferocity that only Jack Dempsey was later to match. He made one believe he wanted to kill; hence his nickname, "the Michigan Assassin," came closer to reflecting his style of fighting than most ring nicknames.

Called by Philadelphia Jack O'Brien, a man he twice rendered *hors de combat*, "an example of tumultuous ferocity," Ketchel had raced through the middleweight division, denuding it of competition, knocking out forty-seven of his sixty opponents. Only once had he been knocked out, by Billy Papke in defense of his title when, as Ketchel reached out to shake Papke's hand at the commencement of hostilities Papke responded by catching Ketchel in the windpipe with a murderous right. Still, even though Ketchel went down four times in the first and was literally beaten to a bloody pulp, it took Papke fourteen rounds to finish this man who possessed what some called "the soul of a bouncer." With the words "Shake hands and come out fighting" now part of boxing's lexicon as a result of his loss, Ketchel came back just eighty days later to knock Papke out, taking one less round to avenge his loss—a loss that would have forced most fighters into retirement. But not Stanley Ketchel.

In Ketchel the fanatics had finally found their hope, the man they believed could reclaim their heavyweight championship. But an air of improbability surrounded the fight. On the one hand there was the middleweight champion of the world, only five feet, nine inches tall, and weighing all of 154 pounds. On the other, was the man known as "the Galveston Giant," a strapping six-foot-plus, 200-pound tree of a man who had made short work of all served up to him of equal size, let alone smaller men, like Tommy Burns. In order to minimize the size and weight differences, all publicity shots between the two had Ketchel posing in over-stuffed greatcoats, and wearing five-inch heels to lend some stature to the dimensions.

But if there was an aura of improbability to their dimensions, it was heightened by the rumors of the improbability of the fight itself, one which was suggested to be less than on the level. It was widely believed by many that Johnson had agreed to carry his smaller foe for the sake of the movie cameras. And Johnson himself, who was not above spinning a good tale, later wrote that he had to do something to make the fight interesting, like "pretending" to go down and then getting back up to knock out Ketchel.

Regardless of the recurring rumors, a watchful nation held its collective breath as Johnson defended his title for the first time on October 16, 1909 against Ketchel and more than ten thousand hopeful fans crowded into the Colma, California arena to see Johnson get his due. Ketchel, sure of himself and his destiny, sat in the dressing room smoking a cigarette and regaling all in attendance with a funny story, until one of his handlers told him it was "time to go to work." The Panlike Ketchel blissfully ignored the summons and finished his story and his cigarette unhurriedly. Then, and only then, he stood up. "Come on," he told his entourage, "let's go out there and finish that skunk!"

But whether Ketchel did not know that he was merely a bit player in a scenario especially made for the movies or had merely forgotten his part is not known. What is known is that he didn't settle for his role as second banana and started to ad lib his part. And only when he did so did Johnson react, three times to be exact. For the remainder of the fight, it was quite evident, as the reporter for *The New York Times* noted, that "Johnson appeared to be holding himself back all the time."

Finally, after eleven rounds of what could charitably be called sparring, the two combatants answered the bell for the fateful twelfth round. The minute it rang Ketchel jumped from his stool and went out to meet his rival. Johnson, with his hands held high to catch Ketchel's forays, met his assault with a straight left, momentarily arresting Ketchel's movement, then grabbed and wrestled Ketchel to Johnson's corner. As the two men broke away, Johnson poised and, with a pantherlike leap, sprang to meet Ketchel. Ketchel, reacting to Johnson's sudden move as well as to a verbal prod which came from his corner in a singsong voice pleading for him to "Come on now, Stanley!" threw a sweeping right hand up over the top. Johnson ducked and Ketchel's right serpentined around the back of Johnson's neck, looking as if it hit him on the ear. Johnson lost his balance and toppled toward the canvas, holding himself up with his outstretched left glove and never really hitting the floor. Johnson leaped up, a malevolent grin on his face as Ketchel raced in to put the finishing touches on his partially completed work. As Ketchel leaped forward, Johnson shot out his right fist, catching the oncoming Ketchel on the jaw. Simultaneously, he threw a left to the pit of the challenger's stomach. Ketchel fell heavily, as if he had been poleaxed, his arms and legs outstretched in a perfect five-point star.

The momentum of his efforts carried Johnson through and over the stricken Ketchel, forcing him to stumble on the fallen form. He hurriedly jumped up and, picking two of Ketchel's teeth out of his right glove, stood legs crossed, with one hand on the ropes, the other on his hip, content with an afternoon's work. An excellent movie "take." When asked later how he felt being knocked down, Johnson gave further substantiation to the prefight rumors by answering, "Far better than Ketchel did thirty seconds later. He crossed me and I made him pay for it."

As the now-silent crowd filed out of the Colma arena, its hopes as crushed as Ketchel's teeth, the call went out for Jim Jeffries. He was the one man who could beat Johnson, and, the faithful held, the "real" champion because he had not been beaten in the ring, but had turned over his title to Marvin Hart for safekeeping. Hart, of course, had lost it to Burns, who had, in turn, lost it to Johnson. But they were not the *real* champions: Jeffries was. And he would beat this pretender to his throne—this black man wearing the white man's crown.

Only the invincible Jeff, the chosen representative of the white race, could answer for the real and imagined slights the Caucasian psyche had suffered at the hands of this black who was living life to the fullest and flaunting his color in the white man's face. Not the white hopes and the white hopeless. It had to be Jeff.

Now he heeded the clarion call to arms. He would return from his alfalfa farm and recapture "his" crown, even if he had to shed close to a hundred pounds to do so. He became the Great White Hope, the Great White Prayer. And he would do his duty as his public saw fit.

This was more than a classic match-up. This was a morality play. Black versus white. Invader versus avenger. And no one grasped the marketing potential of the match better than Tex Rickard. He eagerly sought to become its architect, but he was not alone. Others saw its inherent drama and profit. Representatives of both fighters met and agreed to a bout to be held in July 1910. They stipulated that all bids for the bout must be submitted to them on December 1, 1909, in New York. The "promoters" came out of the proverbial woodwork.

It was Rickard who saw that whoever had the champion had the fight as well. He made a pilgrimage to Pittsburgh, like one of the faithful visiting Lourdes hoping to be blessed, to catch up with

Johnson. There he found the champion, whose big spending had left him broke, taking his turn on the vaudeville circuit—skipping rope, punching the bag, amusing audiences with stories and playing a bull fiddle. When Rickard approached him backstage, Johnson greeted him with, "This is the situation, Mr. Tex. No matter what the papers say about the big money for the fight, nothin' is set. Now, what would be helpful to me is about twenty-five hundred to settle up some bills and damn all." Seeing his opening, Rickard reached into his greatcoat and peeled two thousand-dollar bills and a five hundred from his roll and handed them to the wide-eyed champion whose face broke into the golden smile Jack London—and all the world—had come to abhor. There was no signature, no handshake. But from that moment on Rickard had the champion, and the fight—a fight he nailed down by offering a $170,000 purse, seventy-five percent to the winner, which Jeffries later changed to a sixty percent-forty percent split, and $10,000 under the table to each man.

Now he had to find a site. Originally he planned to have the fight in California, which, at the time was the mecca for big-time boxing, especially championship fights, the Johnson-Ketchel fight having been held there only the year before. But reform was on the move in 1910. State after state passed legislation forbidding drinking, prizefighting, and just about anything else that smacked of fun. Even the pedestrian painting "September Morn"—later to become a logo for White Rock beverages—had been banned by Watch and Ward Societies for promiscuously showing a nude young lady standing on a rock. But Jack Johnson gave the reformers a cause greater than most. White against black was unnatural, or so the reasoning went. Intimating that no white woman was safe in her own boudoir—intermingling choice words like "miscegenation" and "mongrelization"—the reformers set upon California's Governor James J. Gillette to ban the fight.

Coupled with the invasion of their borders by the black champion was something equally pernicious—rumors of a fixed fight.

The betting crowd was convinced that the "fix was in." It supposedly had been arranged for Jeffries to win, with the black champion to take a "dive." As rumors of fix and the rumbles of the reformers reached his ears with an ever-increasing din, the governor saw political wisdom in throwing the fight out of his state.

But if California didn't want him, Richard's old home state of Nevada did—especially Reno, which Rickard selected "because more railroads junction here." And Reno it was, where, on a hot, sultry Independence Day, 1910, the first "Fight of the Century" took place.

Everyone who was anyone was there, and some nobodies as well. One journalist noted, "Pugs, gamblers, newspaper reporters, scrubs, whores, and sons of bitches in plenty" roamed the streets. They were there to witness the day when all would be set right, when Jeff would once again prove to be invincible.

In the name of solidarity, Jim Corbett and John L. Sullivan shook hands and ended their eighteen-year feud to both back Jeff. Bettors, too, backed Jeff, to the tune of 10–7, believing the Easter Bunny-esque tale that he was, as the press would tell its believing public, "in the best shape of his life." But the man who had been coaxed out of retirement and who had shed almost a hundred pounds bore little resemblance to the man who had last put on gloves some six years before; his vaunted left was now only a memory, his once-great strength now a victim of the passage of time. In short, he was a sham. But nobody wanted to believe it. They took as an article of faith that a white man, no matter how old or out of shape, was superior in every way to his obviously inferior counterpart—especially this one, the one with the infamous golden smile.

But Jeffries knew, all too well. The man who had been supremely confident in each of his previous fights could not sleep the night before the bout, pacing his room like a caged tiger. He also knew something nobody else could have even guessed. When the fight moved from California to Nevada, the "arrangement" that Jeffries would win was called off. Johnson had sent him word that he was no longer bound by the secret prefight agreement to "go into the tank." Now it was "best man wins," and Jeff knew before he entered the ring that Johnson was that best man.

But, for the hopeful crowd of 15,760 jammed cheek-by-jowl into the amphitheater of yellow pine—and the 2,000 plus members of the press corps from every corner of the white man's world—the hoped-for never came. As they roared their support of Jeff, and cornerman Jim Corbett exhorted his friend and charge to "Use the one-two, Jeff, the one-two," Johnson showed his mastery by stifling everything Jeffries did, then, pushing him back and keeping his opponent at cautious arm's length, all the while taunting Jeff, the press and his cornermen, singled out Corbett for special abuse. Tied up and frustrated, Jeffries began to take on the look of a boxing version of Dorian Gray, aging right before the eyes of his faithful. The realization that their hero was not the man he had been slowly began to dawn on the crowd. Their disappointment took voice in their pleas, "Jeff, it's up to you."

Finally, in the fifteenth, Johnson ended their hopes forever, flooring Jeff for the first time in his career with a right uppercut and three lefts and then beating him through the ropes with one thunderous left. After being gingerly helped to his feet by his cornermen and shoved back into the path of the advancing panther, Jeffries sank to the canvas under the collective onslaught of five left hooks. He hung on to the ropes and gasped for breath. Amid screams of "Stop it! Stop it!" from the disheartened, Tex Rickard, now acting in his capacity as referee, walked over and held up Johnson's hand. The crusade had failed. The Greek drama had turned into a tragedy.

The defeat of Jeffries sparked riots in many American cities, riots that left almost thirty people dead. In New York, Washington, Omaha, Little Rock, Houston, and all points, north, east, south, and west, whites watched in stunned horror as blacks paraded through the streets proclaiming *their* superiority. It was a terrible blow to a society dedicated to "keeping *those* people in their place," a wound to their psyche which was now ripped open and rubbed raw by the ostentatiousness of Johnson and those who celebrated his victory.

Had there been a Nobel Prize for dividing the races, Jack Johnson would have won it, gloves down. After winning the title from Burns, he had told his then-manager, Sam Fitzpatrick, "I'll make them [the whites] kowtow to me. I'll make them small beer." He outraged both races by making his own rules. He married three white women, one of whom, Etta Duryea, took her own life. Johnson later lamented, "She was murdered by the world, by spiteful tongues, by my enemies, by racial hatred." But this firebrand also fueled the fires of racial hatred himself. Booker T. Washington, one of the black leaders of the time, told an audience, "I'm sure that they [Johnson's actions] do not meet the approval of the colored race." Still, he *was* the cock of the walk, and it wasn't the "coon walk," or the dirt area bordering the street where blacks were required to walk in many cities; it was the center of the street, the main walk. He was one "uppity nigger" who didn't know his place, "ten miles of bad road," in the black vernacular of the day. And that hurt. Both races.

When, only two years earlier, Theodore Roosevelt had Booker T. Washington at the White House for lunch, "Pitchfork" Ben Tillman, the senator from Mississippi, had said, "Washington is a good man, but his going to the White House means we're going to have to lynch a few more nigras to keep 'em in their place." Now they were going to have to lynch Jack Johnson to keep him in his.

And so, what man couldn't do, the government now attempted to do: get Jack Johnson. Declaring that Independence Day had been dishonored and disgraced by a brutal prizefight and that the moral sense of the nation had been outraged, state-after-state took the pathetic stand of banning the exhibition of moving pictures of the fight on the stated belief that their showing would incite further rioting. And, as if to complete their paroxysm of anger, they enacted legislation designed to forbid interracial fights and interracial marriages as well.

But the final blow to be struck against Johnson and his antisocial ways was the enforcement of a law passed in 1910—originally intended to prohibit the transportation of women across state lines for immoral purposes—called the Mann Act, or more familiarly, the White Slavery Act.

Casting about for a likely prospect to testify against Johnson, they found Belle Schreiber, a self-acknowledged prostitute whom Johnson had taken to California for companionship during his training for Jeffries. Based on her testimony, a jury deliberated less than two hours before finding Johnson guilty of transporting the unfair Belle across state lines for the stated purposes of "prostitution, debauchery, committing a crime against nature, and unlawful sexual intercourse," despite her admission that she had gone willingly. The heavyweight champion was sentenced to one year and one day in Joliet prison and a fine of $1,000.

Released to settle his affairs, Johnson jumped bail. Vowing never to return to the United States, he began a less-than-grand tour of Europe. There, a man without a country, *à la* Edward Everett Hale's famous literary figure, Johnson soon found himself out of money, out of contact, and out of sorts. He took anything in order to afford himself the manner to which he had become accustomed. He played the vaudeville circuit, wrestled a Russian, and fought Frank Moran in a lackluster 20-round fight in defense of his title. But when he was unable to collect his portion of the purse because of litigation, wanderlust set in, and he lit out again, this time for South America. And ultimately, Havana.

The "White Hope" movement, born out of the belief that, as novelist Rex Beach wrote, "the ignorant black man is no match for the educated white man," had begun to run its course. The anonymous mediocrities and yawning overdoses served up during the plague years in which Johnson held the title had risen and mercifully then vanished without a trace. Now one emerged called a

"White Hope" for the same reason an aging lady of the streets applies rouge to her cheeks—to gussy up his credentials.

Jess Willard was an ordinary fighter, at best. He had had a recent series of uneven performances, including no-decision fights against fellow "White Hopes" Luther McCarty, Carl Morris, and Arthur Pelky, beaten George Rodel and Bull Young—who died as a result of a ponderous right hand cantilevered by Willard—and lost to the "White Heavyweight champion" Gunboat Smith.

Still, this Leviathan of a man was awesome, not for his record so much as for his size. Standing six-foot-six-and-one-half inches tall and almost as much in circumference at 250-plus pounds, Willard was the sort of man one would expect to meet at the top of a beanstalk. Hailing from a place just about an axle-greasing away from Pottowatamie, Kansas, he became known as "the Pottowatamie Giant." And he became Jack Johnson's next opponent.

This addition to the long list of so-called standard-bearers for the white man's crusade was one of the rawest recruits ever pressed into action for Armageddon. Twenty-seven before he ever saw a boxing glove and 29 before his first professional fight—that a ten-round loss to one Louis Fink in some one-horse town named Sapulpa, Oklahoma—Willard was derisively referred to as "Cowboy Jess," a reference to his previous life, where he had been a cowpuncher, rodeo rider, and plains teamster.

The year after he started, 1912, he determined on a course for himself—and, unbeknownst to him, the white race—when he visited Professor O'Connell's gym in Chicago "to take a gander" at Jack Johnson, then in training for a bout with Fireman Jim Flynn, a fight he would win easily in nine rounds. After Johnson had done some pulling of chest weights, he looked around and said, "Anybody heah want to do a little boxing?" Nobody responded to his call to arms and Johnson went over to where the big cowboy was standing. "Come on." "No," Willard replied, "I'd better not." Johnson tried to coax him. "Don't be afraid," he laughed, "I never hurt a green boy." "It isn't that," responded to Willard. "I mean to fight you someday, and I'd rather wait until I meet you in the ring." The flustered Johnson just looked the big kid over and then grinned, saying, "Say, if these White Hopes keep gettin' bigger I'll have to buy some stilts."

Willard watched Johnson work, knowing in his heart, as he put it, he "could whip him. He had cleverness, all right enough, but the whites of his eyes weren't clear. His left hand was fast as a flash, but a roll of fat dropped over his belt." Willard went home determined he could beat the man who had mastered all his white masters. And every time Willard read "about Johnson tucking away wine," he'd figure, "just one round less."

Finally that time came, not so much because Willard had earned it but because Johnson figured he was just another White Hope. And because promoter Jack Curley had promised he would pose "no threat." Curley also made other promises to induce Johnson into a Havana ring in defense of his championship, some he could keep and some he was in no position to keep. But Curley really didn't care; he was merely indulging in a promoter's perogative, issuing illusory promissory notes in search of an event. He promised Johnson $35,000 as well as something about getting him a pardon from the United States government.

Johnson bought all of it, lock, stock, and pardon, and put his title on the line for the sixth time against this enormous but clumsy fighter, whom he thought so little of he barely trained.

Johnson entered the ring first, under a hot, blistering Havana sun blazing down on Havana's Oriental Park. It was apparent to all that he was out of shape. Not only was he no longer lean, but the 37-going-on-42-year-old champion was no longer the man-eater he once had been, mentally wearied from his travails with the law, and age and inactivity having taken a greater toll than any opponent ever had.

Promised first by Curley that his money would be forthcoming at the prefight weigh-in—which took place in the ring immediately before the fight—and then amended by Curley to read that it would be delivered to his wife, seated ringside, Johnson reluctantly went on to the fight. The bell sounded and Willard came out cautiously, throwing the first punch, a long left that penetrated Johnson's defenses, the first time any opponent had ever dared lead—or worse, land—on the great Jack Johnson. It was a portent of things to come.

As the bout wore on under the 103-degree-and-rising heat, Willard seemed to get stronger. And Johnson weaker. The enormous but clumsy opponent standing in front of Johnson continued to bear in on the champion, using his long, 83-inch reach to get through what had heretofore been Johnson's proudest possession, his defense. By the end of the tenth round Willard threw his long arm avuncularly around Johnson's shoulders, now sure that he couldn't be hurt and that the fight and the crown would ultimately be his.

As round after round passed, the sand began running out of Johnson's heavyweight hourglass. By the twenty-second, with Willard still as strong as he was in Round 1 and his wife still indicating Curley had not as yet made his promised visitation, Johnson sent one of his cornermen to "fetch Curley" and get his money. Then, he returned to the action at hand, action that saw Willard continue to press forward, continue to take Johnson's best, and continue to stalk the rapidly aging champion.

By the twenty-fifth Curley had finally made his way down from the box office to ringside, where he gave an envelope to Johnson's wife. After being informed personally by Curley between rounds 25 and 26 that she had finally received the promised money, Johnson told the promoter, "Tell my wife I'm tiring . . . I wish you'd see her out," so sure was Johnson now that he was on the last leg of his eight-year reign as heavyweight champion.

Then came the fateful twenty-sixth. It started like most other rounds, with Willard swinging his pole-axe right. Johnson, feeling his strength ebbing, tried a last-ditch effort to dislodge his great bull of an opponent. After blocking Willard's right, he unleashed a fusillade of punches—a left, a right, another left and right, and still another series of lefts and rights—all driving Willard across the ring into Johnson's corner. Willard held up under the punishment, finishing the exchange in better shape than the now-exhausted Johnson, spent from his efforts. Willard surmised that the offensive outburst was the last, spasmodic gasp by an expiring champ, and, moving back toward the center of the ring, threw a powerful left to the body, followed by an overhand right with all of his 260 pounds behind the blow. Johnson tried to grab Willard to stay his fall, then slowly slipped beneath his bulk, falling full-length to the floor, his arms over his eyes, shading himself from the noonday sun, almost by instinct. Referee Jack Welsh tolled off the fateful "ten" and raised a white arm in victory.

The longest heavyweight title bout in Marquess of Queensberry history was over—along with dreaded reign of Jack Johnson. Almost as soon as Johnson was hauled erect by his cornermen, he mumbled between puffed lips, "It was a clean knockout and the best man won. It was not a matter of luck. I have no kick coming."

Within months, however, this spitfire would burn up with spite, and through the spontaneous combustion of pure fury and shame ignite into a "confession," one he wrote and sold to Nat Fleischer of *The Ring* magazine. He claimed that, as part of a prearranged agreement, he had agreed to lose between the tenth and twentieth rounds, but because of Willard's "poor performance" had had to wait until the twenty-sixth. It was a sad postscript to the shame of a man who had let his inner anger and arrogance consume him, but who was in the eyes of many the greatest heavyweight champion of all time.

Regardless of how he rationalized his loss, he had lost. That was all that mattered. He was now the ex-champion. The "Dark Ages" of boxing were over, at least in the minds of white America. Little did they know boxing was now on the threshold of something far greater: the "Golden Age of Boxing."

100 Years of Boxing, 1982

Jack Dempsey and Boxing's Golden Age

With the end of World War I and the promised millennium of world peace still unfulfilled, disenchanted Americans began to feel that their privations and principles had failed to gain them anything. They turned from the rigors of problem solving to the rituals of pleasure seeking, embracing, in their free-wheeling mood, any excitement and escapism they could find. Heading the gigantic menu of available diversions was the sport of boxing.

With the title safely tucked under his enormous arm, Jess Willard joined a Wild West show and went on a triumphant tour, luxuriating in his newfound celebrity status. With the crown all but invisible, boxing fans, who had thirsted for action during all those years Jack Johnson was a fugitive from American justice—and American rings—now began clamoring for a title bout.

But the list of legitimate challengers for Willard's crown numbered only four: Fred Fulton, an awkward, six-foot-four-and-one-half inches former plasterer from Minneapolis who had boxed an exhibition against Willard two years before; Jack Dillon, a five-foot, seven-inch battler who weighed but 158 pounds and regularly fought middleweights, although he had knocked out enough heavier men to be known as "Jack the Giant Killer": Sam Langford, the Boston Tar Baby, who had repeatedly challenged Johnson, but who had been sidestepped and was now long in the tooth and coming off a loss to Gunboat Smith; and Frank Moran, a redheaded ex-sailor who lived the life of a playboy, regularly squiring around such leading ladies as Pearl White of *Perils of Pauline* fame. Of the four, Willard immediately dismissed Dillon, invoked the "color line" against Langford, and opted for Moran, who had lost to Johnson two years before.

The fight between Willard and Moran—held at New York's Madison Square Garden under the auspices of Tex Rickard on the night of March 25, 1916—was noteworthy only from the standpoint that it went the full ten rounds to a "no decision" with only one punch of any consequence, a vicious left to the head by Willard in the seventh round. Moran's vaunted "Mary Ann" haymaker was strangely quiescent. And so was the packed house.

It was obvious that they would have to look to other divisions for excitement—and they found it in the lightweight division where Benny Leonard reigned supreme. Called "the White Hope of the Orthodox" by resident boxing wit Heywood Hale Broun, Leonard was a ring scientist, a classicist, whose perfection in offense and mastery in defense were epitomized by his smooth style and his smooth looks—unruffled hair, perfect complexion, and unmarked features. The darling of the Lower East Side, he single-handedly brought boxing back to New York. They also found it in the welterweight division, where Ted "Kid" Lewis and Jack Britton ruled the roost, exchanging wins and the title in alternate years like a loose electrical connection. But the fans found neither the excitement they sought in the heavyweight division, nor in Jess Willard, at best, a transitional character in the history of boxing.

There were no other bonafide challengers on the heavyweight horizon after Willard disposed of Moran. But just below the horizon and rising like the morning sun was a man named William Harrison Dempsey. Fighting under the name Jack Dempsey—taken from the former middleweight champion Jack Dempsey, the "Nonpareil"—he would focus the nation's attention on the sport of boxing and give color to the Twenties and a name, the Golden Age of Sports.

Dempsey's appearance heralded the heroic era of American sports. In an age soon to be surfeited with sports giants, Jack Dempsey stood taller than most and would receive more adulation from press and public alike than all the other famous names of that Golden Age of Sports, combined. He was, to quote one writer, "Red Grange, Babe Ruth, Al Jolson, Paavo Nurmi, and Man o' War rolled into one." His name became synonymous with the sport of boxing. To people who had never seen a boxing match, he was the only name. Dempsey was half-man, half-myth. The question was: Which half was myth?

Born in the tiny mining town of Manassa, Colorado, and bred in the hobo camps of the West, this man who embodied the tough, individualistic spirit in America at the turn of the century was destined to become a fighter—and a great one—that is, if a mother's dreams are ever fulfilled. For his mother, having bought a biography of John L. Sullivan from a door-to-door salesman soon after Dempsey's birth in 1895, took to reading it aloud to her babe-in-arms and felt it held the promise of the good life for her son. She told him, "I want you to be the next John L."

Given his destiny by his mother and his nickname, "the Manassa Mauler," from the town he was born in by Damon Runyon, Dempsey was soon, like the rest of America, on the move, hungering for adventure and advancement, the boom town he was born in becoming a ghost town with the collapse of the silver market the year after his birth.

By the age of 15, Dempsey had left school. Using his hands, which would eventually become famous as the tools of another trade, he found work in one of the many silver mines which pockmarked the topography of the state. There, like Sullivan before him, he was tormented by one of his co-workers, the camp bully, who threw dirt in his face. Dempsey answered in the only manner he could, with his fists, ending the bully's taunts and his mining career with one swing.

Taking the name "Kid Blackie," testimony to his penetratingly dark features, he next found work in neighboring miners' saloons, where, in the style of the man his mother had fashioned him after, John L. Sullivan, he challenged any and all comers—for a price.

Shortly thereafter, when his brother Bernie, fighting under the name Jack Dempsey, suddenly pulled out of a fight in the wonderfully named town of Cripple Creek, Colorado, Kid Blackie filled in for him. Whether it was altitude or the prospect of going up against a tough 200-pounder named George Copelin that caused brother Bernie to excuse himself from the program is unknown; but whatever the reason, the younger Dempsey borrowed the name, won the fight, and thereafter continued as *the* Jack Dempsey.

But being Jack Dempsey was no more an "open sesame" to success than being Kid Blackie. The fights did not come and Dempsey once again struck out for new worlds—not to conquer, merely to survive in. It was while he was working in the Oakland shipyards that fate stepped in. More accurately, Jack stepped in and fate intervened. For one afternoon Jack chanced upon a saloon fight in which one little fellow was being beset by two strapping bruisers. Jack went to the aid of the beleaguered bar patron, downing the two ruffians with two well-directed blows. The man he had saved from a beating was little Jack Kearns, subsequently called "Doc" by Dempsey, as in "Ask Kearns, he's the doctor." Kearns offered him a partnership in the ring and, after some consideration, Dempsey accepted. From that point on, the boy-man who had ridden the rails and lived in the hobo camps of the West had found both a future, and a manager.

Together, this tandem would blaze a searing path across the West, stepping over the prone bodies of heavyweights as they made their way up to the ladder to greatness. Starting with Dempsey's very first recorded flight, against One-Punch Hancock in Salt Lake City—whom he prophetically dispatched with his very first left hook—through his first four years in boxing (three with Kearns), Dempsey scored more first-round knockouts than any fighter in history, twenty-six.

Dempsey left behind him a trail of broken bodies and broken dreams, all leading to the championship as sure as Hansel and Gretel's breadcrumbs had led them. He had dispatched Fred Fulton in just eighteen seconds in July 1918, and then, incredibly, bettered that mark with a fourteen-second knockout of former "White Hope" claimant Carl Morris five months later.

But the record was only part of the Dempsey picture; the rest was style and looks. Both were those of a warrior. Approaching his opponent with his teeth bared, bobbing and weaving to make his swarthy head with the perpetual five o'clock shadow harder to hit, his black eyes flashing and his blue-black hair flying, Dempsey more often than not combined his amazing hand speed and lethal left with an anything-goes mentality bred of necessity in the mining camps. Every bout was a war with no prisoners, no survivors. Later admitting that "three-minute rounds with gloves on and a referee is not real fighting," Dempsey delivered his own definition of survival any way he could—low, after the bell, behind the head, while a man was down. "Hell," he said, "it's a case of protect yourself at all times." But he didn't have to, his opponents did.

This warrior, who took on the look of an avenging angel of death, now stood on the threshold of boxing's biggest prize. His talents and his record, together with fast-talking Kearns's publicity campaign, made him the only challenger to the man, who stood between them and fame and fortune, Jess Willard. Willard and promoter Tex Rickard, that is.

Kearns had long harbored a grudge against Rickard for what he considered his high-handed acts in "stealing" a promising fighter from him, Australian middleweight champion Les Darcy. Even though the man he contemptuously called "Rube" had merely one-upped him, Kearns patiently awaited the opportunity to get his harpoon into Rickard. Now the time had come.

Rickard had signed Willard for a guaranteed $100,000 to defend his crown against *any* warm body the promoter could produce. There was none warmer than Dempsey. Rickard knew it. Kearns knew it. And each one knew the other knew it.

But Kearns played his hand carefully, making noises to the effect that his tiger would fight for nothing, or just expense money. "Just get me Willard!" he shouted. And so, without bothering to reduce Kearns's pleas and "please" to writing, Rickard announced the match. The next day Kearns sprung the trap: "Okay, sucker, now you can pay me fifty thousand dollars." The matter went to arbitration and, although a group of newsmen ultimately decided on a guarantee of $27,500 for Dempsey, both men thereafter were to swear less by each other than at each other.

Nevertheless, Rickard had his bout and Dempsey had his chance. Both were to make the most of it.

The fight was set for July 4, 1919, the first major postwar sporting event. The site was Toledo, Ohio, near as Tex Rickard put it, "the center of population," which was one of his underlying principles of promotion.

The Dempsey-Willard bout generated more interest than any fight since Rickard's previous outdoor promotion, the Jeffries-Johnson match nine years before to the day. Buoyed by the postwar economy and the close proximity of Toledo to the major population centers of the East and Midwest, all linked to Toledo by the network of railroads that honeycombed the area, Rickard foresaw his first million-dollar gate. To house the expected throng, he commissioned what one reporter called, "the most remarkable structure of wood ever erected for a sporting event," an eighty-thousand-seat stadium, with room for another twenty thousand standees. The giant stadium, which made the Reno bowl look like a teacup by comparison, was built from more than one-and-three-quarter million feet of lumber at a cost of $100,000. It stood proudly just outside the city limits on the shores of Maumee Bay.

However, the million-dollar gate never materialized. The railroads, which had been "Hooverized" during the war, had not yet been returned to private hands, and accommodations, especially Pullmans, were in short supply. Those who made it to Toledo were gouged by local merchants. For thousands of others, there was literally no room at the inn. Coupled with these problems was the release which came from Rickard's press agent stating that "seats were going fast," an old carny come-on that backfired and kept many hopefuls away.

As the day of the fight approached, everything was in a state of confusion—especially the concessions. Rickard had sold these profitable ancillary sidelines to "Professor" Billy McCarney, who, in turn, farmed out peanuts, opera glasses, cigarettes, candy, cushions, chewing gum, and condiments to willing sub-concessionaires. Through some administrative oversight, he assigned the lemonade franchise to two different vendors. When confronted with the seeming duplication, he bulled through by telling them, "Look, I sold you the *pink* lemonade concession, and I distinctly remember tell you that you were buying the rights to the *yellow* lemonade."

Battling Nelson arrived, complete with ghostwriter, to theoretically cover the fight for the Chicago *Daily News*. Seeking respite from the sweltering 100-degree heat, clad only in his underwear, he took a running dive into a mirage that resembled a swimming pool. Unfortunately, Nelson, in his overheated state of mind, had mistaken the pink lemonade tank for the swimming oasis of his dreams. Upon hearing about Nelson's "tank job," Rickard paid the pink lemonade concessionaire to dump the contaminated contents of his vat into Maumee Bay. But the concessionaire, already the brunt of one double cross, pulled one himself and doled out the pink eau de Battling Nelson, doubling his profits for the afternoon.

Unfortunately, he was one of the few who made a profit, as the ice cream vendor's stock melted, the sandwich concessionaire's inventory fell apart, and the peanut purveyor's proud possessions became worthless in the hopeless heat, which soared to 112 degrees the day before the fight.

Willard, sitting in his training quarters, thought the fight was a joke. "I outweigh him by seventy pounds," Willard told the press, crowded around him awaiting his thoughts. "He'll come tearing into me ... I'll have my left out ... and then I'll hit him with a right uppercut. That'll be the end."

Others, too, considered Willard a sure winner. Not only had the gamblers installed him as the favorite, but Tex Rickard was worried. He was worried enough to seek out Dempsey in his dressing room before the fight in order to express his misgivings. "Jack, this Willard's a big and tough fighter. He just might kill you. Remember what he did with a single punch of his to Bull Young." Dempsey, his facial features showing the steely concentration before a fight he was famous for, grunted in Rickard's direction. Tex went on, giving Dempsey an "out" just in case the worst happened. "If he hits you a good shot and hurts you, go down and stay down before he kills you. I don't want you killed. That's my advice." And with that Rickard turned and, readjusting his straw boater, made his way back into the arena for the expected carnage.

But it wasn't Dempsey's carnage they were about to witness; it was, instead, Willard's. As the two fighters made their respective ways into the ring—Willard bare-chested and Dempsey clad in a gray cardigan sweater—the disparity in their sizes became all too apparent. Willard looked even larger than his announced six-foot, six-inch and 245 pounds because of a roll of surplus flab which girdled his middle; Dempsey looked smaller than his six-foot, one-inch and 180 pounds, even swathed in a sweater.

At the sound of the bell, a tinny sound barely audible above the roar of the anticipatory crowd, the two fighters advanced from their corners warily, neither throwing a punch. Willard kept moving his hands, just as he had in the Johnson fight, ready to meet the on-rushing Dempsey. Dempsey, for his part, merely circled the oxlike

Willard, bobbing and weaving like a tiger as he did, sizing up his opponent, a task that consumed an entire thirty seconds due to Willard's enormity. Finally, exasperated because Dempsey had not come to him as he had planned, Willard reached out his telephone-poll left to find the smaller man, made all the smaller by his crouch.

That one move decided the fight, for as Willard reached in, Dempsey uncoiled from his crouch and, ducking under Willard's left, threw a right to the body and a wicked left to Willard's cheek, caving in the champion's cheekbone and sending him reeling. Greyhound lean and Dempsey mean, the challenger was now on him in a flash, battering the broken hulk before him. Willard sagged against the ropes, down. He staggered to his feet only to find Dempsey, who had hovered above him ignoring all niceties, concerned only with getting at the champion. Dempsey was on him, beating him relentlessly about the face and body. Again Willard fell heavily. And again he struggled upright. With metronomic repetition the scene was completed, resembling less a boxing match than an exhibition of a toy recently introduced in the United States, the yo-yo. Finally, Dempsey dropped Willard in his corner, his hands hanging on the ropes, his back resting on the turnbuckle as the referee counted away. This time he made no effort to arise, this time he stayed down.

The fight was over. Another first-round knockout for Dempsey. Or so it seemed. There, in the middle of the ring, was little Doc Kearns jumping up and down. On one side Dempsey, the apparent victor, was climbing through the ropes, his sweater thrown over his shoulders, heading for the dressing room. But, wait a minute! As the listless hulk of a man who had entered the ring only three minutes before as the champion was placed gingerly on his stool, the officials huddled on one side of the ring. One of them had detected what sounded like the bell during the last count, drowned out by the roar of the crowd. Now referee Ollie Pickard was trying to get Dempsey's attention, get him back in the ring, aided by Kearns, who was waving his cap madly.

And, unbelievably, there would be a second and a third round of the fight, anticlimactic and unnecessary, with Willard, his jaw broken in two places, his rib cage smashed, four teeth missing, one eye closed, his nose splayed all over his face and his face cut, out to do battle again. But the next six minutes were merely pro forma, the outcome already having been decided by Dempsey's first punch. When, at the end of the third, the half-butchered ox once known as Willard moaned through a clenched jaw that would not open that he was through, the result became official: Jack Dempsey had won the heavyweight championship of the world. And Jess Willard, $100,000 richer, sat in his corner sobbing, "I have a farm in Kansas and a hundred thousand dollars . . . I have a farm in Kansas and a hundred thousand dollars . . ."

Later, in his dressing room, Dempsey would add an ironic post-script to the first-round "mux-ip." "Funny thing about this fight," the new champion said, as he rubbed his wire-stubbled jaw reflectively, "was that Doc claimed he had bet ten thousand dollars to one hundred thousand that I'd knock out Willard in the first round. And that's just what I did. The referee had raised my right hand awarding me the fight. Willard's head was hanging over the lower rope. He was practically unconscious from the several knockdowns. I left the ring. The fight was over . . . or it should have been. I must have been twenty-five yards from the ring when they called me back. That was the biggest shock I ever got . . . when I was told the bell had run three seconds too soon . . . suppose it had? My hand had been raised and I had been given the fight by the referee."

It was just the sort of incident to usher in the craziest, zaniest era ever known in sports, the era of giants, "the Golden Age of Sports," as Paul Gallico called it. And Jack Dempsey was the first of a pantheon of greats who would reflect a grateful nation's idolatry and praise—soon to be joined by the likes of Babe Ruth, Red Grange, Bill Tilden, Bobby Jones, and others during those Roaring Twenties. But, as the Golden Age began, Jack Dempsey stood alone.

Hit the Sign and Win a Free Suit of Clothes from Harry Finklestein, 1978

The Reign of Joe Louis,
the Brown Bomber

Joe Louis's exploits are accorded no special place of prominence in *The Ring Record Book*. His seventy bouts are sandwiched between the records of James J. Braddock, the man he succeeded, and Ezzard Charles, the fighter who won the crown in a bout with the "Brown Bomber" the year after Louis had returned from an announced retirement.

Both Braddock and Charles had more professional engagements, as did Johnson, Dempsey, Tunney, and Baer. And there have been men who had more KOs, Carnera and Charles; a higher percentage of knockouts, Marciano and Foreman; or fought longer, Fitzsimmons, Charles, and Walcott. Even Tommy Burns and Larry Holmes have more consecutive knockouts in defense of their titles than Louis. But no heavyweight champion so captured the fancy of the public, fan and nonfan alike, as the smooth, deadly puncher who, at his peak, represented the epitome of pugilistic efficiency. And no man was so admired and revered as this son of an Alabama sharecropper who carried his crown with dignity and carried the hopes of millions on his shoulders.

But the measure of the man was not merely found inside the ring. For to call Joe Louis just a fighter is to not understand the times. Or the man. For here was a man who held his emotions like gold in a fist, his shyness disciplined into courtesy, his quietness ripened into a firm, quiet dignity. He used his words, like his body, as the tender of a flame, which indeed he was for millions of blacks.

But still, for someone who watched his words as though they were hot coals, Joe Louis is remembered for saying a surprising number of things, and saying them in a way we all wish we had. There was his evaluation of his country's chances in the global confrontation with the Axis powers: "We'll win 'cause we're on God's side." There was his enunciation of his opponent's chances in the second Conn fight: "He can run, but he can't hide." And then there was his ability to say what he meant without recourse to subtlety or misdirection, as witnessed by his short dialogue with Muhammad Ali:

ALI: Joe, you really think you coulda whupped me?

LOUIS: When I had the title I went on what they called the Bum-of-the-Month tour.

ALI (shrilly): Ya mean I'm a bum?

LOUIS, unflappable: You woulda been on the tour.

It was no coincidence that the very year Joe Louis first burst upon the fistic scene was not only one of the worst in boxing's long tatterdemalion history, but also, not incidentally, the year when the ban on interstate trafficking of boxing movies, in force since Jack Johnson had humiliated Jim Jeffries and whites everywhere, was repealed. Although he didn't know it then, Joe Louis was in the enviable position of being the right man in the right place at the right time to change not only the history of boxing, but also the sociological history of the world.

Louis emerged from the amateur ranks the winner of fifty of fifty-four fights, with forty three knockouts. Ironically, he was denied the national light heavyweight title in his first try, losing to a Notre Dame football player named Max Marek in the finals of the National AAU. On the strength of his victory Marek obtained a number of celebrity spots on radio before some of Louis's big bouts. He had the good sense, however, not to try to repeat his victory in the pros. In 1934, Louis finally won the crown before turning professional at the ripe old age of 21.

His first professional fight came against Jack Kracken, a name etched in immortality for having been Louis's first opponent, but not one necessarily etched for very long on the night of July 4, 1934, when he lasted just one minute and thirty-plus seconds before Louis felled him.

Louis continued to campaign in and around Chicago, fighting at Beacon's Casino, Marigold Gardens, and Chicago Stadium, against the likes of Willie Davis, Larry Odell, Jack Kranz, Buck Everett, and Adolph Wiater as barrier after barrier against mixed matches fell, most of them vestiges of the riot which followed the unpopular decision in the Young Jack Thompson-Jackie Fields fight some five years earlier. But Louis's popularity and powerful fists—not to mention the sweet sound of the turnstile clicking away—served to convince the powers-that-were that good business far outweighed bad feelings.

By the end of his first year of action, Louis was beating men who had dotted *The Ring's* top-ten heavyweight list the previous year—Stanley Poreda and Charley Massara—and one who was on the top-ten list that year, Lee Ramage. Suddenly, the name Joe Louis was news; and news travels fast. Especially to Mike Jacobs.

Mrs. William Randolph Hearst's pet charity was the Free Milk Fund. Dedicated to providing "helpless infants" with the primary necessity of life, it was underwritten by Hearst's New York *American* and took its own fund-raising nourishment from an annual boxing bout. Starting with a 1922 match between Harry Greb and

Tommy Gibbons—which drew $118,000, with $75,999 of the proceeds going to the Milk Fund—the annual fight benefited the charity to the tune of $1 million over the next twelve years.

By 1934 even the "helpless infants" were caught in the crossfire of one of boxing's perennial wars. The glaring deficiencies of Jimmy Johnston, the head of Madison Square Garden boxing, as a promoter as well as his devious dealings with boxers came under the scrutiny of several newspaper columnists. But none were more savage than Bill Farnsworth and Damon Runyon of Hearst's *Journal-American*, the unofficial matchmakers for the Milk Fund boxing shows. Their attacks brought a swift reprisal; but not from Johnston. The counterattack came instead from Colonel John Reed Kilpatrick, the president of Madison Square Garden. He announced that the rental for the next Milk Fund boxing show would be increased.

Farnsworth and Runyon, joined in their crusade by sports editor Ed Frayne, not only wrote righteously that the Garden was depriving "helpless infants" of milk, but they sought out ticket-broker Mike Jacobs to join them in promoting the next Milk Fund show. Together they formed 20th Century Sporting Club.

And so on January 24, 1934, Mike Jacobs, long a behind-the-scenes promoter, came out of the closet to promote the thirteenth annual Milk Fund fight, an over-the-weight match between lightweight champion Barney Ross and the Fargo Express, Billy Petrolle, at the old New York Coliseum in the Bronx. Fifteen thousand crowded into the Coliseum—another 10,000 were turned away—as Jacobs's 20th Century Sporting Club answered its first bell.

Better known as "Uncle Mike," Michael Strauss Jacobs was one of the smartest men ever to pull strings in the boxing game. The son of an immigrant who hustled other immigrants right off the boat and procured jobs for them for a fee, he had himself become a hustler in the best traditions of New York's West Side. He started on the piers, first selling newspapers, then souvenirs, and then graduating to the concessions on pleasure cruises. Also known as "Steamboat Mike," he parlayed one small concession into a fleet of seven boats running to and from two amusement parks he also owned. That way, Jacobs got his customers coming and going.

But building a fleet of pleasure boats was not Jacobs's ticket of admission into the boxing arena. As a hustling young man, he had supplemented his entrepreneurial education by working for David Belasco as office boy and shill, rounding up entire cheering sections to applaud and laugh enthusiastically in the right places, thus turning potential box-office flops into Broadway hits.

From there it was just a short step to becoming a ticket broker, scalping tickets for shows, sporting events, and just about anything else that came down the Great White Way. One of those who did was Tex Rickard, scrounging for backing just before the Dempsey-Carpentier fight. From that day on, Jacobs served as the behind-the-scenes consultant to Rickard, advising him on the salability of matches. Ticket brokering and working with Rickard were fine training for the sometimes weird machinations that go on in the fight business. Jacobs was easily a match for all of it. In his early sixties he was a man with perpetual squint and false choppers that seemed to have a life of their own. He'd be saying something but the teeth would seem to be following an entirely different script. In his negotiations, Jacobs also had a lawyer, though he scarcely needed one. His name was Sol Straus, and his caper was bad hearing. He always showed up with an elaborately wired earpiece which he proceeded to disconnect whenever he got into a conversation. It was a wonder anything ever got done between the teeth and the earpiece.

But it did. For Mike Jacobs worked almost entirely off the seat of his pants, with a small staff that included a P.R. man, a matchmaker, an errand boy or two, and two women who kept the books, one of whom was his niece, for safety reasons.

He could think five times faster than the normal person and at least twenty-five times faster than the average fight manager. Once a reporter asked him why he had a "nothing" bout going that wouldn't draw beans to his 20th Century Sporting Club operation at the old Hippodrome Theatre where Mike ran shows every week as a counter-attraction to those at the Garden. "Listen, kid," he replied. "When the taxman comes around at the end of the year, he doesn't ask you how much you made on one show on a Wednesday night in October. He wants to know how much you made during the whole damn year."

While in Miami promoting the Barney Ross-Frankie Klick junior welterweight title fight in January 1935, one of Jacobs's many contacts informed him of a black heavyweight fighting out of Detroit who deserved his attention. Jacobs immediately sent his emissaries to Pittsburgh where the new phenom was to make his second start inside of a week. When they returned, they convinced Jacobs that the black heavyweight, known then as Joe Louis—the result of a ring announcer forgetting to mention his last name, Barrow—was all that he was cracked up to be. And more.

That was all Jacobs had to hear. Within a month he negotiated a contract with Louis's managers, John Roxborough and Julian Black, which gave 20th Century Sporting Club exclusive promotional rights for all future bouts involving the Brown Bomber.

In order to show off his new attraction, Jacobs took a press party of twenty-five New York newsmen out to Detroit to see Louis fight Natie Brown in March 1935. Their glowing reports about this unbeatable man from the midwest, then cutting down everything before him like a harvesting scythe, created a public demand for a look-see at the new heavyweight hope. Jacobs brought him back to New York to face the former heavyweight champion, Primo Carnera, who since his public beheading by Baer had won four bouts, including KOs over former challenger Vittorio Campolo and currently ranked Ray Impellitiere. The third-rated heavyweight, he would serve as an appropriate opponent for the so-called "Black Menace."

Jacobs's choice of Carnera was a master stroke. It would be a good little man making his lasting reputation beating a bigger man and upsetting the old bromide that holds a good big man will always beat a good little man. First there was David who came in as the decided underdog for his battle with Goliath. Then there was Dempsey, who stepped over the several times prone body of Willard to fistic immortality. And now it was to be Joe Louis who would give away some six inches and sixty pounds.

Against a backdrop of the Italian-Ethiopian war and ring announcer Harry Balough's prefight warning to the 60,000 fans jam-packed into Yankee Stadium to "please observe fair play," Joe Louis turned the crowd of curious into a crowd of believers. For on that night they saw the closest thing to fighting perfection ever unleashed in the ring.

In the first round Louis watched as Carnera pecked out his rigid left, regarding the stiff treelike jabs with the mild dismay of a man annoyed by an errant fly. Then, as Carnera assayed a left to Lou's ribs, Louis momentarily halted his shuffling forward movement to counter with a right to the jaw, turning the gargantuan's picket-smile into a bloody mess with one punch. Carnera was never in the fight after that, Louis stalking him, patiently waiting his chance. In the sixth, Carnera, stung by Louis's continual blows to the body, tried a desperate right-hand swing for Louis's jaw that missed. Louis caught the stationary target in front of him with a left that jarred Carnera. A right dumped the giant in a head-first heap in the middle of the ring. Up at the count of four, the rubber-legged Carnera, looking like a man peering out from behind a tree, stood defenseless in front of Louis, who leaped in, raining blows to the almost pathetic-looking ex-champion's head. Finally, another right to the head decked Carnera again. Up once more at four, Carnera turned to face Louis, and under another fusillade of blows went down in sections. The fight was over. Mike Jacobs's protégé had taken his first step to the crown.

But Louis's victory was not only a victory for Jacobs, it was a victory for blacks. For Jack Johnson's cocky superiority in the ring and outrageous behavior outside had left a legacy which had hurt blacks in general, and black fighters in particular. From Johnson to Louis, twenty-two long years, no black fighter had been considered as a contender for the heavyweight title. Now there was one.

It was almost as if blacks had been sitting at their radios saying to themselves, "We who are about to hear a miracle . . ." Maya Angelou, in her novel *I Know Why the Caged Bird Sings*, remembers what that evening meant: "'(Carnera's) got Louis against the ropes' said the announcer . . . 'And it looks like Louis is going down.' My people groaned. It was our people failing. It was another lynching, yet another black man hanging on a tree. . . . It was hounds on the trail of a man running through slimy swamps. . . . It was a white woman slapping her maid for being forgetful. . . . We didn't breathe; we didn't hope; we waited. 'He's off the ropes, Ladies and Gentlemen! shouted the announcer. . . . Carnera is on the canvas. . . .' A black boy. Some black mother's son. He was the strongest man in the world."

But before Louis could lay claim to being the "strongest man in the world," he would have to hurdle some other obstacles, ones hand-picked by Jacobs to pave his way to his ultimate destination: the heavyweight championship.

The next stepping stone served up to Louis by Jacobs was recently defrocked heavyweight champion Max Baer losing his title just three months earlier to Jimmy Braddock. The casting was perfect—on the one hand the irrepressible whacko who trained on bleached blondes and beached bottles, the possessor of the "killer" punch and the iron chin, and on the other the man who was already being described by some as "the perfect fighting machine," and by others as everything from the Alabama Assassin to the Brown Bomber or any other alliterative name that worked. The promotion took, some 88,150 jamming Yankee Stadium to see this new superman of boxing. Thousands more were turned away as Mike Jacobs entered into the inner circle of promoters with his first million-dollar game, the sixth richest of all time.

Baer, though, wasn't filled with his usual braggadocio. In fact, if anything, he was filled with fear, as he was half-led, half-dragged up the aisle to the ring. Jack Dempsey, who was in Baer's corner, snarled in his ear, "Do you want me to knock you out in the corner? Or do you want Louis to do it in the ring?" Baer, unfortunately, opted for Louis. He might have had better luck with Dempsey.

Louis, who was so concerned about the fight he had gotten married that afternoon to Marva Trotter, bounded into the ring the 9–5 favorite. But in that first round there may have been several who had wished they had bet on Baer, as the former champion pinioned Louis in a corner and drilled home punch after punch in an attempt to end it early, almost as if he was fearful of returning to his corner and Dempsey.

By the second the spark was gone from Baer. His punches, what few there were, lacked firepower, and hope. As Louis continued to dig to the body with paralyzing blows, the disillusionment became total. By the third Baer was on the receiving end of a volley of right-hand smashes and sank to the floor for the first time since his match with Frankie Campbell. But this time he didn't spring up, but merely made his way up on unsteady pins as a series of vicious left hooks toppled him again to the canvas. At the count of four the bell rang and Dempsey could be seen dragging his charge to his stool, to be led to slaughter again after a minute's duration. The fourth and final round was more of the same as Louis continued his target practice. Finally, a right high to the temple crushed Baer to the ground, where he sat, first on his haunches, then on his knee, giving no indication he could arise before the fatal "ten." Later, when asked by reporters why he hadn't made an attempt to get up, Baer replied, "Sure I could've gotten up, but twenty bucks only entitles people to see a fight, not a murder."

Jacobs, now intent on using Louis's pulling power to stick his nose under the promotional tent that was New York boxing, next put him in against Paulino Uzcudun, the durable Basque who had been around, or so it seemed, for as long as the Pyrenees. In his eleven-year career, Uzcudun had been in against the best and had never been knocked down, much less out. For three rounds the expressionless Louis stalked his prey, hardly bothering to venture a punch. Then, in the fourth, Uzcudun peeked out from his gloves to find out what was going on. He found out. And quick. For the second the sturdy Basque showed even the smallest portion of his face, Louis let fly with a flattening right that lifted him off his feet and halfway through the ropes, driving two of Paulino's teeth right through his lips.

Now there seemed to be only one man between Louis and the championship: Max Schmeling. No one gave the former titleholder much of a chance, the bettors included, who made Schmeling a 10–1 underdog. But Max was an underdog with a plan.

He had been an onlooker at the Louis-Uzcudun fight, and after the fight had only smiled a Mona Lisa-like smile and muttered something that sounded like, "I zee zometings." Everyone in attendance laughed and joked about his English. It was to be no laughing matter for the Louis camp, though, because that "zometings" Schmeling had spotted was a fault line in the otherwise perfect fighting machine known as Joe Louis. Schmeling had spotted Louis making a questionable move, one that a young, inexperienced fighter might be prone to if he wasn't constantly warned about it. Schmeling had noticed that Louis dropped his left arm preparatory to delivering a hook. It was a sort of giveaway, like a pitcher shifting his feet before he delivered a curveball.

Another who had seen this defect was former heavyweight champion Jack Johnson, who went to Louis's training camp and offered up his services to Joe. But whether it was because it was Johnson doing the offering and Louis wanted nothing to do with this man his people called "ten miles of bad road," or because one of Johnson's demands was that he'd work with Louis only if Louis would fire his beloved trainer, Jack Blackburn, Johnson was sent on his way. And Louis went back to his training regimen, such as it was, his overconfidence showing itself in his spending more time on the golf course than he did in the sparring ring.

Louis wasn't the only one having trouble preparing for the upcoming fight. Mike Jacobs was also experiencing more than a few difficulties himself. For at that magic moment there was a groundswell of bitter resentment growing in the United States, and in New York in particular because of its large Jewish population, over the treatment of Jewish citizens by the Nazi government in Germany. The American Jewish community threatened to boycott the fight, and the organized opposition to Nazi Germany, directed as if by lightning conductor at the fight, threatened the advance-ticket sale, if not the fight itself. Added to everything else, a natural storm postponed the fight for a day.

Finally, the dual storms abated, the skies cleared, and the pickets left. The fight was on. Schmeling, determined to take advantage of the chink he had found in Louis's armament, came out with his own left arm stuck high in the air, his chin tucked deep into his left shoulder, his right eye exposed to Louis's rapierlike left jabs. In order to better deliver his right, he was prepared, as one of Schmeling's handlers told the press, "to lose" that eye if necessary.

By the end of the first round, that right eye was almost closed, so virulent was the assault on the optic by Louis. Its closing also signaled an unwarranted overconfidence in Louis, who, when he returned to his corner between rounds, told Blackburn that Schmeling would be easy; that he could take him out with a left hook any time he pleased. The ring-wise "Chappie" warned Louis that it was still a little early; to wait until the third or fourth round.

But Louis didn't listen. When, in the second, he initiated his first left hook, Schmeling came over with a smashing right to the chin. It dazed Louis, but he recovered and kept stalking Schmeling, all the while pecking away at his fast-closing eye. In the fourth

Louis once again started a left, and Schmeling, who had given up even the pretense of using his left, again came across with his own right, landing fully on Louis's jaw. Louis went down for a two-count, the first time in his brief career he had gained anything resembling familiarity with the canvas.

That was the fight right there. Schmeling went after him, the ring-wise veteran teaching the new kid on boxing's block a lesson. By the sixth he was administering such a beating that one of Louis's friends escorted Joe's mother out of the park so that she wouldn't have to witness any further battering of her boy.

Schmeling gave Louis a systematic battering for the remaining eight rounds of the fight, Louis finally being counted out at two minutes and twenty-nine seconds of the twelfth, his face at one with the resin. Carried back to his dressing room, Louis could only tell his mother, "The man just whupped me, that's all." The only humor Louis, or Jacobs for that matter, found in the fight was when one of Louis's handlers asked him the next day if he wanted to review movies of the fight. "No," he replied, "I saw the fight."

But the world of boxing goes on. And a 22-year-old kid with Joe Louis's obvious ability always gets a second chance. In fact, he got a year's worth of second chances as Mike Jacobs made him his personal reclamation project. He brought him back just two months after the Schmeling debacle to face another former heavyweight champion, Jack Sharkey. Louis made quick work of Sharkey, leaving him both prone and with a special niche in the boxing trivia hall of fame—the only man to face both Dempsey and Louis and be knocked out by both. Louis then ran through Al Ettore and Jorge Brescia before facing Eddie Simms in Cleveland. With the bout eighteen seconds old, Louis pulled the trigger on a devastating left hook. Simms went down and rolled over. Apparently listening to the count, he was up at eight. Instead of facing his opponent, Simms turned to referee Arthur Donovan. "Let's take a walk up to the roof," he said less than coherently. Ten minutes later, back in his dressing room, Simms was still incoherent.

The comeback was almost complete now, and aside from Schmeling, only one man remained who had even an outside shot at Braddock's title: Bob Pastor. Pastor's backers, a loosely formed group known as "the Joe Louis Detractors"—with Jimmy *Himself* Johnston, Madison Square Garden matchmaker, in the driver's seat—were formed with the sole purpose of discrediting Jacobs's attraction. And they almost did it with a fighter who was Bill Robinson's only peer when it came to running backward. For ten rounds, Pastor, who had placed $2,000 at the juicy odds of 3–1 on his being on his feet at the finishing bell, made sure of it by breaking all backward speed records. At the end of ten Pastor had his money and Louis had his win, as well as Jacobs's assurances that he would get him a title shot against James J. Braddock, who for two years had not even cared to risk his title against the heavy bag.

Not everyone thought so, especially not Max Schmeling, who had destroyed the Black Destroyer less than a year before. Now rated the logical contender in most quarters, including Madison Square Garden, Schmeling signed to fight Braddock for the title on June 3, 1937, at Madison Square Bowl in Long Island City. Tired of their bath in red ink, the directors of the Garden tried to protect their flanks by making Mike Jacobs a partner in the promotion, hoping not only that Jacobs's promotorial prowess would ensure success but also that his association with the Garden—no matter how tenuous—would assure them of future successes, most notably with the fighter under Jacobs's control, Joe Louis.

Jacobs, however, had plans of his own. He completely outflanked the Garden. Approaching Braddock's manager, Joe Gould, he offered him a best-of-all-worlds contract for a Braddock-Louis fight. Jacobs not only bettered the guarantee offered by the Garden, but offered Gould ten percent of all Louis's earnings as champion for ten years should Louis, in the words of ring announcer

Harry Balough, "emerge victorious." That was all Gould had to hear. He almost sprained his wrist reaching for a pen to sign the contract which called for Braddock to defend his title against Louis on June 22 in Chicago, sidestepping the Garden, Johnston, and Schmeling completely.

The Louis-Braddock fight found a home in Chicago's Comiskey Park, home of the White Sox. Only it wasn't much of a home for Braddock. Unafraid and carrying the grittiness that had made him champion, Braddock came out fighting, as he promised he would. With 45,000 fans cheering him on, Braddock hardly looked like the 1–3 underdog, as he landed a short right-hand uppercut that caught Louis as he came in. But the blow had little effect other than to knock the pins out from under Louis. Almost as soon as he had gone down, the challenger was up and began his relentless, un-emotional pursuit of Braddock, keeping his razor-sharp left in his face and following up with a variety of combinations—left and rights to the head, body punches heard at ringside—and quick one-twos.

When Louis returned to his corner, his trainer, Jack Blackburn, scolded him. "You should have stayed down for nine," Blackburn told him. "You can't get up fast enough those folks won't notice you was down."

The second was the beginning of the end as Louis had the champion reeling under the power of his blows, Braddock's eyes closed, his face ripped open. At the end of the seventh, Braddock's manager, Joe Gould, had had enough, even if Braddock hadn't, and told him he was going to tell the referee to stop it. "If you do," Braddock said through battered lips, "I'll never speak to you again as long as I live. If I'm going to lose it, I'll lose it on the deck." In the next round one right-hand punch, driven to the point of Braddock's jaw in much the manner a carpenter would hammer a nail ended it as the now-ex-champ toppled over in a pool of his own blood, counted out at 1:10 of the eighth round.

The Reign of Joe Louis, the Brown Bomber

Joe Louis was the heavyweight champion of the world, the first black to ascend that supposedly unassailable mountain since Jack Johnson had been deposed lo those twenty-two years before. And almost before the fatal "ten" had been tolled, thousands upon thousands of blacks were marching up and down Lenox Avenue in Harlem and U Street in Washington, and in hundreds of other cities across the nation, all sharing in the accomplishments of this young man from Detroit. Unlike the celebrations that took place after Johnson beat Jeffries, however, these were not riotous marches, they were merely celebrations, and an outlet for the deep personal satisfaction that was theirs after so many years of being society's invisible people. Now the heavyweight champion was indeed, as Maya Angelou had written, "A black mother's son . . . the strongest man in the world."

Part of the ritual of becoming the heavyweight champion is the promise to be a fighting champion. But although almost every champion since time immemorial had promised to be one, the promise normally turned out to be a vacant one as the title and the titlist went into hibernation almost immediately after winning. Joe Louis promised it; and he meant it. Two months after dethroning Braddock, he was back in the ring, fighting the scrappy Welshman, Tommy Farr. Despite injuring his hand, Louis decisioned Farr. He then went on to knock out a couple of journeymen, Natie Mann and Harry Thomas, in two more defenses of his title.

Now Louis, who after every fight had acted like a man possessed, telling everyone within earshot, "Bring on Max Schmeling. Bring him on. . . ," got his wish. His obsession would become a reality as Jacobs finally cashed in a due bill with Schmeling and gave him a shot at the title.

By this time Schmeling had become the more or less the official representative of the National Socialist, or Nazi, Party, whether he wanted to be or not. His victory over Louis in 1936 had been hailed as a victory for Aryan Germany. *Angriff*, the official party organ, heralded his accomplishment with the following political marzipan: "He succeeded against world opinion. And he says he would not have had the strength if he had not known what support he had in his Homeland. He was allowed to speak with the Fuehrer and his Ministers, and from that moment his will for victory was boundless." Forget that the same Nazi paper had derided Schmeling for not discharging his Jewish manager, Joe Jacobs, "in the interests of Germanhood," especially after Jacobs was seen giving the Nazi salute "with a smoking cigar between the fingers of his saluting hand," or that Schmeling refused to join the Nazi party. He was their hero, the man who would carry the banner of the master race into the ring.

Because most Americans viewed the contest as a battle between two political ideologies, Louis bore the colors of Americans of all colors. Franklin Roosevelt invited Louis to the White House and tenderly gripping his flexed muscle for conspiratorial news photographers said, "Joe, we're depending on those muscles for America."

Louis trained with a fierce intensity and a single-mindedness previously unseen in his normally placid makeup. When sportswriter Jimmy Cannon got him alone on the porch of the farmhouse up at his training camp the night before the fight, Louis merely said, "You make a pick?" Cannon answered, "Yes." Louis, a man of few words, answered Cannon's one in kind, "Knockout?" "Six rounds," Cannon responded. To which Louis held up one of his fingers and said, "No, one." Then as if to reinforce his prediction, he repeated. "It go one."

The next day, June 22, 1938, as more than 80,000 fans passed through the picket lines set up outside Yankee Stadium by the Anti-Nazi League, most carrying posters reading, "Oust Hitler's Agents and Spies" or, "Down with Hitler and Mussolini," Louis warmed up in his dressing room for thirty minutes instead of his normal ten, ignoring Chappie's advice to "Take it easy." He was in no mood, not after waiting for this moment for two years and three days.

Whatever Schmeling stood for, he didn't stand for long. Almost before the reverberating echoes of Harry Balough's prefight oratory had died down, Louis emerged from his corner to meet Schmeling more than halfway across the ring and within five seconds had landed a spearing left, the first of what ring mathematicians counted as fifty blows. Schmeling got in his first licks, an arching right to the jaw that landed. But this time, instead of reeling under its impact, Louis merely sneered and stepped in with his own right to the jaw, propelling Schmeling back into the ropes, his body half-turned. Louis leaped in and landed a thudding right to Schmeling's unprotected rib cage, causing the challenger to let out an audible shriek. Then came a bewildering succession of powerful rights and lefts to Schmeling's head as the German began to crumble, his face twisted into a grotesque mask. Suddenly Louis sent in a murderous right and Schmeling toppled, like a tree felled.

Somewhere between that first knockdown and the third knockdown, the radio broadcast of the fight back to Germany was mysteriously interrupted, courtesy of the propaganda officer personally assigned to the broadcast by Herr Doctor Goebbels. No one in Germany was to know the outcome, at least officially, until the papers black-bordered it the following morning.

But the millions of listeners surrounding their radios in America heard it loud and clear, the gravel voice of ringside commentator Clem McCarthy shouting into the mike, "A right and left to the head . . . A left to the jaw . . . A right to the head . . . And Donovan is watching carefully . . . Louis measures him . . . Right to the body, a left hook to the jaw . . . And Schmeling is down . . . The count is five . . . five . . . six . . . seven . . . eight . . . The men are in the ring . . . The fight is over on a technical knockout . . . Max Schmeling is beaten in one round . . ."

It was over in only two minutes and four seconds, but it was to be seven months before Louis climbed back into the ring, this time against light heavyweight king John Henry Lewis. Lewis had only recently been shorn of his crown by the New York State Athletic Commission for reasons known best to the commission. But Garden matchmaker Jimmy Johnston had gone to court to have Lewis's title reinstated. Johnston had made a deal with the commission: if they would allow Lewis to fight for the heavyweight crown, he would gracefully abdicate the light heavy title. And so, on January 25, 1939, John Henry Lewis went the way of Schmeling in one round. Not long thereafter he retired as undefeated light heavyweight champion, never to fight again. But the last laugh was on the commission; Lewis couldn't have fought again even if he wanted to. His vision was impaired, his career over. He had suffered the only knockout in his long career for a pay day. Knowing of his adversary's disability, Joe Louis followed Blackburn's advice. As a favor to a fellow champion, instead of carrying him and inflicting additional punishment to his already damaged eyes, the Brown Bomber dispatched him in less time than it takes to say John Henry Lewis.

Five months and two defenses later, Louis climbed into the ring with a contender who looked like he stepped right out of a Hans Christian Anderson story gone wrong: Two-Ton Tony Galento. Galento had the body of a butcher's block and the vocabulary of a barroom burgher, calling everybody he met a "bum" and promising to "moider" Louis.

Louis didn't know what to make of the man who had once wrestled an octopus for practice. Louis took more than mild umbrage at being called a "bum," complaining to Blackburn, "Why he say that 'bout me?" But Blackburn was more concerned about the fat little man's style than his manners, and cautioned Louis that Galento "fights in a crouch and throws that left hook from the floor. If you let yourself open, he'll tag you."

And tag him Tony did, springing up from his squat crouch to catch Louis with a stunning left in the closing seconds of the first round. In the second, Louis returned the compliment, decking Galento for the first time in his ring career with a well-placed left of his own. But Galento was far from through and, in the third, caught Louis with yet another left sprung from his almost-to-the-floor crouched position. Louis, "dazed and wobbly," hit the floor, rolled over, and got to his feet at the count of one. Galento went after the unsteady champ, but his awkwardness betrayed him as he threw inaccurate lefts for the rest of the round, the wind undoubtedly reviving Louis, who took control in the fourth to batter Galento into submission.

Louis now began to take on all comers, disposing of contenders in every city with a Jacobs connection. Interestingly, Louis avoided only one man on his way to the top—Slapsie Maxie Rosenbloom. Veteran boxing trainer Cus D'Amato probably agreed with this decision since he once said of Rosenbloom: "You couldn't hit him in the backside with a handful of buckshot."

Although the steady succession of stiffs was dubbed "the Bum of the Month Club" by the press, most were, in the words of Harry Balough, "highly regarded contenders" who were not allowed by Jacobs to fight each other, saving them and their best efforts for Louis. Whatever they were, they began to take on the sound of one of Cab Calloway's scat songs: "Musto, McCoy and Godoy."

Then came Louis's fight with Billy Conn, hardly a "bum" in any month, and assuredly not in the month of June, 1941. Conn, the classy light heavyweight posing as a heavyweight, looked like the heavyweight champion for twelve rounds. But in the thirteenth, under the accumulating weight of his crown-to-be, he tried to trade punches with that most deadly of cornered animals, a champion in danger of losing his title. It was popgun versus howitzer. And instead of becoming the sixteenth heavyweight champion of the world, Billy Conn merely became Louis's sixteenth knockout victim in defense of his crown; his eighteenth victim all together.

Later, when Conn was to ask Louis why he didn't lend him his crown for twelve months so he could make some money with it, Louis merely smiled at the man who had taken his best *and* taken him into the thirteenth and replied, "I lent it to you for twelve rounds and you didn't know what to do with it."

The winds of war were beginning to gust over the country and everybody, athletes included, was getting caught in the ensuing draft. Louis was as much a target for induction as any young married man. His camp, Mike Jacobs, and some deep thinkers at the Pentagon decided that the best time for Joe to go was during the early part of 1942, which wasn't turning out to be much of a year for the Allies, all things considered.

But first there were a couple of financial items. Louis's accountant advised him that he was in arrears on taxes to the tune of $81,100. "Pay it," said Louis, just as though someone at the golf club had asked him whether they could have a sawbuck. The accountant explained that that wasn't quite the way it worked; that you don't pay Uncle Sam what you owe until there's a nice big pile of what you owe. Then you make a deal, so much on the dollar.

It was probably the worst bit of advice since a Crow scout told Custer there wouldn't be much trouble along the Little Big Horn. Louis fought twice in 1942, easily defeating two contenders who had previously extended him, Buddy Baer in one and Abe Simon in six. But neither Baer nor Simon came off worse than Louis did. For Louis, now an Army sergeant, had donated the purses to the Navy Relief Society and the Army Emergency Relief and was reduced to submitting a Statement of Financial Condition to the Internal Revenue Service averring that his sergeant's pay was "barely enough to support wife and parents." IRS agents began pulling straws to see who would handle his case.

Sandwiched between the Conn fight and the 1942 bouts in the name of charity was one against the master of the "cosmic punch," Lou Nova. Nova, relying on the advice of a swami named the "Omnipotent Oom," went *into* the fight braying, "I shall insist upon the return of the million-dollar gate," and went *out* in six.

But it wasn't the Nova fight that Jacobs envisioned as his next million-dollar fight. Instead, it was a return bout between Louis and Conn.

Jacobs began orchestrating the planning and publicity for the rematch. Without fully bothering to explain to Louis how a fight with the entire proceeds going to Army Emergency Relief would help defray his then $117,000 tax liability—except to pay off a "loan" he had taken from Jacobs—Jacobs scheduled the bout between "Sgt. Joe Louis" and "Pvt. Billy Conn" for Columbus Day, 1942.

However, Secretary of War Henry Stimson didn't quite see it Jacobs's way and ruled against the fight just seventeen days before it was scheduled to take place. Jacobs had to call it off. For four years.

In 1946, with the war over, the dream bout materialized, this time between citizen Louis and citizen Conn. Jacobs allowed neither contender a tune-up fight, lest his promotion lose its glamour. He resorted to having high-priced "experts" visit the fighters' training camps and plant newspaper stories calling Louis "dull" and Conn "sharp." Everything was in place and working toward a million-dollar gate.

But nothing worked better than an idea Jacobs had long cherished: charging the elitist price of $100 for a ringside ticket. Only twice before—Jackson versus Corbett and Corbett versus Sullivan—had $100 been charged, and both times for front-row seats only. Now, with the first flush of the postwar boom at hand, Jacobs wanted $100 for *all* ringside seats—including his disguised rows at ringside, numbered 5A and 26A and so on, interspersed with the official rows running from 1 to 37. During an interview with a "friendly" reporter who received an envelope of Christmas cheer from Jacobs's office every week, Jacobs floated a trial balloon. When "asked" what the top-priced ticket would be, he offhandedly responded with a bit of dialogue as carefully conceived as an Abbott and Costello routine, "Oh, I don't know . . . Maybe I'll charge one hundred bucks for ringside."

The balloon took off and Jacobs sold 10,574 ringside tickets, enough alone to make the magic million mark. Unfortunately, Conn didn't make it, succumbing to rust and Louis in eight rounds.

After Louis disposed of Tami Mauriello in one—although Maureillo had clocked Louis with the first punch and then, as Tami admitted into an open mike, "I got too goddamned careless"—Louis ran out of opponents. The sound of the bottom of the barrel being scraped could be heard when they came up with the name of his next opponent: Jersey Joe Walcott.

The 40ish Walcott was so poorly thought of that the fight was originally scheduled as an exhibition, but the New York State Athletic Commission forced Jacobs's hand by holding that it had to be for the championship. On that December night in 1947, Walcott, a 1–20 underdog, dropped Joe for a two-count in the first and a seven-count in the fourth, both times suckering him into a right-hand lead by turning away and walking a step before pivoting back to plant his punch on Louis's jaw. In the final rounds, relying on his corner's assessment that he only had to stand upright to win, Walcott backpedaled his way out of the championship. A disheartened Louis, believing he had lost, started to leave the ring before the decision was announced. Restrained by cooler heads, he was rewarded with a split decision for his efforts. For the first time in his career, Joe heard the crowd boo him.

Six months later Louis would redeem himself, as he had against everybody in return bouts, knocking out Walcott in eleven. However, the tired and overweight Louis had looked anything but good. Properly assessing the encroachments made by Father Time, he announced his retirement on March 1, 1949. The records were in the book, his place was assured in ring history forever. Why bother with the chores of training, fighting, staying in shape?

It wasn't to be, however. In hock to the IRS, Louis tried a "comeback," that most dreaded of all words for boxers. Louis was put in the unfortunate position of feeling compelled to answer the bell like a firehorse retired to a wagon—with the same result. He was soundly defeated by Ezzard Charles, who not only clearly outpointed the former Destroyer, but actually carried him in the final rounds so as not to embarrass his former hero.

Louis fought on against second-raters—men who couldn't carry his jockstrap in his youth. The fire was gone, but the fuel bill from the IRS was still there. Finally, after taking the measure of such marginal men as Cesar Brion, Lee Savold, Omelio Agramonte, Freddie Beshore, and Andy Walker, Louis was matched with a young, up-and-coming brawler out of Brockton, Massachusetts named Rocky Marciano.

Although it was five days shy of Halloween, 1951, the fight was a cruel Halloween trick for the once great Bomber, as Marciano hammered Louis through the ropes in the eighth, leaving the hulk of what once had been great. But by then many of the crowd at Madison Square Garden had left rather than witness the sad inevitability of what was to come, cherishing in their minds' eyes a younger Louis, a rare individual whose likes wouldn't be passing their way again. At least, not wearing trunks and boxing gloves.

100 Years of Boxing, 1982

Thomas Hearns: A Four-Time
Champion Stands Foursquare in History

Their names are as indelibly etched on boxing's landscape as the faces on Mt. Rushmore. They are the eleven men who have accomplished boxing's version of the "hat trick"; those who have writ large their names as masters of all they surveyed in three different weight classes. Those triple champions, in order of their winning their third title, were: Bob Fitzsimmons, Tony Canzoneri, Barney Ross, Henry Armstrong, Emile Griffith, Wilfred Benitez, Alexis Arguello, Roberto Duran, Wilfredo Gomez, Thomas Hearns, and Sugar Ray Leonard.

Now one of those eleven, Thomas Hearns, has scaled his own personal Everest, a hill from which he can look down on the other ten three-time winners as the only man ever to win world titles in four different weight classes.

Oh, sure, there are purists—members of boxing's hardened artery—who hold that the Alphabet-Soup organizations who control boxing have trivialized the historic worth of winning three championships with those halfway houses known as "Junior" or "Super" something-or-other. Even so, Thomas Hearns now joins two other greats as one of only three men ever to win three classic divisional championships, the welterweight, light heavyweight, and middleweight titles—thus joining Fitzsimmons (Middleweight, Light Heavyweight, and Light Heavyweight, in that order) and Armstrong (Featherweight, Welterweight, and Lightweight, in that order) on a tiny island of greatness.

For those who may have taken up residency alongside Rip Van Winkle and do not recognize the greatness that is Thomas Hearns, let us backtrack for a second and give you a quick thumbnail of the man they call "The Hit Man." Thomas Hearns looks like a fighter built by committee. From the wrists to the shoulders, the committee has dictated he be heavily muscled, possessing the physical build of a wide receiver, complete with shoulder pads, and, with a seventy-eight-inch wingspan, the look of a basketball center. They gave him huge hamhock hands, all the better to make his opponent one with the resin. But this quasi-heavyweight upper body sits atop a slender thirty-inch waist poised on spindly, praying mantis-like legs, giving him the appearance of someone who works in an olive factory dragging the pimentos through. But to his opponents, this six-foot-one-inch string bean—his shadow further lengthened by his achievements—looks just like the man met at the top of the beanstalk. And just about as dangerous.

Throughout his ten-year, forty-seven-bout career, Thomas Hearns has desired only what he could accomplish. And he has accomplished much, capped by winning his fourth championship, the middleweight title—the other three merely parsley on the plate called "greatness."

Denied that fourth championship once in his take-no-survivors war with Marvelous Marvin Hagler—and becoming one of the five three-time champions to fail in their quest for a fourth title along with Canzoneri, Armstrong, Arguello, and Duran—Hearns made up for arrearages by filling his inside straight versus a fire-plug known as Juan Domingo Roldan. On Thursday, October 29, 1987,

Thomas Hearns passed through that door to boxing history in an exciting moment—one of more than minor interest to numerologists, winning as he did on the fourth knockdown in the fourth round for his fourth championship.

Now Thomas Hearns had become part of boxing history. No longer enshrined with a mortgage of having lost the big ones, but with having won the big four: The welterweight, junior middleweight, light heavyweight, and middleweight titles. For that alone he is now entitled to another belt, one reading "Boxing Great."

Boxing Illustrated, 1987

Oscar De La Hoya: Bringing Back the Glory of the Welterweights

Ask any boxing fan the definition of the word "welterweight" and they'll stare at you with the eyes of a meditative fish. Even that most punctilious of wordsmiths, Noah Webster, drawing on his fine command of the English language, comes up empty, explaining it in his tome as deriving "prob. fr. 'welt': to thrash, beat."

But if the definition of the term "welterweight" is lost to etymologists, so too are the many who have toiled in the 147-pound vineyard, their efforts hidden under the twin bushel baskets of the heavyweight and middleweight divisions and commanding less attention than the international trade balance.

While many of the greats and near-greats in the welterweight catalogue of constituents have begotten no more than a small lake of print around an islet of illustration, several have been able to step forward, center stage, and stir the boxing fan. And the press.

Usually those rare moments when the welterweight division becomes the center of the boxing world's attention come when the heavyweight division is on the cusp of being called off on account of lack of interest, the fans turning their attention elsewhere while waiting for action, any action, to erupt amongst the heavies—a theory no doubt related to some hypothesis about the watched pot.

The 1930s were one such time, the heavyweight division a joke and the champion, Primo Carnera, a clown. In fact, it has been said that if the heavyweight division had been a wake, it would have been an insult to the deceased.

Into boxing's vacuum stepped two men who stood taller, much taller, than their respective heights of five-foot-five-and-one-half inches and five-foot-seven inches: Jimmy McLarnin and Barney Ross. Together they gave the boxing fan something to cheer about, something great that made everything else in the thirties pale in comparison.

In as thrilling a fight as boxing had seen in many a year, Ross threw both caution and punches to the wind. Discarding the efficient, careful style that had seen him victorious in all but two of his previous fifty-five fights, Ross carried the fight to McLarnin, matching punch for punch with the master puncher, wading into the dynamite-fisted welterweight champion. Time and again he got away with it. He even got away with a split decision and the championship.

Two more times these two greats were to battle. And when the final tabulation had been made, it read: two wins for Ross; one for McLarnin; three for boxing.

Jump-skip, dear reader, to the early '80s when, again, the heavyweight division had become about as exciting as the sight of paint drying and fans looked elsewhere to feed their boxing fix. They found it in the welterweight division, its ranks filled to overflowing with the likes of Sugar Ray Leonard, Thomas Hearns, Wilfred Benitez and Roberto Duran. Once again the division came front and center, pulling boxing out of its doldrums.

And now, today, as the heavyweight division grinds down to a bore-snore, its so-called headliners either too old in the tooth, too pacifistic or not even household names in their own households, it is the welterweights who again breathe life back into the old sport—giving it so much that its very breath could becloud a mirror.

This time around, it is its two superstars—not only of the welterweight division, but of all of boxing—Oscar De La Hoya and Felix Trinidad, who have made the welterweight souffle rise yet another time. Together these two warriors give one of boxing's most overlooked divisions the recognition it so richly deserves. And so rarely receives.

But, then again, the story has always been there, story-size Triple-E. And maybe, just maybe, it takes potential greats like De La Hoya and Trinidad to make us sit up and take notice of the welterweight division and bring us back, one-by-one, like carrier pigeons over a stormy sea coming back to our home base.

No matter. The temporary hiatus will be worth the wait.

Fight Game, 1999

Roy Jones Jr. vs. The Light Heavy Greats . . . Who Would Have Won?

Roy Jones Jr. has more than established himself as the best of the light heavyweight class. In a ranking of one through ten, he might well be able to spread-eagle the field and be all ten, so far superior is he to the rest of those fighting in the division that it looks like Roy Jones and the seven dwarfs.

While the boxing media has worn down a carload of lead pencils to stubs writing about his exploits, there is great difficulty comparing him to the greats of the past since his present-day competition is made up of a group of life's losing stuntmen posing as light heavyweights, many called contenders only in the same way raisins are considered fruits—technically and only in a manner of speaking.

For this, Roy Jones is penalized in any assessment of his greatness, both in terms of his current greatness on a pound-for-pound basis or historically.

And so, we at Fight Game have decided to do what all bar arguments do: Put him against the best that history has to offer, the ten greatest light heavyweights of all time.

To properly do our research into just who those "greats" in the 175-pound class were, we repaired to our favorite watering hole and asked those in concert assembled for their nominees. And in no time at all were assaulted with names, many times over the union scale of ten as we found ourselves scribbling down name-after-name on official bar stationary (read: napkins).

Now, normally, when we hear someone utter those deathless words, "I remember," we reach for our coats. This time, however, we reached for our pens and took down every one of the names, using more napkins than Rosie used *Bounty* during her commercial career, continually adding, deleting and refining the selections as they tumbled out. From someone we got the name Archie Moore; from someone else, applauding their childhood memories much as an audience at a concert hall will applaud a song they recognize more than the performer rendering it, came Matthew Saad Muhammad. Then came Bob Foster, Maxie Rosenbloom and scores of others, up to and including Mike Rossman and Dick Tiger and Victor Galindez. The names of Georges Carpentier and José Torres were also offered, as were Bob Fitzsimmons, Billy Conn, Dwight Muhammad Qawi, Harold Johnson and John Henry Lewis. But no one so much as breathed the name Ezzard Charles, probably because he is best remembered as a heavyweight and not as a light heavyweight. But he belonged on any list and so was added as a write-in candidate.

Next problem: What exactly defines "greatness" and qualifies one of our final ten to be on our list of historic opponents for Roy Jones Jr.? It was a combination of their overall record, their domination of the division and their overall excellence—excellence that illumined their greatness almost as smoke defined light in the movie houses of our youth.

All that said, or unsaid, the next question was "when," as in "when" should so-and-so have fought Jones. This is tricky because some of the fighters mentioned had careers that were longer, it seemed, than boxing itself, like Archie Moore. But you couldn't judge Moore 200 fights into his career. Fighters have to be picked at their primes, much like fruit.

And so, after winnowing the list down to ten—and then checking it and re-checking it like someone touching the paint to see if it was really dry—and then ascribing the fighter's so-called prime years to him, give or take a year, we had the ten we would match-up against Jones.

And after all that it came down to one thing, and one thing alone: Styles, because styles make fights. And Jones' style is almost as undefinable as the word "Selah" in the Bible, his movements eloquent in their execution, delivered with a touch of specialized intelligence.

So now, to cop a phrase from radio, return with us to those thrilling days of yesteryear to see Roy Jones Jr. up against the greatest light heavyweights of all time in their primes, many of whom have been pressed between the pages of time and trotted out for this one-time-only great match-up.

BOB FITZSIMMONS (Peak years: 1891–'93) vs. Roy Jones Jr.

Called a "fighting machine on stilts," Fitzsimmons looked like one of nature's irregularities, muscular shoulders and upper body resembling that of a village smithy set atop a twenty-eight-inch waist with spindly legs that hardly looked like they could uphold the obligation they were sworn to uphold. And yet "Ruby Robert" possessed a left hook, the first recorded one in boxing history, that separated many an opponent from his senses and three men from their crowns. It was this left, thrown by shifting his feet, that enabled Fitzsimmons to win, in order, the middleweight, heavyweight and light heavyweight titles—the last, twenty years into his boxing career. One of the all-time greats, Fitzsimmons fought in the manner of the day except for that left hook, straight up and with little or no movement, and would have been no match for Jones, historic greatness or no.

OUTCOME: Jones by early-round KO.

TOMMY LOUGHRAN (Peak years: 1927–'29) vs. Roy Jones Jr.

Loughran was rightfully labeled the "Phantom of Philly," a wraith-like presence in the ring who made it almost impossible to get to. It was that complete mastery of the ring—and of his opponents—that caused one of those just beaten by him, Jimmy Braddock, to ask: "Loughran? Has anybody here seen Loughran? I was supposed to fight the guy tonight." Throwing a left that was almost independent of conscious effort, and one of the best in the history of boxing, Loughran combined it with ring skills unimaginable today. In one of his fights, against the heavier Max Baer, Baer merely stopped chasing the elusive Loughran and turned to the crowd with arms extended and a "What-the-hell-can-you-do?" expression on his face. He was that good. In a chess match, almost one of reverse polarity as the two great ring tacticians tried to get the upper glove, it would have been this close.

OUTCOME: Jones by decision.

MAXIE ROSENBLOOM (Peak years: 1929–'32) vs. Roy Jones Jr.

The man called "Slapsie Maxie"—the term "Slapsie" deriving from the sound his open glove made when it hit an opponent—was a bona fide "cutie." So cute, in fact, that according to trainer Cus D'Amato, "You couldn't hit him in the backside with a handful of buckshot." With a shake of the leg here, an open glove there and a *tush* thrown in for good measure, Rosenbloom, Public Enemy #1, was virtually unhittable. And a guarantee to make every opponent look bad—so much so that Joe Louis' braintrust backed out of a fight with the over-the-hill Rosenbloom because even though the up-and-coming Louis was virtually assured of beating him, he wouldn't look good in the process. As tough as he was to hit, "Slapsie Maxie" was impossible to knock out, only twice KO'd in his 289-fight career—and both times as a result of "doing business." Jones would win in as terrible-looking a performance as one could imagine him giving, but that would be Rosenbloom's fault more than Jones'.

OUTCOME: Jones by decision.

JOHN HENRY LEWIS (Peak years: 1936–'38) vs. Roy Jones Jr.

The name John Henry Lewis has been relegated to the dustbin of history. Which is a shame because he was *that* good: 116 fights, 105 wins, 64 by KO and KO'd himself only once, by Joe Louis in a title shot, hardly a disgrace since he was one of twenty-one challengers to go that route—and it was his last fight. But before his loss to Louis he had established himself as a great ring mechanic and all-around great fighter, good enough to beat Maxie Rosenbloom twice and Bob Olin three times, plus several ranking heavyweights such as Elmer Ray, Al Ettore, Marty Gallagher and Johnny Risko. However, while boxing had rarely seen an executant as skillful as Lewis, his style, straight up and always coming forward, would make it an easier fight for Roy than it looks on paper.

OUTCOME: Jones by decision.

BILLY CONN (Peak years: 1939–'41) vs. Roy Jones Jr.

Billy Conn was a Tommy Loughran with brashness, almost with the balls of a cat burglar. Constantly told he couldn't do something, Conn would continually turn the odds on their head, defeating no less than ten men who held titles at one time or another—from A to Z, Apostoli to Zale and Zivic. With Conn, it was always a case of referring people to A. Lincoln's sonnet on "fooling all the people," etc. After virtually retiring the light heavyweight division single-handedly, Conn stepped up to the heavyweight division and, de-spite being outweighed by thirty-five pounds by the champion, Joe Louis, took the fight to Louis, almost pulling off one of the biggest upsets in heavyweight history. Conn could forge almost anything in the smithy of his soul, and the bet here—against all reason—is that he could do it head-to-head against Roy Jones Jr. in a battle any dues-paying fan would appreciate.

OUTCOME: Conn by decision.

ARCHIE MOORE (Peak years: 1947–'49) vs. Roy Jones Jr.

At an age when most men are already planning what to do with their Social Security checks, Archie Moore finally won the light heavyweight championship. But, truth to tell, by that time, 1952, Moore was already three years past his prime, his career having started somewhere right after the stampede of apple salesmen first chased Adam out of his Garden. Still, the man they called "The Old Mongoose" would go on to establish homesteading rights to the light heavy crown and fight another eleven years, his legend enlarging itself in breadth and width, largely through his own efforts. But what wasn't mere legend was the fact that 145 of his opponents succumbed to gravity as a result of his handiwork, most of those victims of Moore's powers, both physical and psychological. However, Archie, who always had trouble with movers, would not even be able to strike up a waving acquaintance with Jones whose moves are so fast you almost need an odometer to measure them.

OUTCOME: Jones by decision.

EZZARD CHARLES (Peak years: 1948–'49) vs. Roy Jones Jr.

Ezzard Charles was one of the great boxers of all time, heavyweight or otherwise. However, his exploits as a light heavyweight are as overlooked as those of the second man to fly cross the Atlantic, being remembered only as the man who succeeded Joe Louis as the heavyweight champion. This is unfair to Charles, who is held by many, including Ray Arcel, to be the greatest light heavyweight of all time. But this beautifully tooled machine, who used an economy of effort to achieve an efficiency of results, fought and beat Archie Moore three times and ditto Charles Burley twice. And to further his credentials, also defeated light heavyweight champion Joey Maxim and Anton Christofordis. In short, he was a Swiss movement to be watched and would have more than given Jones a tough fight, but would have won handily.

OUTCOME: Charles by decision.

BOB FOSTER (Peak years: 1967–'70) vs. Roy Jones Jr.

Despite a body that made him look like the poster boy for Missing, Bob Foster could generate a left hook from hell from that thin-as-a-whisper frame, one which ended with the sound of an explosion that fells six or seven bystanders. Its very presence was such that most of his opponents entered the ring looking like all they wanted was to catch the first train going south. And yet, in a match-up between Foster, one of the heaviest hitters in the history of the light heavy division, Archie Moore included, and Roy Jones Jr., Jones would hardly be vulnerable to the quaking knee factor. Moreover, his speed and know-how would enable him to move away from that dynamite-laden left for twelve rounds—though maybe not for the fifteen of Foster's day.

OUTCOME: Jones by decision.

MATTHEW SAAD MUHAMMAD (Peak years: 1978–'80) vs. Roy Jones Jr.

The man who started out as Matt Franklin and gained everlasting fame as Saad Muhammad fought as if he were two men: Demonstrating a great capacity for taking hurt in the beginning of every one of his contests, then coming back from the brink of destruction to put his own "hurtin'" on his opponent. Fighting with reckless disregard for his own comfort and safety, Saad was there to be hit. And be hit again. Despite his reputation as a slow starter—belied by his second performance against Montell Griffin—Jones would not give Saad a chance to stage one of his patented comebacks, scoring early and often.

OUTCOME: Jones by KO.

MICHAEL SPINKS (Peak years: 1982–'84) vs. Roy Jones Jr.

With a rubber-filleted frame and a style that made him look as if he were going three more ways to catch up with a four-way cold tablet, Michael Spinks was still able to deliver his patented knockout punch, the "Spinks Jinx," to rule the light heavyweight roost for four-plus years. And then do something no other light heavy had ever done: capture the heavyweight title. Still, for all his cuteness, Spinks would more than meet his match in the lightning and thunder of Roy Jones, who could match Spinks in both moves and power.

OUTCOME: Jones by decision

FINAL TALLY: Jones 8, Greats 2.

Fight Game, March 2000

By Unanimous Decision, Prince Naz is the Best Boxer Today, Sound-for-Sound

Willie Pep . . . Kid Chocolate . . . Henry Armstrong . . . Abe Attell . . . Alexis Arguello . . . Salvador Sanchez . . .

Not to worry, these great featherweight champions' place in boxing history is still secure, unchallenged by the man who, upon his arrival in America, brashly announced to one and all that he was "the greatest featherweight of all time."

The utterer of that verbal puffery was none other than Prince Naseem Hamed. And so far all he has proven is that he is more pretender than contender to the title of "great" he so boldly designated for himself with two less-than-pound-sterling performances here on this side of the Atlantic.

In his first fight in the States, against Kevin Kelley, Hamed went down a total of three times—including getting knocked on, as Eliza Doolittle would have it, his "bloomin' arse" with the first punch thrown by Kelley—and looked like he was having less fun than Napoleon at Waterloo before Kelley met his after getting "too anxious."

145

With his claim to "greatness" still incapable of standing up to even the vaguest sort of examination, especially against the likes of . . .

. . . *Tony Canzoneri . . . George Dixon . . . Sandy Saddler . . . Harry Jeffra . . . Johnny Kilbane . . .*

. . . Hamed now decided to dip his toe in the waters this side of The Pond again, this time against former bantamweight champion Wayne McCullough, whom Hamed, with his usual peacock-proud blathering said would take "such a beating it's probably going to be his last fight." And then, in his best imitation of Muhammad Ali, not only predicted the round such a beating would culminate in a knockout, the third, but pinpointed the exact time, 2:28 of the round.

As he shamelessly dithered on—"You know as well as I do, I have a gift from God"; and "These are weapons (holding up his fists) of aggression, of destruction"; blah . . . blah . . . blah—the media began to view him as the second most unpopular import to come to America from Britain since tea was shipped to the Colonies some two centuries ago.

One could only hope that he would just shut up. Or, at least, take a breath.

But Naz had no intention of doing either. And as the days leading up to the McCullough fight wound down, the Prince's motor-mouth wound up, going into high gear.

"This country has to be broken," he declared. "There is an Arab-Sheffield-Yorkshire-Yemini-English banging machine who's going to rock the house." And on . . . and on . . . and on. . .

Naseem's pre-fight carryings-on were less like those of feather greats . . .

. . . *Azumah Nelson . . . Davey Moore . . . Eusebio Pedroza . . . Chalky Wright . . . Wilfredo Gomez . . .*

. . . than those of Bert Lahr's swaggering lion in the *Wizard of Oz*, delivered in a baritone vibrato: "I'll fight you with one paw tied behind my back! I'll fight you standin' on one foot! I'll fight you wit' my eyes closed!"

Bert Randolph Sugar (Turner Classic Movies)

Splendid in plaid with Alexis Arguello.

With Roberto Duran. (Sandy Goldberg)

Sharing a laugh with Evander Holyfield.

A gathering of the greats at a testimonial for Sugar Ray Robinson: From left: Jake LaMotta, Sugar Ray's wife, Millie, Ken Norton, Joey Giardello, Floyd Patterson, the author, Rocky Graziano, LeRoy Neiman, Alexis Arguello, Joe Frazier. (Fred Roe)

Cheek-to-cheek with Jose Torres.

With The Greatest.

Ringside with the Yankee Clipper, Joe DiMaggio. (James Dombrowski)

Squeezed by two of the best, Sugar Ray Leonard, left, and Marvelous Marvin Hagler. (Pat Orr

Close, but no cigar, with the always perfecto Bo Derek.

And with the always recognizable Don King.

Sparring at Deer Lake with Muhammad Ali.

Finally, however, Naz had to pause long enough to fight the fight he had been talking the talk about all week. It was a fight that almost hadn't come off, pulled off life-support systems at the last second by HBO, which had rescued it from the entangled legal underwear of British promoter Frank Warren.

Now, on this Halloween night—with the fight, appropriately enough, called "Fright Night"—Naz entered the arena with a four-minute music video-style entrance, gyrating all the while through a make-believe graveyard and, after decapitating one of the cardboard cutouts with a straight right, backward-somersaulting into the ring and proving only that Yeminis have no rhythm. Grinning broadly in the other corner was the party of the second part, Wayne McCullough, who viewed the goings-on with more than a slight measure of disdain and scorn, sure that none of the other featherweights like . . .

  . . . *Hogan (Kid) Bassey . . . Sugar Ramos . . . Johnny Famechon . . . Joey Archibald . . .*

  . . . would have ever burlesqued so much. Or so badly.

After a few pec-*smecks* and a bump-and-grind routine worthy of Gypsy Rose Lee, the Prince turned his attention to the business at hand: McCullough.

For two rounds Naseem attempted to acquit his pre-flight prediction of "beating" McCullough by catching him with straight lefts, overhand rights and who-knows-where-they-came-from punches. But McCullough, buoyed by the presence of more than 1,000 hometown fans who had flown over from his native Ireland and were now screaming like youngsters with green apple colic, walked right through them and continued to take the fight to Naseem.

Come the third, the round singled out by Naseem as the round he would treat McCullough to the same fate as he had his previous eighteen opponents, Hamed stepped up the action, even once seeming to stun McCullough. But McCullough took everything Naseem had—up to and including through the 2:28 mark—and continued to come on. At the bell ending the round, McCullough

147

raised his arms in victory and his fans greeted his minor victory in outlasting Naz's prediction with the din and roar of a patriotic celebration.

And then something curious happened. For Naseem, who had fought for three rounds, now became a fistic break-dancer, backpeddling and throwing backhanded jabs, with McCullough forcing the fight, making what action there was. To Tim Smith of *The New York Times* it seemed that "Hamed was running and backpeddling on his bicycle so much that he completed two phases of a triathlon during the 12-round bout. If there had been a moat around the ring," Smith concluded, "he would have completed the event."

Forget that Hamed won a unanimous decision (by lopsided scores of 116–112, 118–110 and 117–111) or that he ran his record to 31–0, in terms of his much-ballyhoo'd build-up, it was, in the words of James Lawton of the *London Express*, "a deeply embarrassing defeat."

One former featherweight champion who was amongst those in the two-thirds filled Atlantic City Convention Center, Juan LaPorte, could only shake his head at Naseem's performance as a poseur and say, "Naseem earned $2 million for that? I'm going straight back to the gym."

But if LaPorte is going back to the gym to re-assert his position in featherweight history over the man who said he was "the greatest featherweight of all time," he needn't bother. Neither should . . .

David Kotey . . . Barry McGuigan . . . Jeff Fenech . . . Danny "Little Red" Lopez . . . Bobby Chacon . . .

. . . or any of the previous featherweight champs.

Hell, we might even place another clown—but a professional one at that—named Jorge Paez ahead of Prince Naseem on the list of featherweight greats off his two performances here in America.

Fight Game, 1998

Lennox Lewis: Britain's First Vertical Champion

It was Red Smith, the poet laureate of all sportswriters, who penned the immortal lines ". . . the deep, dreamless slumber that comes to small children, the pure of heart, and all British heavyweights."

The subject matter for the piece was Bruce Woodcock, the Doncaster heavyweight who had just been carried to his corner with "eyes full of the wood violets of Doncaster," courtesy of Tami Mauriello's right hand back in 1946. But, truth to tell, it could have been written about any one of a number of Brit heavies, all rendered endwise by their colonial relations, the long list throughout the course of boxing history including the likes of Charlie Mitchell, Jem Smith, Bombardier Billy Wells, Don Cockell, Brian London, Henry Cooper, Jack Bodell, Richard Dunn, etc., etc., *ad nauseum*.

Incurable British boxing fans have always taken great nourishment in those few small accomplishments of their heavies, with memories of Tommy Farr's going fifteen rounds with Joe Louis, 'Enery Cooper knocking down then-Cassius Clay and Frank Bruno momentarily stunning Mike Tyson all dancing in their heads. After all, it's part and parcel of the British mentality to instinctively admire any man who can make defeat sound like a victory. (Don't forget, they view Dunkirk as a victory.)

But all that changed on Halloween eve, 1992, when Lennox Lewis returned the favour (with a British "U") by knocking out Donovan "Razor" Ruddock in sensational fashion in just two rounds. Forget the fact that Lewis was Jamaican-born or that he was Canadian-bred. He was now British-based and that was enough for British writers to enthuse about his ending "almost a century of routine humiliation at the hands of transatlantic heavyweights."

The victory of Lewis over Ruddock not only gave lie to the slander that Brit heavies couldn't stand up to their American counterparts—or stand up at all, for that matter—but all of a sudden established Lewis as the major force in the heavyweight division, the standard bearer for a long list of British heavies from Woodcock on up. Or down, if you will. And all of a sudden, the Brits, who had invented the bloody sport, were on the cusp of having their first heavyweight champion for . . . how long was that? Almost a century?

And then, a few months later, after Riddick Bowe had deposited his WBC belt into a London "dustbin," the WBC retrieved it and presented it to Lewis, retroactively, as *their* heavyweight champion. Lewis was now, as his British supporters hysterically maintained, their "first heavyweight champion since Fitzsimmons," even if he had won the title while relaxing on the beaches of Jamaica.

Don King then rushed in with the mandatory challenger in the person of Tony Tucker, whom Lewis decked twice on his way to a unanimous, if uninspiring 12-round decision. He followed that up with an equally unimpressive showing against Frank Bruno—the first all-British heavyweight title fight in Lord-knows-when.

But still Lewis failed to win over his critics who continually carped about his style, one which found him keeping his lip stiff and upper and his punches a little less of both. It was almost as if they expected him to duplicate his effort against Ruddock with every outing and found his cautious, almost polite, style indicative of someone who didn't possess the requisite "fire in his belly." To hear his critics, of whom there were many—and all, it seemed, were over on this side of The Pond—Lewis had all the appearances of someone who had his pinkie extended when he punched as if he were serving tea in the ring.

After finding himself in a negotiating cul-de-sac, all of his potential opponents finding something else to do on the day of a suggested fight, Lewis signed to fight Phil Jackson—who not only wasn't in anybody's Top 10 list of heavyweights, but to the American sporting public wasn't even in their Top 10 list of people named "Phil Jackson."

The match-up was met with all the excitement of one hand applauding, as thousands of fans showed up as empty seats at the Atlantic City Convention Center—black curtains draped across a portion of the arena to blot out acres of empty space and scalpers on the Boardwalk offering tickets, to no takers, at bargain-basement prices.

From the opening bell it was obvious that the pairing was a mismatch, at least as far as their size was concerned, with the 217-pound, six-feet-one inches Jackson giving away both height and weight to the 235-pound, six-feet-five inches Lewis—a size differential accentuated all the more by Jackson's constant crouching, giving the two the appearance of the 1939 World's Fair symbol, Jackson being the sphere and Lewis the pylon.

And then, just thirty seconds into the first round, Lewis put the punctuation point on the mismatch—and Jackson on the seat of his pants—with his very first right hand.

It was to serve as the leitmotif for the entire fight with Lewis loading up with his right hand and using his left merely as a diving rod and Jackson occasionally leaping in with a vagrant left. In the fifth, after Lewis stumbled embarrassingly off balance, he found both his balance and Jackson's chin with a single right hand that put Jackson face-down. Arising slowly, Jackson was once again bombarded by rights and went down again from another right, this one thrown after the bell ending the round—for which Lewis was penalized one point.

But one point made little or less difference as every round was pretty much the same: Lewis pitching and Lewis catching. By the middle of the seventh, one ringsider commented, "Jackson's eye is closing" and his neighbor retorted, "Both of mine are." It was *that* boring; and *that* mechanical.

And then in the eighth, Lewis enthusiastically ended the festivities by landing a short right and followed that with an uppercut and two hooks that finished the job.

It was enough for referee Arthur Mercante, but not enough for the cynical American press which remained solidly underwhelmed by the lack of fire by the one-third champ.

Still, it might be the beginning of that glorious day when some British journalist could finally write: "and the deep, dreamless slumber that comes to small children, the pure of heart, and all *American* heavyweights."

Boxing Illustrated, 1994

III
The Fights

Jack Dempsey vs. Luis Firpo
Polo Grounds, New York
(September 14, 1923)

If they had been two bull moose, horns interlocked, fighting for their turf, they would have ground each other into fine dust; if they had been two Roman gladiators, replete with tridents and shields, they would have reduced each other into two puddles that could have been borne off by blotters; and if they had fought on a barge, Luis Angel Firpo would have beaten Jack Dempsey to become the heavyweight champion of the world.

Luis Angel Firpo was a great bull of a man. Dubbed by one less than imaginative writer, "the Wild Bull of the Pampas," this Argentinian stood some six feet, three inches tall and weighed some 220 pounds in the days when heavyweights barely scaled 200. His idea of fighting was simple: hit your opponent with a bludgeoning right hand, period. But his skills, or lack thereof, had gotten noticeable results. He had taken on—and beaten—six men since he had landed on the shores of America some eighteen months before, dispatching all of them in fewer than the scheduled number of rounds. His victims included among their number two whom the heavyweight champion of the world, Jack Dempsey, had also dispensed, Jess Willard and Bill Brennan. And Firpo had needed only four more rounds to do away with them than had Dempsey.

So, it was no wonder that promoter Tex Rickard looked upon this walking version of the Andes as the next logical contender for Jack Dempsey. Especially since Dempsey had just practiced mayhem less on his opponent, Tommy Gibbons, than on the little town of Shelby, Montana in his last fight. And, if memory served Rickard correctly, and it usually did, his last Dempsey fight was a million-dollar one, with another foreigner—in that case, Georges Carpentier—serving as the party of the second part. Rickard couldn't think of a better match than one between Dempsey and Firpo in early fall in New York. But the giant Firpo, who, like many immigrants, had come to America thinking the streets were paved with gold and would break the fingers of anybody around him to get to an idle nickel lying on the sidewalk, knew the worth of a build-up almost as much as he knew the worth of a build. He wasn't about to be rushed into a match with Dempsey, preferring, as he told Rickard in his best English—which also was his worst English, almost nonexistent—that he wanted to wait another year before challenging anyone for the title. Rickard eyed the man before him, dressed in a rumpled $15 suit with a yellowed celluloid collar that would have been discarded months before if it hadn't cost another quarter to buy another, and said, "But next year you *may* get a lot of money fighting Dempsey. This year, you *will* get a lot of money." It took no interpreter to tell Firpo what to do. He signed, thereby becoming the first Latin American ever to challenge for a world's title.

But even if Luis Firpo had impressed his victims with his might, Rickard's move had not impressed the New York media as right. One columnist was moved to write, "Has Rickard run out of common sense, as well as contenders? Firpo, without question, is the clumsiest-looking oaf ever proposed as a challenger to a heavyweight champion." The oddsmakers concurred, installing Dempsey—in this, his fourth title defense—as an overwhelming 3–1 favorite.

However, a sports-starved public viewed the battle as a battle of giants and paid no heed to disproportionate odds or a disparaging press, thronging to the Polo Grounds the day of the fight for tickets. With a larger army on hand than Gallieni had led out of Paris to the first battle of the Marne, some 125,000 fans, believing that, like nature, Rickard abhorred a vacuum, tried to fill 82,000 seats. It was a classic case of demand far outstripping supply. In those pre-ERA days, a woman headed the long grey line of people pushing to get general admission tickets. However, despite her long vigil, when push came to shove and the line was broken up by a frantic mob seeking to get the bleacher seats, she lost her place. When the line was reassembled and the tickets actually were placed on sale, the crush of the crowd was so great that she was somewhere on the outskirts of the crowd, unable to get within half a block of the ticket window.

Still, some 85,000 fans came in through the gates, over and under the turnstiles, and even over the fence, to fill the 82,000 seats and give Rickard another million-dollar-plus gate, paying $1,188,603 for the privilege of seeing two men beat the living whey out of each other. They overflowed the aisles, stood on seats and gave little ground to those seeking their rightful seats, especially in the $50 ringside section. The only time the sea of humanity parted was when the two combatants coursed down from their centerfield dressing rooms to be greeted by rousing cheers. It was a crescendo that was never to subside.

Standing in the middle of the ring to receive their instructions from referee Jack Gallagher, the difference in size could be seen. There was a 24-pound difference in their weights, Firpo weighing in at 216½, Dempsey at 192½. But their size differential was measured in more than mere weight, for Firpo stood almost three inches taller than the champion, and his primitive musculature made the champion seem puny by comparison. As referee Gallagher intoned the instructions, an interpreter stood at Firpo's side. But even an interpreter couldn't have given voice to two instructions that never were uttered, two instructions which could have changed the course of the heavyweight division: that upon scoring a knockdown a man must go to the furthest neutral corner; and that a man knocked from the ring must get back in within ten seconds under his own power.

Then there was the bell, seemingly lost in the continuous cataract of sound which 82,000 voices made. Firpo came out in an unusual stance, for him. It was the classic boxer stance, taught him by his American trainer, Jimmy DeForest, who had tried to instill in this South American neanderthal, who knew absolutely nothing about the science of self-defense—his only defense being his right fist—a modicum of science.

Dempsey crouched low, all the better to appraise the giant in front of him and minimize his target. But the champion didn't get much of an opportunity to assess Firpo or his moves. For Firpo's first punch was a thunderous—and ponderous—right which caught Dempsey on the jaw, sending him to the canvas only ten seconds into the fight.

Dempsey jumped off the canvas with no count, more embarrassed by being knocked off-balance than hurt, and went to the attack. As the two flailing behemoths' arms entangled, they fell into a clinch. The referee shouted "break" and, as the trusting Firpo dropped his hands and glanced inquiringly at the ref, Dempsey threw a left hook over Firpo's half held-up right. It landed on the jaw and now Firpo was down. He, too, was up without a count. The first two punches had produced two knockdowns, both all within twenty seconds. It was to set a record. And a pattern. For as soon as Firpo had bounced up, he threw himself into the champion, connecting with a right to the only spot available to him, Dempsey's body. Dempsey continued to sacrifice his body, holding his hands high up, against his chin and against the chance that Firpo would land another of his lethal rights. But Firpo paid Dempsey no mind, just as he had paid no attention to advice from his handlers, and threw another looping right which came from somewhere out in right field. It caught the champion on the point of the jaw. But this time, instead of finding refuge on the canvas—as he had from the first right—Dempsey instead found refuge in returning firepower with firepower, drilling a left uppercut through Firpo's haphazard defense. The Argentinian stood there wavering. Then, with a resounding thud, he crashed to the canvas for the second time.

As the crowd jumped to its feet, yelling, screaming, climbing up on the benches, falling down, clawing at each other, roaring forth a wild, tumultuous cascade of sound in the greatest sustained mass audience-hysteria ever witnessed, Firpo, too, tried to jump up. But Dempsey, like an avenging angel, stood over him, ready to jump on the man as soon as his hands left the resin of the canvas. As they did, Dempsey caught him with a left and a right. But instead of retreating, Firpo came on, throwing three devastating hammer rights into Dempsey's unguarded rib cage. Then, as he sought to bring off yet another booming right to the body, Dempsey stepped instead with his own bomb, a left hook to the chin. Firpo fell as if he had been pole-axed, flat on his face, arms surrounding his head.

Miraculously he arose, only to run into Dempsey who had positioned himself directly over the head of the fallen challenger. Dempsey was off target with a right, grazing Firpo's head. But Firpo was so groggy that its force brushed him back to the canvas for the fourth time. The referee tried to push Dempsey away. As he backed up, Firpo got up. Dempsey was back on him faster than you can say Luis Angel Firpo, and, after another left and right to the jaw, Luis Angel Firpo was back where he had begun that exchange—on the floor. This time, after righting himself, Firpo found Dempsey waiting for him the very second his hands had tentatively cleared the floor. Another right sent Firpo down for the sixth time in the round.

Somehow, either from resolution or instinct, Firpo got to his feet, shaking but still trying to hurl just one of his rights at the on-rushing Dempsey to turn the tide of battle. But before he wound up to throw it a left and a right from Dempsey floored the Argentine giant a seventh time. This time he looked like he was through, his head buried in the mat, his arms stretched out. But unbelievably the giant shook, shivered and then stood up, reaching a standing posture just before the fatal count of "10."

Now, calling on some superhuman effort, Firpo flung himself at Dempsey, bullying him away from him, across the ring. Then, with Dempsey on the retreat, the battle-blind and berserk Firpo threw a clubbing right which landed aside Dempsey's head and the champion, impaled on the ropes, proved Newton's Law—that every action has an opposite and equal reaction—by falling through the ropes into the press section, feet flying and with his arms behind him to cushion his fall. It was the most famous moment in sports, captured for all time by George Bellows's equally famous portrait. In the words of Bugs Baer, Dempsey had "skipped three ropes at once." Somehow, in a stadium where Rickard had built the press benches higher than usual, fate conspired to have Dempsey fall on the typewriter of Jack Lawrence of the New York *Tribune*, who was more worried about protecting the forty-four keys of his typewriter than the 192½ pounds of falling champion. But whatever the reason, the result was the same; Lawrence hydraulically jacked the champ up onto the ring apron by the count of seven. By the count of eight Dempsey could be seen by a handful of people struggling up onto the ring apron. And by nine he had climbed between the middle and lower ropes and was back in the ring.

The rest of the round found Firpo literally hurling right hands at Dempsey, who instinctively rolled slightly under the punches, breaking their force. Had Firpo even had a hint of a left hand, the championship would have changed hands. But such was not the case, and he spent the remainder of Round 1 taking aim at the bobbing head in front of him with an unvaried nonassortment of right-hand swings. The end of the round found Dempsey still on his feet, beginning to throw punches of his own. Even after the bell he threw several punches at Firpo, all of which landed, leaving both men dazed and spent from their first-round efforts.

The bell for Round 2 had scarcely sounded when Dempsey picked up where he had left off, throwing short inside punches and taking rights to the body. Dempsey, hurt slightly by one of Firpo's rib-crackers, fell into a clinch. Then, on the break, he stepped back in and began throwing combinations to Firpo's head. Two left hooks landed over Firpo's by-now limp guard. A left to the body, followed by two right uppercuts and another left to the body. Firpo tried to hold on, but Dempsey pulled away and caught the exhausted challenger with another left and right to the head. Firpo less fell than wilted to the ground, down for the eighth time. Once more he defied gravity and pulled himself erect at the count of five. He pulled back and clouted Dempsey with a wild right to the neck. Dempsey moved in close and found Firpo with a left to the jaw and followed up with a right, literally lifting the Argentine from his feet and hurling him headlong to the floor with the crashing sound of a mighty oak falling from great heights. Firpo lay on the floor, full-length, his gloves covering his head. As the count progressed he shuddered and turned his body, trying once again to will himself up—to get back into battle. But this time he was not to arise. This time it was over.

It had lasted exactly three minutes and fifty-seven seconds, 237 seconds of mayhem, in which 11 knockdowns were scored in the shortest and wildest "great fight" in the history of boxing. It could hardly be called "The Sweet Science," but it was one helluva sweet quarrel.

The Great Fights, 1981

Rocky Graziano vs. Tony Zale

Yankee Stadium, New York (September 27, 1946)

Chicago Stadium, Chicago (July 16, 1947)

Ruppert Stadium, Newark, New Jersey (June 10, 1948)

There have been twosomes throughout history that have gone together like salt and pepper. These twosomes have sprung up in every field imaginable: Biblical, Cain and Abel; mythological, Damon and Pythias; musical, Gilbert and Sullivan; comical, Weber and Fields; political, Franklin and Delano, etc. Boxing has its own twosomes. Perhaps one of its famous pairings was that of Zale and Graziano. Like it says in the song, "Love and Marriage": "You can't have one without the other."

For three years, rivals Tony Zale and Rocky Graziano lit up the skies in the world of boxing with fireworks. And today, a half-century later, their fights are still legendary. They weren't fights, they were wars without survivors.

Their rivalry began the night of September 27, 1946 when Zale, "The Man of Steel," from Gary, Indiana, entered the ring with a record of sixty wins—thirty-six by KO, twelve losses and one draw, plus his middleweight crown—to do battle against Graziano. Rocky, a "Dead End Kid" from New York's Mulberry Bend Ghetto, fought the way he lived, according to the rules of the street, alternately hitting and holding anyone who stood in his way. Graziano had compiled a record of forty-three wins—thirty-two by KO, six losses and five draws, including sensational knockout victories over welterweight champions "Red" Cochrane and Marty Servo the previous year.

In a battle that was more savage than scientific, Zale floored Graziano midway through the first round for a count of four. By the end of the round, however, Zale was on the receiving end of a Graziano bombardment and reeling under the attack. Round 2 saw "The Rock" batter the champion around the ring with rights and lefts to the head, splitting Zale's lip in the process and finally toppling Zale with four successive rights. The bell saved Zale at the count of three and Zale was literally dragged to his corner. In the third, Graziano continued his attack with a maniacal fury, hammering the champion at will. However, Graziano could not finish him. When Zale came out for Round 4, he was amazingly refreshed and began to attack, throwing lefts and rights to the body of Graziano and forcing the challenger to retreat. Early in the fifth, Zale pressed his advantage, concentrating on the body with both hands. Suddenly, Graziano leaped at the champion with a tigerish attack and drove Zale back with rights and lefts to the head. But once again Zale weathered the round and came out for Round 6 renewed in vigor and purpose. Graziano made a final furious attempt to finish off "The Man of Steel," but the tide turned once more as Zale crashed home a thunderous right under Graziano's heart, followed by a left hook to the jaw. Rocky sank to his haunches, unable to catch his breath and was counted out for the first time in his career.

A rematch between the two warriors was a foregone conclusion. Ten months later, on July 16, 1947, the two took part in another seesaw slugfest, this time at Chicago Stadium. Zale immediately took the fight to Graziano, punishing him with a steady body barrage and closing his left eye by the end of Round 1. Zale switched his attack to the head in Round 2, attempting to inflict greater damage to Graziano's injured eye. But by the end of the round Zale was in trouble as Graziano connected with a right to the jaw that straightened up the champion and had him so bewildered that he want to the wrong corner at the bell. In Round 3, Zale split open Graziano's left eye and floored him for no count with another right to the head. He then drove the temporarily blinded Graziano into the ropes for an unanswered volley. Round 4 was more of the same, as Graziano spent more time wiping the blood out of his eye than trying to wipe out Zale—although Zale went to the canvas, more from a slip than a punch. By Round 5, the flow of blood had been stemmed, and Graziano started swinging, connecting with a right to the head that seemed to take the steam out of Zale. The champion took the initiative in the opening seconds of the sixth, but it was short-lived as Graziano threw a right cross and then another right to the jaw that sent Zale reeling. Three more rights sent the champion down for a count of three and when he arose the challenger was all over him, draping him over the middle strand of the ropes and pummeling him at will. The fight was halted at 2:10 of the sixth round, and Rocky Graziano was the new middleweight champion of the world. He won the title on his tremendous punching power, his heart and, as he put it, because "Somebody up there likes me."

The rubber match came eleven months later in Newark, New Jersey—the *only* one that was filmed. Graziano came in as the prohibitive 12–5 favorite. He went out as the ex-champion. The product of the Gary steel mills came out first—and fast—hooking a left to Graziano's jaw and knocking him down with less than a minute gone. The rest of the first round was all Zale's as he banged home his awesome one-two (a right to the body and a left to the jaw) several times. Round 2 was a carbon copy of Round 1 with Zale pounding home his combination. Then, for a brief moment, Graziano flurried, cutting loose with some of his old ferocity and forcing Zale to retreat. The third round continued where the second had left off and then the roof caved in on Rocky as Tony caught the champion with a left hook that floored him. As Graziano struggled to an unsteady position, using the rope as a crutch, Zale was on him again, determined to end it. He caught Rocky with a rib-crunching right to the ribs and followed it up, in perfect tandem, with a left to the jaw. Graziano went down as if pole-axed, and lay there as referee Paul Cavalier counted out "The Rock" at 1:08 of the third round.

Tony Zale became the first middleweight champion since Stanley Ketchel to regain his title. Somebody "Up There" obviously liked him, too.

The Great Fights, 1981

Rocky Marciano vs. Jersey Joe Walcott
Philadelphia Stadium,
Philadelphia, Pennsylvania
September 23, 1952

With one deep-dish beauty of a right at forty-three seconds into the thirteenth round, Rocky Marciano almost tore the head off defending champion Jersey Joe Walcott, knocking off his crown in the process—a crown he had worn securely for the previous twelve rounds.

It was a right hand that traveled no more than six inches, and yet it reached back seventy years, to the first modern heavyweight, "Boston Strongboy" John L. Sullivan. And with it, Marciano became not only the first heavyweight champion to come from the same area as Sullivan, but the first man to ascend to the throne with a perfect record since Sullivan had accomplished the same feat seven decades before.

For twelve rounds the so-called Brockton Blockbuster had hardly seemed like the world-beater the betting society had thought he was when they made him a 9–5 favorite. The same firepower that had ended the career of Joe Louis, stopped Harry ("Kid") Matthews in two, and sent Carmen Vingo to the hospital, was totally ineffective in stopping Jersey Joe—or Father Time, Walcott's greatest ally.

Right from the opening bell, Walcott made a liar out of the naysayers who said that he was too old and "the Rock" too much for the champ. Throwing his powerful left hook—the same left hook that had taken out Ezzard Charles just the previous year and decked Joe Louis three times—Walcott floored Marciano midway through the first round, the first time in his 43-fight professional career that Rocky had ever been down. Up at the count of four ("I got up fast because I was more mad at myself than hurt," Marciano was to say later), he looked hurt. Eschewing his patented shuffle, the 198-pound Walcott went right back to the attack, swarming all over the 184-pound challenger, staggering him again at the bell.

The second round was more of the same, with Walcott on the attack, even planting a left hook somewhere south of the border of Marciano's beltline, further adding to the challenger's discomfiture.

Rocky, trying to stem the tide of battle and turn the momentum, came out for round 3 in a deep crouch as his manager, Al Weill, kept up a staccato of "Keep down low, keep down low." But again Walcott found his way through the challenger's defense, landing another clean left to the chin. But despite repeated meetings of his right chin with the champion's left, Marciano showed that even though he lacked polish and finesse, he possessed a chin of granite and a heart to match as he came back to exchange shots with Walcott after the bell.

By Round 6 "the Rock" had taken the battle to Walcott and made him fight his kind of fight, backing the champion into the ropes and blazing away with lefts and rights. During one of their heated exchanges, Marciano suffered a deep gash on his head and Walcott a cut eyelid. As the bell rang, blood flowed freely from Walcott's damaged left eye and the end looked imminent for the oldest champion ever to defend his crown.

But somehow, someway, somewhere, the solution used to stem the flow of blood (here the story becomes clouded as to whether it was the solution on Marciano's head or Walcott's eye) got into Marciano's eyes. By the end of Round 7 Marciano came back to his corner hollering, "I have trouble with my left eye. I can't see."

Blind for three more rounds, Walcott made the most of them, using everything he knew and threw to beat "the Rock." Marciano missed repeatedly and Walcott countered with his own lefts and rights, cutting Marciano between the eyes and on the forehead.

By the end of the twelfth round Walcott was in total control. Ahead on all three officials' cards (7–4–1, 7–5, and 8–4), all he had to do was "last" nine more minutes. He was to miss by eight minutes and seventeen seconds.

With just thirty seconds gone in the thirteenth round, and with no punches thrown, Walcott unexplainably backed into the ropes. He was caught there with as hard a punch as had ever been seen in a fight—a short right hand that caught him flush coming off the ropes. As a grazing left (thrown for good measure and merely serving as a postscript) swept by him, Walcott slowly sank to the canvas, one arm hanging onto the ring rope, a grotesque imitation of a religious fanatic in prayer. Referee Charley Daggert counted ten over the inert form. He could have counted to 100 for all the difference it made.

Back in his dressing room, where there was more back-slapping going on than could be found at a Shriner's convention, the thoroughly exhausted champ greeted his well-wishers while over in one corner his father, Peter Marchegiano, wept. "I'm proud," he said over and over again.

So were many other well-wishers who wouldn't make it into the dressing room, but still crowded into the ring where their favorite son—twenty-six years after Tunney had dethroned Dempsey in the very same ring—had won the title. They had all won. Everyone, that is, except Marciano, who had lost a new pair of trousers in the confusion to some souvenir hunter and had to leave Municipal Stadium with a bathrobe thrown over an incomplete suit.

The Great Fights, 1981

Carmen Basilio vs. Sugar Ray Robinson
Yankee Stadium, New York
September 23, 1957

There is an old saying that no man walks so tall as the man who has accomplished something. And yet the man who walked the tallest on the morning of Tuesday, September 24, 1957, was the shorter of the two men who had met the previous night in New York's Yankee Stadium to decide the middleweight championship of the world. In fact, he was perhaps the shortest middleweight champion of all time—Carmen Basilio.

Basilio *had* accomplished something. He had won the middleweight crown from the incomparable Sugar Ray Robinson in as grueling a contest as had ever been witnessed. And, in doing so, he had become only the second welterweight champion ever to step up in class and win the middleweight title. But it wasn't Basilio's height—or lack of it—that decided the outcome of the fight. That was brought home to him when the two fighters were called to the center of the ring for their prefight instructions by referee Al Berl.

Basilio, remembering the moment years later, recalled, "I was five-six-and-a-half. I looked up at Sugar Ray. He was sneering at me, trying to scare me. So I started to laugh. I was laughing so hard that the ref had to stop to see if I was OK."

Carmen was not only OK, he was A-OK, and knew then that, to rephrase an old boxing adage, a good little man could beat a good big man if he had one other element to go with it: determination. And that the Canastota, New York onion farmer had, in abundance.

Basilio discovered early on he needed that determination, for, almost from the sound of the opening bell, Robby began a steady ratta-tat-tat tattoo of left jabs into the readily available face of the challenger. By the time the crouching Basilio—whose crouch emphasized further the size differential even more than the five measurable inches and six measured pounds, 160 to 154—was able to penetrate Robinson's defense for the first time, his craggy features had a slightly pink hue, the result of thirteen direct hit by the champion's left jab.

Basilio was trying to go to the body, force the action, score on any part of Robinson that wasn't protected. But first he had to get past that jab, which kept coming at him with pistonlike efficiency. And when Basilio did get in, Robinson tied him up, his shorter arms in against his sides and holding on until the referee could part them and Sugar could escape back into midring again, away from the bull-like charges of Basilio, away from the pressure Basilio was exerting. Far enough away to start the staccato of jabs all over again. But Robinson, who had gone in as the betting underdog—the fourth time in his last five fights he had been the underdog—looked like anything but an underdog for the first three rounds. This was the man they had called "the greatest pound-for-pound boxer" in the history of boxing, a phrase coined especially for him. And he was jabbing, stabbing, and even grabbing at the rough-hewed features of the man in front of him, beating him both with his punch and to the punch.

In the third round Robinson bloodied Basilio's nose with an uppercut. Then, in the fourth, Robby connected with a right uppercut that cut Basilio's left eye. But still the freshly-stuck bull kept charging at his tormentor, throwing caution to the winds and lefts and rights to the body. Maybe it was his battle plan, or just maybe it was his cornerman, Angelo Dundee, who told the challenger before the start of the fourth round, "Go get him." Whatever, it worked. In the fifth, Basilio began to connect. Not that he hadn't before, but now it was more noticeable, attributable in part to the fact that the 37-year-old Robinson was beginning to wind down, the clock in his elder statesman's body beginning to run on a different time. For the first time Basilio was able to rush Ray into the ropes and land a left-right combination, staying in close and beating the Sugar Man to the punch.

Round 6 was a momentary reprieve for Ray as he once again relied on his stock-in-trade, his left jab, catching the onrushing Basilio on the face with six beautifully timed jabs, moving under and over, countering, bobbing, and weaving. But that was Sugar's last draught of the eternal youth elixir, his last taste of what once was. For the 37-year-old body trapped inside the 20-year-old mind was slowly taking over, slowly dictating the actions and reactions of its owner. And no amount of past greatness could will away the tiredness that now was. Nor the determined challenger. Basilio was now pressing the suddenly slower champion, driving him and the body that had been through 157 ring wars through the hells of an intensive body attack.

Robinson continued to use his jab, but starting in Round 7 he retreated behind it instead of using it as the first part of his vaunted one-two. And the shorter Basilio, disdainful of Robinson's left, kept coming in, throwing hooks, sweeping rights, and even straight right leads, catching Robinson with all of them.

As Round 8 opened, Basilio, his eye now covered with grease coating the cut and looking more like a ghostly apparition than a gladiatorial aspirant, continued to press Robinson, landing with lefts and rights to the body and with left hooks to the head. Occasionally he would vary his attack with a left to the body and a right to the head or a right to the body and another right to the body. But no matter what variation Basilio tried, it worked. Robinson, as was his trademark, would attempt to rally right before the bell in his traditional round-winning flurry, all the better to impress the judges, but to no avail. When he started to attack, more in desperation than in deliberation, Basilio would beat him to the punch.

Rounds 9 and 10 were more of the same. By the tenth Robinson was on his bicycle, trying to move away, to rally his forces for one last-ditch attack. But he was paying for his backward flight as the ever-pressing ex-Marine kept atop him, wading in behind left-rights to the head and to the body.

The eleventh opened as the tenth had ended, with Robinson landing his left and Basilio his right. But this time the positions seemed reversed: it was Robinson landing the heavier blows, looking like he had gone to the well and found new life. Instead of waiting for a round-ending rally, he was carrying the action to Carmen from the beginning—a hard right to the body, another counter-right to the body, a left to the body, and rights and lefts to the body in close as Basilio failed to tie him up. Then, with less than a minute to go in the round, it was Basilio's turn. And what a turn it was. He nailed Sugar on the jaw with three rights, propelling him back to the ropes, and then proceeded to use the champion's head for fungo practice, connecting with a fusillade of punches to the head. It looked like Robinson might go down, but right before the bell he came off the ropes and held.

It was hard for even the most dedicated Robinson fan to see how Robby could come back. His legs were working on a different time basis. His body had been ravaged by Basilio's strafing punches. His best was probably not good enough to hold off the challenger. But in a bout that will be remembered for its eddies and flows, the twelfth was to take another turn, with Robinson turning back the clock, getting in two lefts and a right to the head of the challenger, followed by another left and right—all on target. Suddenly Basilio was on rubbery legs, his balance that of a marionette with its strings cut. One minute he was standing there erect, if not tall, the next he was reeling around the ring looking for a place to fall down. But his Leon Errol act was too good. He wouldn't go down. And at the bell he half-walked, half-staggered back to his corner. And the tired Robinson, having shot his bolt and his best, went wearily back to his.

Still the fireworks weren't over. Robinson set out to finish up where he had left off in the thirteenth, landing an entire series of perfectly punctuated jabs to the now-bloody mess that had once been Basilio's face. It was Carmen who was throwing the desperation punches now; Robinson's were accurate and on target. But just as Robinson seemed to have stemmed the tide, back came Basilio with a vicious right to the jaw that shook Ray, followed by a left hook to the head. Then, as if in a kid's game of "now it's my turn," Robby came back with a right and two right uppercuts, again hurting Basilio. At the bell the 35,000 fans at Yankee Stadium were in bedlam, their voices as one, all cheering the two men who were putting on one of the greatest give-and-give battles in the history of boxing.

Robinson continued his assault in round 14, but no man—let alone a 37-year-old wonder—could maintain the pace. Although his left jab continued to work, his motions were slower, wearier, more those of a thirty-seven-year-old. He hurt Basilio again, but couldn't follow it up. By the last round, he was circling and jabbing, experiencing trouble moving as Basilio dictated the pace. Then came the bell, and the fight was over.

When the unassailable sums and straight-angled figures on the three officials' scorecards were tabulated—the referee calling it 9-6, Robinson, and the two judges, 9-5-1 and 8-6-1, Basilio—

Carmen Basilio was the new middleweight campion and Ray Robinson, for the fourth time, wore the title ex-middleweight champion of the world.

Afterward, each man, a winner in his own right, was to lose something. Basilio, the new middleweight king, automatically lost his welterweight crown, unable, by New York State law, to hold both crowns simultaneously. And Robinson lost his $500,000 purse, the IRS attaching it on "anticipated" income.

And yet whatever had happened, it couldn't be said, even by the heartiest of Robinson fans, that their man hadn't given his all. It was just that it wasn't the young Robinson whom Carmen had treated so indelicately. And therein lies the story of the fight, a great fight between two great fighters.

The Great Fights, 1981

Archie Moore vs. Yvon Durelle
The Forum, Montreal, Canada
December 10, 1958

Throughout the ages, old men have been lionized in everything from literature (*The Old Man and the Sea*), to nursery rhymes ("Old King Cole") and song ("Ol' Man River"). But none of them held a candle to the old lion of the ring, Archibald Lee Wright, better known as Archie Moore.

There was only one Archie Moore. He was glib, elegant, quick of wit and of hands, the possessor of more knockouts than any man in history, and holder of a world's championship for a longer period of time than any other champion except two. But the Methuselah of the ring will be remembered not for any of those achievements, but instead for his performance on the night of December 10, 1958—the night he battled Yvon Durelle and proved that you can't keep a good man—young or old—down.

The road to that memorable night was paved with detours and plenty of hard rocks. Born in either Collinsville, Illinois, or Benoit,

Mississippi, on either December 13, 1913, or December 13, 1916 (depending upon who was keeping score, Moore or his mother), Archie was either 42 of 45 years old the night of the fight. When asked about this discrepancy in his birthdate, the quick-thinking champion sidestepped and countered, "I have given this a lot of thought, and have decided that I must have been three when I was born."

Moore's first bout was in 1935 against Piano Mover Jones at Hot Springs, Arkansas. It ended in a second-round knockout for Moore, his first of a record-setting 141. It also began his long career in "bootleg" fights and tanktowns on the so-called Chittlin' Circuit, which was open to "colored" fighters who couldn't break into the big time. By 1936, Moore hit the highways and byways of backwater America, fighting some twenty-one times, mostly in and around his adopted hometown of St. Louis. He won eighteen fights, sixteen by KO, and was ready to make the bridge to the next rung on the fistic ladder, the small town clubs.

However, there were so many gradations to boxing back in the thirties that one boxer once asked his manager when he was booked for a fight in a town he had only a nodding acquaintance with, "Which one is it, small time, medium small-time, big small-time, little big-time, medium big-time, or The Bigtime?" And before Moore could even approach The Bigtime he had to pay his dues in more cities than anyone aside from Messrs. Rand and McNally ever heard of: cities like Keokuk, Quincy, and all points east, west, and south.

Moore fought twelve times in 1936 and won all twelve, ten by knockout, and the middleweight championships of Kansas, Oklahoma, and Missouri in the process. Now, it was on to the bigger time, if not The Bigtime, and Moore set sail for more lucrative boxing pastures in California, where he hoped to meet, and beat, the prominent middleweights fighting on the Coast and establish his credentials. However, as Moore's luck would have it, the day he arrived in San Diego was the day the boxing arena burned down.

This was the beginning of an unlucky streak that ran through Moore's early years: a severed tendon in the wrist here, a perforated ulcer that necessitated an operation to save his life there. If Moore had any luck, one wag suggested, it would have been "all bad."

But Moore, who was to survive more hardships than Job ever endured (including acute appendicitis, organic heart disorder, etc., etc., etc.), clung to his dual dreams that he would somehow come back and some day become a world champion.

Through dedication and perseverance he accomplished his first goal, coming back in 1942 to win his first five fights by KO. His second goal, however, took longer, much longer. It took him more than eleven years and fifty-eight knockouts to get a shot at a title.

Finally, on December 17, 1953, in front of his hometown fans, Archie Moore achieved his second goal, beating Joey Maxim decisively for the light heavyweight championship of the world. But even then Moore got the fuzzy end of the lollipop, earning only $800 for climbing to the pinnacle of his profession.

By now Moore's rocket had flown too close to the moon for him to be content with mere hang-gliding. He sought something more. He had to have something more than the $800 he received for winning a world's title. And, in the strange and wondrous way boxing operates, he got it. For along with Maxim's championship belt came Maxim's manager, the wily old Doc Kearns, the man who had guided Maxim—and, before him, Jack Dempsey and Mickey Walker—to the title.

It would be what Humphrey Bogart told Claude Rains at the conclusion of the film *Casablanca*, "the beginning of a beautiful relationship." Together they would forge a new trail on the fistic horizon, stepping over prone bodies on their way to the top. Over the next six years Moore would go to the post forty-three times, taking on all comers regardless of weight class, and dispatching twenty-five of them in fewer than the requisite number of rounds. His victims began whizzing by with all the rapidity of signs on the San Diego freeway, with names almost as recognizable: Bob Baker, Joey Maxim, Harold Johnson, Bobo Olson, Nino Valdes, James J.

Parker, Eddie Cotton, Willie Besmanoff, Charlie Norkus, and Howard King, among others too plentiful to enumerate.

Only twice during these six years was he to come up short. Both times in heavyweight championship fights. The first time he lost to Rocky Marciano in nine rounds after knocking down the Rock in the second with a short right uppercut. The second time he lost to Floyd Patterson in a fight for Marciano's vacated throne. It was a fight that has never been fully understood.

Beaten, but hardly vanquished, Moore returned to the more comfortable environs of the light heavyweight division, defending his title about once a year. In 1957 he fought Tony Anthony, and in 1958 he fought Yvon Durelle. Therein lies the story of Moore's greatest fight.

Yvon Durelle was a mightily muscled fisherman out of the Maritime provinces of Canada. The third-ranked light heavyweight, he had brawled his way through 96 fights in 11 years, hammering out thirty-eight of his opponents and outstaying another thirty-six. Despite his record, which included six losses—all by KO—Durelle was thought to have two chances, little and none, of becoming the Canadian to win a world's title since Jackie Callura had captured the NBA featherweight title some fifteen years before. Many of the writers—and the betting gentry who had installed Moore as a 3–1 favorite—thought the fight a mismatch. In fact, the local correspondent from the Montreal *Gazette* thought so little of Durelle's chances that he wrote, "People snicker when the name of Yvon Durelle is placed alongside that of Archie Moore."

When Moore arrived at the pre-fight physical resplendent in a midnight-blue tuxedo, a black homburg, and waving a silver-topped walking stick, he looked like he was snickering, too, if not laughing outright as he paraded around in what he called his "morning clothes." But the last laugh that night was almost on ol' Archie.

For that night, at the Montreal Forum, Archie had hardly had time to take off his gaudy red velvet dressing gown with the silver trimmings and show off his trim 173½-pound waistline before the "fit hit the shan." Working inside, Durelle delivered a right hand over the top to Moore's head. Moore dropped to the canvas as if he had been hit with a sledgehammer, which he might have been. The referee, former heavyweight champion Jack Sharkey, started tolling over the inert form of what appeared to be the soon-to-be-former light heavyweight champion of the world.

After what seemed like an eternity—to Moore as well as to the 8,484 fans—the lifeless form beneath Sharkey stirred and righted itself on shaky legs at the count of nine. Durelle fairly flew from a neutral corner, cuffing the champion, and then, with another right, dropping him again. This time Moore was up without a count. Trying to hold on, to use every ounce of guile and mastery mustered in his twenty-four-plus years in the ring, Moore attempted to weather the storm created by the fisherman in front of him. He hid behind his gloves, raised armadillo fashion, throwing out an occasional left. But Durelle was all over him, attempting to end the fight early.

As the seconds ticked off, and the sand in Moore's eternal hour glass began to slip away, Durelle caught Moore with yet another right to the head, dropping him for the third time. Moore looked up at Sharkey as he tolled off the count, thinking, as he was to recall later, "Can this be me? Is this really happening to me?" (Later, much later, on the banquet circuit, he was to "remember" thinking to himself, "This is no place to be resting. I'd better get up and get with it.") And get up he did, at the count of nine, and somehow, someway, got through that first round, his longest round, fighting largely on instinct.

He was also able to take advantage of a mental lapse on the part of the challenger who later admitted that he didn't go for a knockout after the third knockdown because, "I forgot that this was a championship fight and that three knockdowns didn't halt the fight."

Round 2 found a totally different Moore coming out to face his challenger. No longer was he snickering. He was in a battle for his boxing life. He started jabbing and hooking with his left, staying away from the lethal right hand in front of him. He not only managed to hold off the stronger challenger, he won the round on most of the unofficial cards at ringside. But Durelle came back in Round 3, once again applying pressure and once spinning Moore around and catching him with a left and right that had the champion covering up.

Round 4 found both men flurrying, with Moore landing by far the flashier combinations and taking the play away from the challenger. So furious was the pace that their flurries continued far past the bell ending the round, angering both combatants. The fifth was a replay of the first with Durelle catching Moore with a wild left hook, sending him sprawling for the fourth time.

Suddenly, out of the cloud that had enveloped him for the first fifteen minutes of the fight, Moore went on the attack, using his left as a battering ram, keeping it in the face of the challenger and trying to set up the one punch that would end it. Occasionally he would alter his attack, coming up with left hooks and combinations, as he did twice in the sixth when he staggered Durelle and bloodied his nose, and once in the seventh, when he floored the challenger for a count of three. But it was the left, and almost exclusively the left, that won Moore rounds six through nine. That and the fact that the 29-year-old challenger was running out of steam while the 42-going-on-45-year-old champion was coming on stronger.

Moore's systematic attack began to wear the challenger down, and he began to miss with wild punches as the obviously tired Moore reached back into his bag of tricks, if not into his memory, and staggered Durelle with a hard right.

It might have been at that exact moment that the momentum of the fight changed, when the fight went out of Durelle. Or, it might have been between rounds when Doc Kearns wouldn't let Moore sit down in his corner, but instructed him, instead, to wave to his wife in the audience, telling Moore his wife was seated in the opposite corner when, in fact, she was behind him. Durelle, seeing Moore wave, thought he has waving at him, scornfully.

Archie Moore vs. Yvon Durelle, December 10, 1958

In the tenth, the bell began to toll for Durelle's Cinderella story as Moore carried the attack to his tired challenger, hitting Durelle with everything he threw—hooks, uppercuts, overhand shots, and right-hand chops. Near the end of the round Durelle collapsed under the cumulative weight of the fusillade, looking as far gone as Moore had nine rounds earlier. But the bell rang at eight, saving Durelle for one more round.

The eleventh was merely an extension of the tenth as an exhausted Durelle staggered out of his corner and fell down without being hit. Up at the count of nine, he ran into a short right to the chin and went down. And out.

Archie Moore had come back from the dead. The old man had done it again, adding another name to his list of KO victims, number 127 to be exact, breaking Young Stribling's record.

Archie Moore had retained his crown as king of the light heavyweights and became in one night the all-time king of knockout artists. But he had done something else as well: he had seemingly found the secret of longevity.

The Great Fights, 1981

Cassius Clay vs. Sonny Liston
Convention Hall, Miami Beach, Florida
February 25, 1964

No event in recent American history, with the single exception of the assassination of President John F. Kennedy, is more shrouded in myth and mystery than the dethroning of heavyweight king Sonny Liston by Cassius Clay in Miami Beach on February 25, 1964.

Charles "Sonny" Liston was a much-maligned and badly misunderstood man—one who devoted most of his adult life to a clumsy quest for respectability. Jose Torres, former light heavyweight champion of the world and noted author, remembers Liston as "one of the most intelligent athletes I have ever met. He was so smart it wasn't even funny." But most of the world knew him as an ignorant, mean-tempered bully. This sharp difference between the man and his image may have had a great deal to do with his strange behavior on the night that he surrendered boxing's biggest prize.

Sonny was born into the family of an Arkansas sharecropper, a brutal drunkard who reportedly fathered twenty-five children. After an argument with his father, Sonny left home at the age of 13 to live with an aunt in St. Louis. There he drifted into a life of juvenile delinquency. At 16 he was already fighting with the local constabulary—their clubs against his fists. It was no contest, even then. Eventually he tried his hand at armed robbery. He was caught and sentenced to three concurrent five-year terms in the Jefferson City state penitentiary, an extremely harsh punishment for a young first offender.

A Roman Catholic prison chaplain had the foresight to suggest to inmate Liston that he channel his appetite for violence into boxing. Sonny agreed and quickly blossomed into a crude, but awesome talent. The authorities were sufficiently impressed to grant him a parole to pursue a career in the ring. In 1953, he captured the Chicago Golden Gloves heavyweight championship. A few months later he turned pro.

Blinkie Palermo, one of the mob figures who then controlled professional boxing, took an early interest in Liston's ring career. It was a Svengali-Trilby relationship that was at once Sonny's making and undoing. With Palermo's help Liston was given every opportunity to climb up the heavyweight ladder. He began to peak in August 1958, with a first-round knockout of tough Wayne Bethea in Chicago. The fight lasted all of 69 seconds. Just long enough for Bethea to lose seven teeth.

Sonny's first win over a recognized contender came six months later in Miami Beach, where he annihilated huge Mike DeJohn, the hardest-punching white heavyweight around and a darling of "Friday Night Fight of the Week" fans, in six rounds.

During the next four years Sonny Liston marched through the heavyweight division like Sherman through Georgia, leaving few survivors. Cleveland Williams, a ferocious puncher in his own right, fell in three of the most brutal rounds ever fought by big men. Liston, seemingly immune to pain, absorbed a series of the Big Cat's best punches without flinching.

Four months later, in August 1959, Nino Valdes, a man who had beaten Ezzard Charles, was dispatched in three rounds. In March 1960, Williams and Liston clashed again in Houston. In another incredible match, it took Sonny only two rounds to finish the job. A month later Roy "Cut and Shoot" Harris, who had gone twelve rounds in a title fight with Floyd Patterson, failed to survive three minutes with Liston. A third-round knockout of talented stylist Zora Folley in July 1960, and a 12-round decision over Eddie Machen in September of that year, entrenched Liston firmly in the number-one contender's slot, where he would languish for two long years.

The heavyweight division had never seen another man quite like him, a giant compressed into a six-foot, one-inch frame. His fists, fifteen inches in circumference, were bigger than Carnera's or Willard's. He had an eighty-four-inch reach, sixteen inches longer than Marciano's. He strengthened the muscles in his seventeen-inch neck by standing on his head for hours at a time. It was as if some futuristic geneticist had bred him in a test tube for the single purpose of beating up other men. His left jab knocked men out. It was in a class with Joe Louis's. His left hook was a lethal weapon, comparable to Joe Frazier's. He could go to the body with the ferocity of a Dempsey and launch a man toward the roof with an uppercut as powerful as George Foreman's. His right cross was a bit awkward, but he eventually perfected it into a deadly club.

But for all of his raw power and size, Liston's most remarkable attribute was psychological rather than physical. He made a science of inspiring fear in the hearts and minds of his opponents, breaking their wills with a stony stare during the referee's instructions, and stuffing towels under his robe to make his enormous physique look even bigger and more intimidating. In short, he was the meanest "mother" on the block, and not only didn't he care who knew it, he *wanted* everyone to know it.

Liston's carefully crafted techniques of intimidation were never more effective than they were against Floyd Patterson on

September 25, 1963 when Liston finally got his chance to fight for the heavyweight title.

Patterson's super-cautious manager Cus D'Amato had persuaded Floyd to stay clear of Liston for over two years, but pride and embarrassment finally got the better of the champion. Patterson was beaten before the first punch was thrown. He came to Comiskey Park in Chicago with a disguise hidden in a brown paper bag, all the better to slink out of the stadium unnoticed if—or rather *when*—Sonny beat him. The fight lasted all of two minutes and six seconds. On July 22, 1963, Patterson tried again. This time he survived four seconds longer. Both bouts could better be described as muggings than heavyweight title bouts.

The new heavyweight champion was perhaps the least-liked man to hold the title since Jack Johnson. Newspaper editorials cried out for boxing commissions to strip him of his crown. The NAACP made haste to put distance between Liston and the "respectable" portion of the Negro race. And even President Kennedy had called for Patterson to deny him the chance to fight for the title. The title that he had sought for so long, believing that it would magically make him as popular as his idol, Joe Louis, turned out to be an albatross. With few contenders left in the division he had decimated, even Liston's chance to cash in on his crown seemed to be, at best, illusory. At worst, nonexistent.

A desperate search for a fresh face who could create box-office interest in a fight with the seemingly unbeatable Liston turned up a 22-year-old youngster from Louisville, Kentucky named Cassius Marcellus Clay. Clay first gained national recognition in 1960 by winning a gold medal in the light heavyweight division at the Olympic games in Rome. He turned pro in October 1960, under the tutelage of Angelo Dundee, who already had guided three other fighters to world titles.

Clay's early career proceeded apace, as he ran off a string of seventeen victories—including fourteen knockouts—against carefully chosen opponents. His style was a composite of extreme unorthodoxies in and out of the ring. He carried his hands low, some said dangerously low, as he moved in wide circles around an opponent, stabbing out with a long, incredibly quick left jab, and delivering punches in dazzling bouquets of six, seven, and eight at a time. When a punch came at his head, he pulled back instead of slipping underneath it, or to the side as "the book" dictated.

Clay grabbed headlines for himself by stealing a page from a professional wrestler named Gorgeous George. He assumed an arrogant pose that insulted opponents and irritated the working press. To compound matters, beginning with his fight with Lamar Clark in April, 1961, he began predicting, in doggerel, the exact round in which he would knock his opponent out. Incredibly, he made good on his predictions seven times, even disposing of contenders Alejandro Lavorante and 49-year-old Archie Moore in the promised round.

By March 13, 1963 while Sonny Liston was training for his rematch with Patterson, Cassius Clay, the punching poet, was big box-office news. An all-time-record crowd piled into Madison Square Garden, hoping to see an inflated light heavyweight named Doug Jones short-circuit Clay's prediction of a fourth-round knockout. And his career as well. They got more than they bargained for, as Jones, a notorious failure as a heavyweight, fought Cassius to a virtual standoff for ten rounds, only to lose a highly controversial decision.

Three months later Clay traveled to London to fight Henry Cooper, who was, like Jones, a fringe contender. Cooper possessed a heavy left hook and facial tissue as brittle as a 50-year-old coat of paint, tissue that gushed like a geyser when it broke under the impact of a punch.

Late in the fourth round "Our 'Enery" unloaded an exquisite short left hook which exploded against Clay's chin and knocked him on the seat of his pants along the ropes. Cassius wobbled to his feet just as the bell sounded and before Cooper could follow up his momentary advantage. Between rounds Angelo Dundee miraculously "discovered" a tear in Clay's glove, manufacturing an excuse for a new glove which delayed the beginning of Round 5 and saved Cassius from the inevitability of a knockout. He answered the bell for Round 5 and quickly turned Cooper's face into a real-life imitation of raw hamburger.

Even with his tarnished wins over Jones and Cooper, Clay found himself occupying the number-one contender's slot during a heavyweight talent drought. He was eager for a fight with champion Sonny Liston, but few observers gave him the chance of the proverbial snowball in hell. Some gave him even less.

Liston's best punch was a left hook—the same blow that had twice sailed over Clay's low guard and knocked him to the canvas, once by Cooper and once by Sonny Banks.

Clay's chance at the title was the successful culmination of a two-year campaign to get Liston into the ring, a campaign that began moments after Sonny's enormous arm was raised by the referee on the night that he was crowned champion. That night Clay muscled his way through the crush in the ring at Comiskey Park where he stood face to face with Liston and issued a loud challenge. And when Liston set up camp for his rematch with Floyd in Las Vegas, Clay was right there, needling him incessantly during his workouts.

Sonny's training sessions were calculated to inspire fear. He could break a heavy bag with one punch. He juggled a medicine ball as if it was a peanut, to the sultry tune of his favorite song, "Night Train." But Clay wasn't impressed. He taunted Liston in the gyms and haunted Liston in the casinos, issuing insulting challenge after insulting challenge.

By November 1963, Liston had had enough. He agreed to fight Clay in Miami Beach the following February.

The Sonny Liston who signed to fight Clay admitted to being almost 32 years of age, but no official record of his birth existed. Friends placed his age closer to 40. Dating back to his close 12-

round decision over Eddie Machen in September 1964, Liston had engaged in four fights that lasted a total of only six rounds. The fine edge he had honed in his climb to the top had been dulled with ring rust. The one-sided nature of his two first-round knockouts of Patterson had disguised the fact that by the ordinary standards of the ring Sonny was ready to be taken by the right opponent.

In compiling a 32–1 record, with twenty-one knockouts, Liston had traveled ten rounds only three times and twelve rounds once. Virtually all his important wins were quick knockouts. Even at his peak, when he was fighting regularly, he had never had to demonstrate great stamina.

Clay, an avid student of fight films, was endlessly curious about the particular strengths and weaknesses of his opponents. Dundee, his trainer, was perhaps the foremost analyzer of styles in the business. Together, they identified the obvious flaw in Liston's arsenal. Machen, a quick scientific boxer, adept at slipping punches and using the whole ring, had managed to last twelve rounds against Liston at his best and come within a couple of points of beating him. The lone loss on Liston's record had been inflicted by a little-known journeyman named Marty Marshall, who subsequently lasted a full ten rounds in another fight with Liston. Marshall, a defense-minded clown out of the Willie Meehan school, had frustrated Liston where better fighters had failed because he employed lateral movement. If Cassius Clay had mastered anything, it was lateral movement. If he could keep away from Liston until Sonny had depleted what had to be a limited supply of energy anything might happen.

Clay was not content to rely on speed and strategy. He attacked Liston with a well-orchestrated psychological *divertissement*, coming to a rousing climax at the prefight weigh-in.

Weigh-ins are generally uneventful. Both fighters are usually anxious to get away from the press for a few final hours of rest and quiet contemplation of combat. With the moment of truth approaching for Clay, Sonny must have anticipated that he would confront a chastened challenger at the weigh-in, one who would be vulnerable to the usual Liston intimidation.

Clay and his entourage, including Drew "Bundini" Brown, photographer Howard Bingham, Gene Kilroy, Dr. Ferdie Pacheco, and Angelo Dundee, arrived first. They were wearing big cowboy hats and waving placards. Even Dundee, normally a conservative man, was wearing a hat. Clay and Brown, his court jester and resident witch doctor, were chanting like lunatics: "Float like a butterfly, sting like a bee! Rumble, young man, rumble!" The mob of reporters in the room pressed forward, trying to make some sense out of the nonsense.

Liston walked into a madhouse. At first he couldn't even get close enough to Clay to fix his cold stare on him. When the two fighters were finally face to face, with the international media crowding around them to record the scene, Clay actually taunted Sonny and Brown had to "restrain" him. When commission doctor Alex Robbins took the challenger's blood pressure it registered at 200/100—an alarmingly high reading.

A confused press rushed back to their typewriters, still trying to figure out exactly what had happened. Relying heavily on what turned out to be a case of self-induced high blood pressure, they reported that Clay was gripped by fear. The press might have been fooled, but Liston wasn't. He knew the look of fear on a fighter's face and this wasn't it. Madness, perhaps, but not fear. And if there was anything that vibrated Liston's strings, it was someone "acting crazy."

Like most confirmed practical jokes, Liston hated nothing worse than being made a fool. After the final travesty of the weigh-in, Sonny was determined to make Clay pay dearly for his fun, which was exactly what Cassius had hoped for.

That night, in front of a disappointing crowd of 8,297 fans rattling around Miami's spacious Convention Hall, a more composed Clay met Liston again. This time, face to face in the center of the ring for the prefight instructions, it became apparent to Liston, for the first time, that Clay was larger, much larger, than he was. This would be no confrontation between a Jack and a giant—like the Liston-Patterson fights. Clay, although outweighed by eight pounds, 218 to 210, and giving away four inches in reach, stood a full two inches taller than Liston. It was a psychological victory for Clay, Liston never having fought anyone taller.

Liston tried once more with his famous death-ray eyes. *Six* towels had been stuffed under his robe, so that he looked like a wall of terrycloth. Clay met his gaze squarely. As referee Barney Felix gave his instructions, Clay hissed, *"Chump!* Now I got you, *chump!"* The shock must have hit Sonny harder than any punch he ever absorbed in the ring.

Liston was a somewhat mechanical fighter—a George Foreman trying to imitate Joe Louis. He had learned how to jab and feint and vary his punches. He knew how to cut off a ring. But his basic technique never changed: two steps forward, step again, and jab. Hook off the jab or follow it with a right. Two steps forward and so on and so on. Clay had studied films of Sonny's fights, taking note of his ponderous, patterned footwork and the heavy jab that packed enough power to knock down a wall.

As the bell sounded Liston lurched out of his corner, an energized Frankenstein coming to life. He nearly ran at Clay to begin the first exchange, but as soon as Sonny started his jab, Cassius slid gracefully to his left, away from the punch. Clay almost seemed to be running as he circled around the champion at a speed unheard of in a heavyweight contest. Liston jabbed and jabbed again, missing Clay's head by wide margins. The challenger's hands were almost dangling at his sides, leaving his head exposed to all kinds of mayhem. But each time Liston reached for it, it was gone, faster than you could say Cassius Marcellus Clay. As Clay moved to his left, Sonny made the correct adjustment, trying to decapitate him with a right hook. The punch missed. Liston kept shuffling forward moving quickly enough for Sonny Liston, trying to maneuver Cassius into a corner, but not quickly enough to catch him. Clay didn't throw one punch in anger until the round was almost over. A left jab, like a switchblade knife pulled out from under a coat, snapped into Sonny's face. Clay stopped moving and unleashed a flurry of lefts and rights to the champion's face. Liston seemed frozen in time. By the time he woke up and surged forward, Clay was on his bicycle and the bell had sounded. Liston stomped back to his corner, snorting mad. By surviving the first round, Clay had already won an important psychological victory.

For all of his anger and anxiety, Liston still remembered what he had been taught by his trainer, Willie Reddish. After only one round of chasing Clay, he concluded that he would not be able to take him out early with a single left hook to the head. First he would have to slow him down by clubbing his body, a process that Sonny was able to accomplish against most fighters in one or two rounds.

As the bell sounded to begin Round 2, Liston charged out of his corner, throwing heavy punches with both hands. Quickly he forced Clay against the ropes, where he dug brutal blows to Clay's liver and kidneys before Cassius could wriggle out to ring center. Still moving, almost galloping, to his own left as Sonny came straight at him, Clay picked his openings with the care of a master craftsman. His jab never missed and he always followed up with a fast combination before gliding out of danger. Each time he was hit, Liston froze, unable to counter Clay's blows.

A tiny cut, barely perceptible, opened on the champion's left cheekbone, under his eye. It was the first time in thirty-four professional fights that Liston had shed even a drop of blood. Sonny retaliated with a long left that was like a 2×4 coming out of a basement window, catching Clay with a meaningful punch for the first time in the fight. The challenger recalls, "It rocked me back. But either he didn't realize how good I was hit, or he was already getting tired and he didn't press his chance." In fact, it would be many years before anyone would be able to tag Clay with *two* damaging blows to the head in quick succession, and his ability to absorb punishment to the body would become legendary.

Round 3 saw Liston still pressing forward, hacking away at air, and Clay revolving clockwise around him. Sonny was moving just a little bit slower now. Still he was able to jolt the challenger with punches to the body that appeared to be inconsequential, but were, in fact, painful. "After the fight Clay's ribs and flanks were one big angry red welt," remembers the challenger's physician, Ferdie Pacheco.

Midway through the third session, Clay inflicted the first real damage of the fight. He feinted with his left and then drove a right uppercut into Sonny's cheek. The punch landed like an ice pick, and the once-tiny wound gaped open, spurting blood. Liston pawed at the cut, not completely believing what was happening. At the end of the third round he walked back to his corner, a weary man. For the first time he sat down.

During training for the fight Liston had sustained a very minor injury to his left arm or shoulder—the kind of slight damage that athletes habitually ignore when there is a big payday at stake. Liston's handlers had prepared for a possible aggravation of this minor injury by including a solution of alcohol and oil of wintergreen in their corner kit. During the early rounds, Sonny unleashed dozens of full force punches at Clay's head that missed everything. Swinging at air is more fatiguing to the muscles than hitting a target. Inevitably Liston's sore shoulder began to ache under the strain. Between Rounds 3 and 4 Sonny's corner was a busy place, as they worked to close the deep cut under his left eye and massaged his left shoulder with liniment.

Round 4 was the least eventful of the fight. Clay allowed Liston to work inside, sometimes covering up instead of moving laterally. The challenger, who had gone ten rounds only three times, was pacing himself for a 15-round bout. And, as Cassius walked back to his corner at the end of the round, he was squinting and blinking. A bit of Liston's liniment had gotten into Clay's eye. As Dundee wiped the fighter's face with a sponge, more of the fiery substance went into both of his eyes, leaving him momentarily blind. He was frightened. No man, however brave, would willingly take on a wounded beast like Liston without full sight. In the challenger's corner they were unaware that the liniment had caused the problem. Clay wondered if Dundee hadn't put something in his sponge. He looked to Drew Brown, holding up his gloves, and screamed, "Cut them off!" Referee Barney Felix came over to see what the confusion was about. Dundee, halfway down the steps leading out of the ring, came back up, pushed Clay out into the ring with one hand, and snatched the stool out from under him with the other. "This is the big one, daddy!" he shouted as he launched his fighter into action.

All of this had not gone unnoticed in the champion's corner. Indeed, in two of his previous fights, Liston's opponents had complained about their eyes "burning." Liston now looked at Clay "like a kid looks at a new bike on Christmas," remembers Ferdie Pacheco. He came at Cassius with renewed energy, swinging his big fists like a pair of meat cleavers. How clearly Clay could see is still not certain. He walked out on unsteady legs, holding out his left hand like a blind man's cane. Sonny quickly backed him against the ropes. Clay leaned back, pushing his left glove into Sonny's face, slipping those punches he could see. Referee Barney Felix thought seriously about stopping the fight.

At first Liston's punches got through—agonizing wallops to the midsection and a couple of left hooks to the head. Clay began to move blindly around the ring on instinct as his corner tried to guide him and Liston tried to tear his head off. Then his eyes began to clear just as Sonny was slowing down and not throwing so many punches—and missing most of them. As the round drew to a close, Clay began lashing out with needle-sharp jabs, raising red welts under both of Liston's eyes.

Referee Barney Felix had the ring doctor take a precautionary look at Clay's eyes between Rounds 5 and 6. On the other side of the ring, Liston's corner was a somber place. The champion was clearly tired now, having already boxed just one round less than he had fought in the preceding three-and-a-half years.

Like a man trudging off to the guillotine knowing what fate had in store for him, Sonny Liston shuffled out in the sixth round to face the fastest and perhaps the greatest heavyweight fighter in history. Quickly Clay went on the attack, missing with a left hook, but scoring with a wicked right-left combination to the head. When Liston failed to return the fire, Clay machine-gunned him with six consecutive unanswered punches—three lefts, followed by three rights. Sonny jabbed back listlessly and Clay ripped home a pair of lefts into the soon-to-be ex-champion's lumpy face. Clay then moved out to long range, circling and jabbing with surgical precision. The punches made a loud, painful thud as they wacked into Liston's sad face. There was a purple lump under the champion's right eye and a four-inch gash under his left one. Cassius missed with a big right that drew a rise from the crowd. He drilled holes in Sonny's head with his left, driving it into his face four times in succession. Sonny responded with a solid, short right that was his last hurrah, but Clay made him pay for his folly with two more razor-sharp lefts. The crowd roared its approval at the bell.

As Clay went back to his stool he shouted at the press section, "I'm gonna upset the world!"

Both corners worked feverishly on their fighters for fifty seconds of the allotted minute between Rounds 6 and 7. At the ten-second buzzer Clay was on his feet, glaring across the ring at Liston who was slumped on his stool, the sand slowly sifting out of his championship glass. Some observers claim that a tear coursed down his wounded cheek. Liston opened his mouth and spat his mouthpiece out onto the canvas, as if it had a bad taste. Suddenly, the fight was over. Liston's manager, Jack Nilon, had stopped it because of what he said was "the severe pain in Liston's left shoulder."

Clay, looking like his feet were afire, leapt around the ring. "King!" he bellowed. "Eat! Eat! Eat your words! I am the king! I am the *king!*" he shouted to the forty-six newspapermen at ringside, forty-three of whom had picked Liston.

It was anyone's guess what really went through the bruised, confused head of Sonny Liston as he sat on his stool between the sixth and seventh rounds. His was a head that had been hit with policeman's clubs and filled with the strange paranoia of the underworld. Being the champion couldn't have been much fun for Sonny, not with the leaders of his own race, the press, and even the President of the United States lined up against him, and God knows what kind of creatures crawling out of his shady past to claim repayment for old favors.

You sensed that when Sonny Liston spat out his mouthpiece, he was spitting out the rotten, bitter fruits of a success that was really just one more disguised failure in the life of this unlucky man.

Hit the Sign and Win a Free Suit of Clothes from Harry Finklestein, 1978

Muhammad Ali vs. Joe Frazier
Madison Square Garden, New York
March 8, 1971

Just as the making of a great martini must be the correct mating of gin and vermouth at precisely the right moment, not a second too early nor one too late, so too is the making of a great fight, one made at precisely the right moment.

Such was the case with the Muhammad Ali and Joe Frazier on that night of March 8, 1971, a fight which possessed all the right ingredients of a great fight: two undefeated heavyweight champions, fighting for the most money ever earned by an athlete, let alone a boxer, fought in the midst of a turbulent debate over the Vietnam conflict with one of the participants adopted by those in support of the war, the other by those opposed, and held in the mecca of boxing, Madison Square Garden, in front of a riotous assemblage.

It was a fight that captured the imagination not just of the fight fans, but of the entire world. It was not merely another of the "Fights of the Century," which, according to the boxing historians, had already totaled up to centuries far beyond Flash Gordon's twenty-fifth, but, as boxing scribe Barney Nagler dubbed it, "The Fight."

The weeks leading up to the fight had writers everywhere reducing their pencils down to stubs covering it like the Creation of the World, part II, chronicling everything and anything about it and its participants. Ali's pre-fight doggerel had him saying, "They call Joe Frazier 'Smokin' Joe' because he talks about he's hot. He always talks about he's gonna come out smokin'. So I wrote a poem and it describes what happens:

> *Joe's gonna come out smokin'.*
> *And I ain't gonna be jokin'.*
> *I'll be pecking and a-pokin'*
> *Pouring water on his smokin'.*
> *This might shock and amaze ya,*
> *But I'm gonna re-tire Joe Frazier."*

On the other glove, Joe Frazier made no such request upon the art of conversation, instead saying only: "He calls me 'Uncle Tom' and I call him a phony." No match for Ali in their pre-fight hoopla, Frazier had hung up the phone on Ali during a commercial being filmed for the hair tonic *Vitalis*, not wanting to put up with Ali's "jive." He would save his talking for the ring.

The scene that Monday night in '71 would have done justice to the worst excesses of the French Revolution. Hours before the doors officially opened at 7:30, thousands, both with and without tickets, milled around outside Madison Square Garden, there to be seen and obscene. Amongst the crowd could be seen scalpers offering one-hundred-and-fifty dollar tickets for seven hundred a pop, men preening and prancing around in full-length white mink coats and women in extreme clothes, sporting everything from twelve-inch-down-the-knee slit skirts to low-cut blouses and five-inch heels. And everywhere more fur than could be found on an Alaskan range.

When the doors to the Garden finally opened, many went through hell just to make their entrance. Even those with tickets had to wait an hour as the crowd surged toward the doors. One woman, in tears, had just given her ticket to a ticket-taker when a mysterious hand materialized out of nowhere to snatch it from her. The doorman, a witness to what happened, was powerless to redress her loss.

As the 17,000-plus filled the cavernous arena, there, at ringside, could be seen the celebrities *du jour:* the notables, quotables, and even those who weren't household names in their own households, all of whom created a stir once identified. At ringside could be seen Burt Lancaster, doing the commentary for the closed-circuit audience; LeRoy Neiman, sketching the goings-on; and the photographer for *Life* Magazine, Frank Sinatra. And up in the balcony, (the balcony for Chrissakes!) was former vice president, Hubert Humphrey.

Finally, after what seemed an eternity, the house lights go down and the people rise to their feet in one noisy mass. For there he is, emerging from the shadows, clad in red robe and red tasseled shoes, throwing punches in the air as he dances down the aisle: Muhammad Ali. Commotion! Chaos!

As he steps into the ring, he extends his arms in the air, and the crowd, now his congregation, let out with a two-syllabic chant: "Al-li, Al-li, Al-li!" He rewards them with his famous "Ali Shuffle" and the crowd goes wild.

Then, almost as if a choirmaster had waved off the noise, the crowd begins to settle back in their seats only to rise again as another familiar figure comes down the aisle: Joe Frazier. His entrance is more subdued, his pace more measured, as Frazier, berobed in a velvet-brocaded outfit, green and gold, shuffles toward the ring, throwing punches, his eyes straight down, all business. The crowd, recognizing him, lets out with another cheer, almost equal to the one given Ali just seconds before.

Now the two fighters are in the ring, attended by their entourage—Ali by Angelo Dundee and "Bundini" Brown and Frazier by Yank Durham—as ring announcer Johnny Addie reaches for the microphone coming down from the ceiling. The crowd hushes, bursting into wild applause only when the fighters' names are announced. Referee Arthur Mercante then brings the two fighters to the center of the ring for their last-minute instructions and they return to their respective corners to hear last-second advice and exhortations from their handlers.

And then, the bell! Frazier walks straight in, Ali comes in a circle, both meeting almost in the center of the ring. Ali feints with a left, Frazier walks in, missing his own jab. Frazier misses with another jab and Ali counters with one of his own. Frazier keeps coming, a one-dimensional machine, his body weaving, his hands moving up and down, his chin buried in his chest, pursuing Ali. Ali stops and throws a jab. Another jab. Many of his punches are missing and Frazier keeps coming. Ali stops again, throws a jab, steps back, feints, throws a fast jab and follows with a right cross, then an even faster left hook/right cross combination, many of the punches missing the crouching Frazier, who keeps boring in at the same pace. Frazier connects for the first time with a right to Ali's chest. Ali keeps moving. He moves straight back and Frazier follows. It is relentless pressure. They go inside now and Ali pushes Joe to the side and hits him with a jab. Ali smiles. Frazier throws a left that falls short again. The bell.

Round 2. Again Ali comes to the center of the ring in a circle. Again, he feints. Frazier jumps back and jumps back in, but is unable to reach the taller Ali. Ali stops and throws a barrage of punches. Now Ali moves with Frazier chasing him, maintaining the same exact pace. Ali's eyes seem transfixed on Frazier's forehead; Frazier's on Ali's chest. Ali circles Frazier, first to his right, then to his left, throwing jabs. Frazier is following him, not cutting off the ring, his pace turtle-like compared to Ali's. Frazier connects with a jab to Ali's head. Another falls short as Ali comes back with one of his own that misses. The bell ends Round 2.

Ali stands in his corner, his mouthpiece still in place, listening to Dundee—and occasionally to Bundini, who remains quiet when

Dundee talks—while, over in the other corner, Frazier listens to the calm, soothing tones of Durham, who alternately wipes down his face and doles out advice.

The bell for Round 3. Frazier starts out of his corner per normal invoice, walking straight to Ali. But this time Ali doesn't circle, but instead meets Frazier in his corner, then retreats two, three steps back into the ropes. Frazier begins to work Ali over. A wild left by Frazier. Ali pulls back his head at the last second and the air generated by the blow air conditions the first two rows. Ali remains on the ropes and Frazier continues to look for openings, connecting with a right to the body and then launching another long, left hook, which misses its mark again.

Ali is still on the ropes and Frazier hits him with a vicious left. A right hits Ali's face as it moves away. A fast hook grazes Ali on the right side of his face. Ali tries to move, but Frazier won't let him. Joe pushes Ali back to the ropes. Ali smiles. Now Frazier smiles. Another hook by Frazier lands on Ali's face, but Ali sees it coming and rolls with the punch. Ali gets off the ropes, Frazier pursuing, coming forward, like a tank. Frazier throws some vicious punches, but Ali shakes his head "No," signifying to the crowd that he is not hurt. His fans laugh and cheer. Ali now smiles at the crowd. Again, his crowd laughs and applauds. Meanwhile, Joe is punching furiously: a left hook, a right, another hook. Frazier is making the fight. Ali retaliates with a flurry, almost pitty-pat punches. Now Frazier is the one who laughs. The "other crowd" laughs with him. A mean left hook that Ali never saw just misses and the round ends where it began: with Ali on the ropes.

There had been a change in the momentum of the fight. The transition was being forced on Ali by Frazier, with Frazier pinning Ali on the ropes and banging away with murderous punches while Ali, on occasion, responded with combinations, catching the oncoming Frazier. But Ali's responses were just that: occasional, not often. For Ali, he may well have experienced the worst round of the 204 he had fought in his pro career.

The fourth and fifth rounds would be more of the same. If you were writing footnotes, you could write *ibid.*

Ali has now begun sitting on his stool between rounds. His breathing is heavy, but no more so than Frazier's in the opposite corner, both fighters working under tremendous pressure.

In the sixth, Ali seems to move more. Jabs and moves. Jabs again. Frazier hasn't changed, he's still coming in. Ali begins throwing uppercuts at a head that doesn't stop moving. Ali retreats to the ropes and jabs at Frazier, who doesn't look like he has the same drive. The momentum swings again. Ditto, round seven.

In the eighth, two seemingly tired fighters face off against each other. Ali again goes to the ropes and Frazier tees off, missing his target with seven punches. Ali drops his hands, daring Joe to hit him. Frazier, too, drops his, and Ali accommodates him, throwing a one-two combination that hits Frazier flush on the face, above the jaw. Now Frazier is the one laughing. Frazier's tree trunk-like legs push him toward Ali and Ali goes back to his favorite spot: the ropes. Frazier lashes out with another of his attacks. The round ends.

Ali is welcomed back to his corner by two open mouths. They are telling him off. He's fooling around. And fooling himself as well. For every time Ali invites Joe to come and punch, Joe accommodates him, Ali doing nothing in return. And, in doing so, Frazier is showing both the confidence *and* the will to win.

Round 9 has Ali moving beautifully again, looking like he has found his "second wind" and snapping his jab off in Frazier's face. When Ali moves and punches he makes the slow-moving Frazier seem amateurish and slow. It's now that kind of fight for Ali.

But, in Round 10, Ali reverts to the Ali of old, the Ali of Rounds 3, 4 and 5, retreating to the ropes where Joe begins his work again. He is throwing fewer punches than before, but making more contact. A wicked left hook lands to Ali's body. A right to Ali's forehead. Ali seems to be resting, Frazier chasing. Frazier missed a lot, especially with wicked left hooks, but he was doing *something;* Ali, *nothing.* Then, in the last twenty seconds of the round, Ali tried to steal it, throwing one . . . two . . . three jabs. All direct hits. Then a left/right combination of his own. The bell. The fight is two-thirds over and Ali is seemingly in command of his own destiny with the "championship rounds," Rounds 11 through 15, to go.

But then comes Round 11. And everything changes again. For as Ali goes back to his favorite resting spot, like a tiger remembering its favorite place, Frazier is on him. And then a left hook from hell catches Ali on the button. His legs shake, he can't control them. Frazier goes on the attack. He rakes Ali's body with vicious punches. A right to the body, a left to the body, now Frazier pushes Ali back against the ropes. Another sinful left hook! Ali's legs, strangers to each other, buckle. His eyes are glassy. He looks like he's going to the canvas. In his entire career he has never been hurt this badly. Ali's will struggles to keep him on his protesting legs. Frazier is punching, his muscles forcing his arms to move faster, stronger. Ali begins playing games, pretending he is hurt worse than he really is, momentarily halting Frazier's forward movement as he considers whether his opponent is playing possum. Then it's back to the attack. Finally, the bell ends the one-sided round.

Bundini is up on the apron of the ring, throwing water at Ali who walks slowly to his corner. Water splashes some of the newsmen at ringside. Ali slumps on the stool. Dundee works on his weak legs. Bundini pours water over Ali's head and back.

Round 12 finds Ali moving slowly out of his corner, using his damaged legs, trying to overcome the beating he got in the previous round. He moves to his right, now to his left. Frazier resumes his attack, pinning Ali against the ropes once again. Ali keeps his right hand close to his cheek, all the better to avoid those savage hooks to his chin. The round plays itself out with Ali trying to recover from the horrific beating he took in round 11.

The thirteenth begins like all the previous three rounds: Ali, with back to the ropes, Frazier, applying more pressure than an army of acupuncturists, on the attack. Frazier now looks like a man who has been pushing a loaded truck uphill for thirty-six looooong minutes, but shows no signs of stopping short of his goal as long as his energy holds out. For three more minutes he's everlastingly at it, backing Ali up, beating on him, dealing out more punishment. And Ali's taking it. The noise at the end of the round tells it all with Frazier's crowd, some of them having backed *their* man with money at the 7–5 odds he commanded as the favorite, aroar, and Ali's constituency murmuring with concern.

The bell for the fourteenth quiets the crowd. A little. Ali is again pulled by the magnetism of the ropes. Frazier swings twice with wild lefts. And misses. Now, somehow, someway, Ali escapes from his self-made prison of ropes to come out to the center of the ring and is the one doing the swinging. He connects with a vicious left hook to Frazier's head. A right. He pushes Joe back and hits him with a one-two combination. Ali looks like a new man, a revitalized man, as he explodes with punches to Frazier's head. Ali is now a moving target; a moving target leaving punches to be remembered by.

Could it be that Ali has once again changed the course of the fight? That he still has a chance to pull it out? That Frazier has punched himself out and that Ali has found new life? These were the questions going through everyone's mind as the bell sounded, ending Round 14.

Last round! Expectation is still the word to describe the excited crowd. No one is sure who is ahead. Some say Ali, some say Frazier. But nobody, nobody, is yelling one-sided now.

Both meet in the center of the ring for the ritualistic touching of the gloves, Frazier coming out of his corner in a determined gait, Ali a little more deliberately. Ali moves back, toward his corner, with Joe almost on top of him. Ali moves to his left. He now moves to the center of the ring. He moves straight back to the south side of the ring. He moves his left foot back, as if to throw a punch. Joe starts a left hook. He pulls it back and reloads, then leaps off the floor to launch it, getting all 205½ pounds behind it. Ali is moving his head back slowly, looking away from the punch. The left hook explodes on Ali's exposed jaw. For only the third time in his career Ali crashes to the canvas, his eyes glazed.

One second passes and Ali's eyes are trying to focus desperately. Mercante's count goes to "three" and Ali, by force of will, lifts himself off the mat, taking the mandatory eight-count. He walks toward Joe on unsteady feet, the right side of his face distorted from the power of Joe's malevolent left hook. The damage from that one blow is irreparable. Frazier has just won the fight. The impact of that one blow took everything Ali had left. He is there strictly to finish the fight on two feet. Moments later, Frazier, on the attack, jolts his 215-pound rival with another left hook. But Ali holds on. With a minute remaining in the round, and the fight, Ali tries to go for a knockout. But his punches have no effect on Frazier. With the crowd roaring, the bell rings and Frazier playfully cuffs Ali across his head, hung in acknowledged defeat.

The decision, read by Johnny Addie—Judge Bill Recht, eleven rounds to four, Frazier; Judge Artie Aidala, nine rounds to six, Frazier; and Referee Arthur Mercante, eight rounds to six, one even, Frazier—merely verified what everyone already knew: that Joe Frazier had won "The Fight."

But even though Frazier had won "The Fight," the people's hearts had been won by Ali. In subway after subway leading away from Madison Square Garden that chilly March night, signs could be seen etched in the artistic medium of the "little" people, spray paint reading: "Ali Lives."

Sting Like a Bee . . . , 1972

George Foreman vs. Joe Frazier
Kingston, Jamaica
January 22, 1973

A funny thing happened to Joe Frazier on his way to a multi-million dollar return bout with Muhammad Ali: He met George Foreman in a match called "The Sundown Showdown." And, in a blowout as elementary as any since Jack Dempsey had annihilated Jess Willard some half-century earlier, the young challenger dissembled "Smokin' Joe" in just 275 seconds.

With shoulders like those of a blacksmith and arms like battering rams, Big George was unbeaten in thirty-seven fights, thirty-four of those knockout wins. But common wisdom asked, "Who'd he ever beat?" and installed him as a 3–1 underdog to the supposedly "invincible" Frazier, winner of all his twenty-fix fights and conqueror of Muhammad Ali. Still, Foreman thought he could do it, and that was all it was to take.

At the opening bell, "Smokin' Joe" came out in his patented bob and weave. Pressing the attack, he set up shop in midring, all the better to work his way under the seventy-eight-and-one-half inches-reach of the challenger and throw his potent left hook. But Foreman met him head-on, never taking a backward step, and started probing at the champion's head with a left.

One of those in Foreman's corner, Doc Broadus, had scouted Frazier during his training sessions to look for secret moves. He told Foreman, "I didn't see any. He just led with his head, same as always. George, drop that hammer on him." And that's just what George did, frescoing him with a thunderous right to the head as Frazier waded in, head up and unprotected.

Falling base over apex, Frazier's seat had barely touched the canvas before he jumped up and once again tried to work his way back inside. But after an exchange of punches, Foreman unloaded with a series of rights to Frazier's head. Once again, Frazier went to the canvas. Wearing the look of a man who had eternally been put upon, a dazed Frazier arose quickly. But just as quickly, he was deposited back on the canvas by a howitzer shot of a right that Foreman delivered just as the bell sounded to end the first round.

Frazier rushed out for the second round, trying mightily to land his left hook. But Foreman picked off the punches, and in return, landed a woodchopping right and left to the champion's jaw, sending Frazier to the mat for the fourth time. Frazier, with powers barely those of respiration and locomotion, got up only to be knocked down yet again. Frazier struggled to his feet once again, where this time, he ran into a series of punches, punctuated by a pluperfect right uppercut. The punch lifted the fireplug form of Frazier straight up in the air, defying gravity, like a tree stump pulled out of the ground.

And still he tried to regain his feet. As he stood there, unsure of what was going on—or going wrong—referee Arthur Mercante Sr. signaled the end of Frazier's reign at 1:35 seconds of the second round and six knockdowns. Now, to those who asked, "Who'd he ever beat?", George Foreman could answer "Smokin' Joe" Frazier. Badly.

The Great Fights, 1981

Aaron Pryor vs. Alexis Arguello
The Orange Bowl, Miami, Florida
November 12, 1982

Belief is a funny word. It's made up of one part hope, one part per-ception, and one part realization—with a sprig or two of bias thrown in for good measure. And boxing has more than its share of beliefs-cum-biases, especially where great matches such as the Pryor-Arguello match are concerned.

When the fight itself was announced you had to believe that this would be one helluva match-up: The unflappable, almost un-beatable Alexis Arguello going for his fourth title—something even the immortal Henry Armstrong could not bring off—versus the undisciplined style of Aaron Pryor, a Waterpik out of control, running amok in the trappings of a boxer. The match-up was so good, in fact, that writers converging on Miami before the fight had already ceded it "Fight of the Year" honors before the first punch was thrown in anger.

Belief dictated that Arguello would be the matador, Pryor the bull, with Arguello, one of the fiercest body punchers in the history of the sport—so fierce, in fact, that when he hit Cornelius Boza-Edwards a shot to the *la bonza*, Boza-Edwards lost control of his bodily functions and actually soiled his trunks—implanting his bondaleros into the unprotected gut of Pryor until the final kill. Unless, of course, Pryor was to get to him early.

The beliefs, and the theories, went on and on. Pryor early, Arguello late went one. Pryor was easy to hit, even knock down, especially if KO Kameda could knock him head-over-belt, went another. Legs, went still another, tend to rebel against an older fighter's wishes and in the later rounds have a mind of their own. And, the ropebirds suggested, champions from lower divisions fail more often than not in their upwardly-mobile challenges across the divisional Rubicon. Finally, there were many from the good-little-man-good-big-man school who held that punchers cannot take their power with them when they transcend a division's boundaries, the weight displacement working against them geometrically rather than arithmetically.

But, for forty minutes and six seconds, belief was in a constant state of suspension, as first one and then another of the preconceived beliefs were knocked into someone or other's cocked hat.

The evening at Miami's Orange Bowl had started in a strange manner, destroying any belief anyone put into local boxing commissions. Starting with the absence of a bell (because, as one commissioner put it, "The man who had the bell was a timekeeper who was not assigned to the main event and I guess he told everybody to 'go to hell' and took off,") down through the lack of stools for fighters, the Miami commissioners paid an amazing lack of attention to details. With six inspectors assigned to cover the two dressing rooms, five fewer than the number assigned showed up, meaning that one of the two dressing rooms would always be uncovered. With the psyche running about as rampant as the flu on a cold winter's night, this oversight allowed those in the Pryor camp to try to throw a pre-fight intimidation into Arguello, much as they were trying to pump up their own man, screaming in unison, "It's Hawk Time" in response to their own exhortation, "What time is it?" But the inspector's absence almost took on tragic overtones in light of the pre-fight hysteria surrounding the presence of Nicaraguan Sandinista forces in the audience who would try to "get" at expatriate Arguello. (In fact, one man with a gun was apprehended near the Arguello dressing room, with the three-time champ hurried into the shower.)

Despite the boxer commissioners acting like anything but, the two fighters somehow made it into the ring, fighting their way through the crowd at ringside and even through their own hangers-on, now filling every corner of the ring, proving that nature and pre-fight championship fights both abhor vacuums. In fact, it was a similar pre-fight mob scene before the Pryor-Kameda fight that caused the predestined loser, KO Kameda, to complain, "I had no room to warm up, that's why I lose fight."

Now the two warriors stood still, at least momentarily, Pryor frozen with his newly-wrapped hands extended in his menacing hawk pose, Arguello transfixed, staring at the mob scene across the ring while doing a little hop, skip, and jump in place. Two national anthems later, the dim bell somewhere in the bowels of the Bowl rang and the long-awaited match was underway.

As predicted, Pryor came out blazing, throwing lefts and rights to the head, the shoulders and any other anatomical part of Arguello that might have been visible. Arguello, for his part, pawed back with a left hook, throwing it in the general direction of the hurricane hovering around his head. Then, after Pryor forced him to give ground, Arguello threw his first right of the fight, catching Pryor with a straight right. Suddenly Pryor staggered backwards. Momentarily. And came back firing. It was a pattern that would be repeated time and again, as he caught Arguello with two punches that caused the three-time champ to lift his foot from the canvas, stung by the fury of the attack.

In Round 2, Pryor came out at Arguello in so many directions it looked like he had just taken a four-way cold tablet and decided he had three more ways to go to catch up to it. Lead rights, rights following rights, and left-rights, all the while changing his positioning and angles on Arguello. The latter was reaching out and beginning to find the now-he's-there-now-he's-not Junior Welterweight Champion with an occasional left and even two rights, which landed flush and would have, under normal conditions, started an avalanche. Only they didn't. Pryor took them and, after brushing them off as one would a pesky mosquito, went back on the attack.

Round 3 found Arguello beginning to land his vaunted one-two, a left to the body and a right to the head, once forcefully enough to drive Pryor's head and torso out between the ring ropes. After referee Stanley Christodoulou had saved him, Aaron went back to work. Only this time he added something new to his already fully stocked arsenal, a left jab and a right uppercut. Still, Arguello caught him in a toe-to-toe slugging match off the ropes and won his first round.

By the fourth, Aaron's punches-in-bunches had produced a long, angular cut alongside Alexis's eye and once again established his control of the fight; again despite getting caught with a punch that later Arguello's personal manager Bill Miller would describe as having the force to "fell King Kong." As the rounds continued at their breakneck pace, one had to begin wondering when either one of the following two scenarios would play out: (1) Pryor would wind down, like a toy whose spring has been wound too tight; or (2) The ageless legs of Arguello, which had carried him to seventy-six wins in eighty fights, would begin to show the inevitable erosion of pressure.

Throughout the middle rounds, Alexis continued to pursue Pryor, his one-two landing more frequently; but unfortunately for him, Aaron's center of balance, as unpredictable as the man possessing it, carried him out of harm's way every time. Arguello tried to press his advantage, reducing Arguello to a two-shot fighter.

Pryor now admitted he was "worried" about the stretch drive, having heard so much about Alexis' killer ability in the final rounds. Indeed, when the fight came into Arguello's "turf," the lightweight champ began to take charge, driving the plucky junior welterweight champ back with one and two punches. But never more, his ability to follow up negated by the fact that Pryor's footwork took on the look of a Ray Bolger with St. Vitus.

In the thirteenth Arguello, now nicked both above and below the left eye, took a bead on his opponent and caught him repeatedly with his patented left to the body and right to the head. Exhorted by his corner to keep coming at him, "You're the champ," Pryor would come back in, usually with a lead right, only to find Arguello's own right placed against his nose. Twice Arguello caught Pryor with right hands that would have folded any other fighter within the next six weight divisions that night. But not Pryor. Maybe it was just that Aaron, who came back in with a vengeance every time he was hit, found that every clout had a silver lining. Or maybe it was that Arguello, at 138½, couldn't displace the 140-pound Pryor as he had so many lesser weights. Whatever, after thirteen the fight was even on *Ring's* card, 124–124, reflecting the closeness of the fight as seen by the three officials, two of whom had Pryor ahead by three and one judge Arguello ahead by two.

A funny thing happened on the way to the fourteenth round. In Aaron's corner, at least. For toward the end of the sixty-second break, and after breaking yet another spirit of ammonia capsule under Pryor's nose, his trainer, Panama Lewis, abruptly grabbed the water bottle handed him by cutman Artie Curley and demanded something that sounded like, "Give me the other one . . . the one I mixed . . ." and proceeded to give the second bottle to Aaron, who swallowed it rather than spit it out.

With the swig and snort under his belt, Aaron charged right back to the fray, landing a left and a right, another left and a left hook. Then, in the center of the ring and with Arguello trying to set up another of the one-two that had been taking their toll of Aaron for the last three rounds, Pryor put his punching machine into high gear and rattled off a volley of six punches, the last of which, straight right, caught Arguello flush, sending him straight back into the ropes and aging him instantly.

Pryor, known as a "finisher" *par excellence,* was on him in a trice, raking him with punch-after-punch as Arguello's mouth fell open, his black mouthpiece giving him the eerie look of a grotesque jack-o'-lantern as his head lolled on his neck and his eyes sought their sockets. Twenty three punches, accentuated by three devastating rights coming one after another, prompted referee Christodoulou to jump in, his arms waving like the wings of a giant pellican, and signal the end of Arguello's dream.

As Alexis slumped to the canvas, his dreams behind him as well as ahead of him, the majority of the 23,800 fans in the Orange Bowl fell silent, their fears with him, their hopes shattered, their beliefs as crumbled as the form on the floor. When, after some four minutes, he finally stirred, they did too, feeling as he felt, now believing that Aaron Pryor was the better man.

Gone now were their second guesses, the questions about what was in the bottle. ("Peppermint schnapps" answered Artie Curley when he happened by the table of a *New York Times* columnist and yours truly after the fight. "He had a late meal and he was burping when hit in the stomach.") They knew, as all did, that the gods of chance were against Alexis in his try for a fourth championship. Aaron Pryor was the better man. And that was all they had to believe in the fight that *was* indeed "The Fight of the Year."

Ring Magazine, 1982

Roberto Duran vs. Sugar Ray Leonard I
Olympic Stadium, Montreal, Canada
June 20, 1980

Vince Lombardi, sport's premier winner, was so sure of his success that his strategy consisted of but one tactic: "I'll give the other team my game plan and plays. If they can stop them, they'll win; if they can't, I'll win."

Sugar Ray Leonard tried the exact same approach. Only this time, Roberto Duran stopped it. And won.

The difference between Lombardi and Leonard reduced itself to one distinction: Lombardi was talking about using *his* strength(s), not the other guy's. Challenging his opponent to make the mistakes, and taking advantage of him when he didn't respond correctly. Leonard, on the other hand, was determined to use his opponent's strength, not his own. Therein lay the underlying weakness in Sugar Ray's battle plan.

And so, he of the lightning fists and well-defined moves, inexplicably took on the man with the hands of stone and the straight-forward, but subtle, moves in a deadly game—a game of "Machismo." And, as he must, he lost. Not only because the word "Macho" is a Spanish word meaning "courage and aggressiveness"—today given new meaning by a Spanish-speaking Panamanian, whose forebears had invented the word Duran was to perfect—but because he was destined to lose playing another man's game; a game which played into Duran's hands—"of Stone."

The battle plan against Duran was Sugar Ray's idea and his alone. "I surprised a lot of people with my tactics . . . ," he was to say after the fight. "I fought Duran a way I thought I could beat him." Angelo Dundee concurred, saying only that, "It was his plan. He had it in his head that he was stronger than Duran." Even before the man with the plan entered the ring, Roberto Duran had scored the first punch, psychologically. Entering the ring a full two minutes before the-then WBC welterweight champion, Duran had beamed to the crowd and his handlers-followers had unfurled the Quebec Liberation flag. It was to be his last smile of the night. He would waste none on the Sugarman, who entered the ring to the shouts of the $20 patrons, sitting somewhere North of Moose Jaw in the upper reaches of the same Olympic Stadium where just four years before, Leonard had become the darling of the 1976 Olympics. Now, in his best laid-back manner, he bowed respectfully to all four corners—Nord, Est, Sud et Quest—as the sounds of adulation fell like the cloudburst which had just drenched the 46,317 Fightophile fans who had turned out to see what was billed as the "Fight of the Decade," just six months into the decade. It was a build-up soon to be acquitted by the fight to follow.

But, if it did rain on the 46,000-plus, it was not to rain on Roberto Duran's parade as very shortly after the first bell it became evident he intended to dominate the action, and that Sugar Ray intended to allow him to do so.

The man who had subordinated so many other fighters to his own purposes rushed, bulled and grabbed inside, all the better to tie up the fast-moving Leonard and land his own body punches.

Before the fight, the fight mob had wondered about the selection of Carlos Padilla as the referee. His historic approach to a fight had been to break the two combatants whenever they got close enough to touch. Now, probably stemming from Ray Arcel's impassioned plea before the fight ("You're good . . . I only hope you let my boy fight his fight inside.") Padilla employed a "hands-off" policy, letting the bull bull and the matador get gored. It was Duran's kind of fight.

In the second, Duran bulled Leonard back to the ropes and landed one *bonito* right to Sugar's head. He then fell inside to follow up his advantage.

Round 3 looked much the same: Duran inside and Leonard landing underneath. But Duran was the aggressor at all times, aggressor being the operative word in the definition of "Macho."

By Round 4 Leonard, for the first time, held his distance and forced Duran back to the ropes. But the rest of the round—if not the rest of the fight—found Duran crowding in, following Arcel's directive "not to let Leonard do anything, to keep him up against the ropes." Dundee's advice to Leonard ("Slip in and out, in and out") went unheeded.

As the middle rounds progressed, both battlers went at it toe-to-toe. And even though this was Duran's type of fight, now Leonard was landing more often, and with more telling punches. The non-stop action—made even more non-stop by Padilla's refusal to break while there was anything resembling a loose hand showing—incited the fans to constant screaming, the Panamanian delegation shouting "Arriba, cholo" (or upstairs) and the Leonard followers shouting "Pour it on, Sugar."

Leonard was scoring, sometimes heavily underneath as he caught Duran charging in. Several times he landed his patented flurries and once even got away with an accentuated bolo. But it was Duran's aggressiveness that dictated—and, at times, even dominated—the fight, as he charged, pushed, punched and even butted Leonard in the ninth round.

Coming down the stretch, Leonard fetched many a good right solidly on Duran's "Macho"—and untrimmed—jaw. But all he got in return was a sneer from the Satanic-looking Panamanian, who then tore back into Leonard for more of the same. The pace and the noise continued unabated throughout the last two rounds, two rounds Duran conceded to Leonard, so sure was he now of his imminent victory.

When the final bell sounded, Leonard extended his hands in friendship. Duran, "Macho" to the end, did the only thing a Machoman could: he disdained them, walking past the man he hated with a passion that burned deep within him and throwing up his hands in exultation.

That exultation was premature, but correct. For when the decision was announced—148–147, 145–144 and 146–144, including 19 "draw" rounds amongst the three officials—Duran was the new "Champeon del Mundo" in as close and exciting a fight as boxing has ever seen.

Roberto Duran, as always unhumble in victory, said after the fight, "I proved myself the better fighter." His interpreter, Luis Enriques, boastfully added, "Duran over Leonard, (General Oma) Torrijos over (President) Carter and Panama over America."

And so, just as the Panama Canal passed to Panama in 1979, the welterweight title passed to Panama in 1980. Maybe that's what the two stars on the Panamanian flag truely symbolize: the blue for the waters of the Panama Canal and the red for the machismo of Duran.

Roberto Duran vs. Sugar Ray Leonard I, June 20, 1980

For Leonard, there will be another day, another fight with Duran—Montreal Redux. And for that he'd better remember Vince Lombardi's one underlying theory: "Winning isn't everything, it's the *only* thing."

Ring Magazine, 1980

Sugar Ray Leonard vs. Roberto Duran II
Superdome, New Orleans, Louisiana
November 25, 1980

It was as unbelievable as Santa Claus suffering vertigo, Captain Kidd sea sickness, Mary having a little lamb. The "it" being Roberto Duran giving up, crying out *"No más . . . no más."*

The first time I saw machismo die a little came when, as a kid seated in the front row of the old Savoy Theatre in Washington, D.C., I saw John Wayne kiss a girl instead of his horse. The second time came when Roberto Duran told the whole world to "kiss off" in the eighth round of his fight with Leonard.

Before that unmagic moment it was thought that there were but four immutable laws which governed the universe: That the earth goes around the sun; That lawyers always get paid first; That every action has an equal and opposite reaction; And that Roberto Duran would have to be carried out on his shield, blood streaming out of his ears, before he would ever quit. Now you can scratch one of the above.

It was an unthinkable act. As unthinkable as Ted Williams throwing away his bat with two strikes; as unthinkable as O. J. Simpson, unable to find a hole, suddenly stopping and falling down; as unthinkable as Secretariat or Alydar quitting at the top of the stretch.

Here he was, one moment the man who in another life would have notches in his gun rather than knockout victims on his record, the toughest hombre on the barrio block, boxing's noblest savage. And the next, a beaten man waving his hands in a cross between "Get lost" and "Something's wrong." But whose intentions were made perfectly clear by his repeated utterance of those deathless words "*No más . . . No más,*" which translate, in any language, into "I give up!"

What had happened to turn the legendary "Manos de Piedra" the man without a heart and the sneering model of male machismo, into a quitter?

To understand the "why," first you must understand the "what." Boxing is a sport where everything comes in tidy little packages, is labeled and then put away. When something is divorced from reality, as the boxing fan perceives it, then it thwarts that desire to be pigeon-holed and filed away neatly. Boxing, more than any other sport—or human activity—puts full faith in its belief that the past is father of the present. However, in cases where there is no prologue, or it is illegitimate, with no history to rely on, then the moment is memorable, at best; controversial, at worst. Take the case of the Tunney–Dempsey celebrated "Long Count," or the Schmeling–Sharkey foul. Both were controversial because both pushed beyond expectable human experience and were inexplainable in any but new terms.

In a sport rife with memorable and controversial moments, few, in forthcoming years, will rival the moment when Roberto Duran called out "*No más . . . No más,*" and held out his hands. There was no past experience for the boxing crowd to call on. And without that, they must resort to coming up with new answers to the perplexing question: "Why"—no matter how farfetched.

It soon became a field day for the so-called "experts." And the Roshomon theory put into practice—a reference to the classic 1950 Japanese movie in which four different people involved in a brutal rape and murder each give their own version of the crime. Each differing radically. So, too, did Roberto Duran's mysterious surrender become the subject of a long laundry list of theories. They, too, differ radically.

To many of the thousands of fans seated in the spacious Superdome—some, in the upper tiers, as far away as Hattisburg, Mississippi—and a large proportion of the millions watching on closed-circuit TV, the first thing which came to mind was the most popular three-letter word after "sex": the word "fix." But it was an unthinking, knee-jerk reaction, one neither thought out nor worthy of those who rendered it; a simplistic response to their hurt at not seeing their hero win or, more deeply, the cynicism that pervades today's society and thinks that all activities are pre-planned to take advantage of them.

However, while this writer will not deny that there have been such things as "fixes" in the history of the "Sweet Science," this was *not* one of them. For what purpose? Money couldn't have swayed Roberto Duran, inasmuch as he was set even before the first Leonard match. And, if, for argument's sake, "the fix" was in, how could one have been executed more clumsily or more inelegantly than merely waving one's gloves at 2:44 of the eighth round and crying out "*No más . . . No más*"? No, it wasn't a "fix." But boxing is a sport that suffers fools—and their reasoning—gladly.

Nor does the real answer to the question "Why" lie in the spoon-fed rationalizations that were handed out after the fight, all revolving around something called "stomach cramps." Hell, this was the same Duran who had fought the first Leonard fight with a bad liver and the flu. How could stomach cramps disable this man called "El Animal" by his followers? Especially when, supposedly rendered nolo contendre by those same cramps in the ring only an hour-and-half before, Duran hosted a big post-fight "Victory" party, eating and drinking like any other man who comports himself like Roberto Duran should—in an animalistic fashion.

Most of the other theories are as airtight as domestic swiss cheese. Take, for instance, the supposed excuse that Duran had ballooned up before his rematch with Leonard and had to take off mucho weight in a short period of time. Granted that Duran had added more than thirty-three pounds living the easy life he had merited by winning the title in a hard-fought fight five months previous and had to find shortcuts to rid himself of all vestiges of easy living. Those searching for answers came up with several, all revolving around those supposed shortcuts to reducing his weight: Romantics cited "hard training," others "diuretics," and some even had the indelicacy to mention cocaine as an appetite suppressant. None of these explanations had ever been brought up before, although Duran had continually had to fight weight as well as opponents during much of his professional career. Why now? As a rationalization for the inexplainable behavior of Duran at 2:44 of the eighth round, that's why! But none bears up under the light of reflection; none qualify as answers for Duran's unfathomable act of quitting.

If these reasons don't wash, then the answer must be found elsewhere. For, as Agatha Christie's master sleuth Hercule Poirot was wont to say, "When a thing arranges itself so, one realizes that it must be so, (and) one only looks for reasons why it should not be so. If one does not find the reasons, why it should not be so, then one is strengthened in one's opinion."

Having looked at—and dismissed, for good reason—all other possible answers, one is left to look at the only place left: Roberto Duran's mind, one which apparently has more connecting locks than the Panama Canal.

All of which serves as a table-setting—albeit a long one—for the fight itself, billed as "Stone versus Sugar." It was the much-awaited rematch of the Montreal bout which already had been heralded as the twelfth greatest fight of all time in a recent poll.

Starting from the moment the bout was announced, Duran began to spew out his contempt for Leonard. "This time I will keel him," he was to say time and time again, attempting to belittle the man he had beaten in Montreal. And, to punctuate his remark as well as his dislike for the man he called "a clown," he would at times extend his middle finger in the half-peace sign. Other times, just to vary the act, his wife would extend the same pleasantries to Leonard's wife, Juanita. It was a family act with all the subtlety of a community bedpan.

Leonard, on the other hand, ignored his trainer—soon to become his ex-trainer—Dave Jacob's advice that such a rematch was "too soon" and that, instead of taking on Duran, he should take two warmup fights. Eschewing the warmup fights, and Jacobs as well, Leonard went into serious training to reverse the only defeat in his professional career—and recapture the crown he had come to look at as his own private property.

This time Leonard was determined, burning with the same intensity that had once burned deeply within the soul of Duran. He was also determined not to fight Duran's fight, not to let Duran dictate the pattern of the fight nor control the action as he had in Montreal. In short, Sugar Ray Leonard was prepared, which is more than Roberto Duran could say.

As the countdown continued and the crowds began to congregate in New Orleans—well-wishers and hangers-on alike, including some eighty-one Panamanians who followed Duran everywhere—something seemed to be amiss. The live promoters blamed it on everything from Thanksgiving to the football season. But a new element had been introduced to the equation: WBA champion Thomas Hearns. No longer could it be argued without fear of contradiction that the two best welterweights in the world were fighting in New Orleans the night of November 25th, 1980. However, at least one of the two best welterweights in the world showed up that night in the person of Sugar Ray Leonard. The other, Roberto Duran, looked like he was just playing through.

If there was one omen that was to foretell the outcome of the fight, it came at 9:01 CST, just before the fight actually started. For at that moment the Panamanian national anthem was rendered, sounding for all the world like the noise made by two gypsy wagons rolling over their own violins. It not only failed to stir the hearts of the twelve Panamanian hangers-on who had taken Duran's corner as a beachhead, but stimulated them to talk to each other and to anyone else they could find at ringside. That was followed by a boffo rendition of "America the Beautiful" by Sugar Ray's namesake, Ray Charles, which was to do for Sugar Ray what Kate Smith's "God Bless America" had done so many times before for the Philadelphia hockey Flyers. Round 1 to Leonard—and the fight hadn't even started.

Then came the opening bell. And Sugar Ray, wearing different colored trunks than he had sported in Montreal—black and yellow—soon began to show that he came equipped with other new trappings, including a new battle plan. This time, instead of leaving a wake-up call for Round 5, as he had in the first fight, he immediately moved out to the middle of the ring and landed the first punch, a left that caught Duran flush. After a brief moment when both tried out tentative left jabs, Duran put on one of his patented bullrushes. But Leonard, instead of standing in harm's way, moved quickly backwards, out of reach.

It was like that for most of the first two rounds, Leonard moving out of the way and Duran barreling in. Occasionally Leonard would catch Duran to the midsection, coming under with uppercuts. But his battle plan seemed to be one of getting off first and his weaponry seemed to be a telling left jab, one that seldom missed. Duran would frequently respond by throwing his right—catching air most times and Leonard's left almost as often—and an occasional sneer.

As Round 3 began, Duran, who had missed more punches in the first two opuses than he had in his previous fifteen rounds against Leonard, became much more aggressive. He began mauling Sugar Ray into the ropes. But this time, instead of Leonard standing his ground, he either tied up Duran, caught him coming in or spun him off and moved out of danger. This time the pattern was different. And Duran's eyes began to tell more of the story than his fists as he stood in the middle of the ring, befuddled by the moth moving around the flame that burned within him, but never getting close enough to become scorched.

It was becoming woefully obvious to all but the most foolhearty Duran supporter that Leonard, who had gone to school for fifteen rounds in Montreal, was now putting in some post-graduate work—as well as some well-placed lefts. Instead of bullying Leonard to the ropes, Duran found himself shoved to the floor on one occasion, spun off on others and even suffering the ignonimity of having his head pushed down, a la Ali with his opponents, on several more.

And then there was Leonard's movement of foot, something not seen since Fred last danced with Adele. By moving backwards and forwards, alternating direction and spinning Duran off continually—a strategy devised by trainer Angelo Dundee, who told Sugar Ray to "move 'em, spin 'em"—Leonard had Duran mesmerized. He followed Leonard's movements with his eyes, much like a beginning student would follow a foot outline at Arthur Murray's. And while he was watching, Duran was made to pay an entertainment tax, taking more than a few hard lefts to the nose for his efforts—or lack thereof. Between Rounds 5 and 6, Duran complained to his interpreter, Luis Enriquez, that something was wrong. Enriquez relayed the message to Duran's manager, Carlos Eleta, seated at ringside. But before Eleta's message, "Can he go on?" was relayed back, the bell had rung. Duran had a good round, negating most of the concern for his welfare.

Then came Round 7, one of the most memorable in the long history of boxing. It started out with Duran landing the first punch of the round for the first time in the fight. But that was to be the extent of his attack. For now Leonard, sensing that he "was in control" as he later was to say, began taunting Duran, first sticking out his chin and then his tongue. Duran looked at him with disbelieving eyes, unsure of how to handle this new threat. For the man who had been through 73 previous fights had met every threat head-on—punchers, runners, counterers, etc., but never taunters.

And, if that wasn't traumatic enough for Duran, he had yet to suffer one of boxing's most crushing and devastating psychological blows, a trick not dissimilar to a little kid's throwing one snowball in the air and catching the other kid looking at it with a second one, right in the puss. Leonard wound up with a mocking copy of Kid Gavilan's bolo punch. And while Duran stood transfixed, Leonard popped him a good one with his left. It was humiliating. It was worse. The man who had fought 441 previous rounds was made to look like a novice; like a fool. And many at ringside laughed. It was enough to make a grown man cry. Or quit.

That was the moment when a seed began to take root. And grow. And inspired Duran's act of submission sixteen seconds before the end of the eighth round.

For that was the moment Roberto Duran cried out, more in anguish and frustration than in resignation, "*No más . . . No más.*"

It was as if he had heard a mention of E.F. Hutton. Everything stopped. And with one contemptuous gesture, more of the "I'm-going-to-take-my-ball-and-go-home" variety than "I quit," he had, like the schoolyard bully who, when his prey ran, caught him, when he stood to fight, beat him, but when taunted, merely held up a middle finger and hollered, "So's your old man," or "Your mother wears tennis shoes." Only this time, the finger was encased in a glove.

It was a shame. A shame for Roberto Duran, whose seventy-three previous fights would be subjugated in memory to that one second when he cried out "*No más . . . No más.*" A shame that a magnificent performance by Sugar Ray Leonard had to be tarnished and that his victory would be less than complete.

And it was a shame for the millions-upon-millions of people who idolized Roberto Duran, many of whom couldn't fill their bellies with food but had looked upon "Manos de Piedras" as someone who could fill their souls with hope, the hope of machismo. "*No más.*"

But even though Roberto was to say "I fight no more" immediately after the fight, the realization and the magnitude of what he had done to his image and to boxing with that one gesture had not yet set in. It soon did. And rather than go home to Panama, where he had been a demi-god, he retreated instead to Miami, where he hid in seclusion for eight days.

There his conscience—as well as the advice of his manager, Carlos Eleta—began to play on him. He would come back, he announced, and as a form of penitence for his irrational act of telling everyone from Sugar Ray Leonard on down to "kiss off," he would donate his next purse to charity.

But if Roberto had told the world to "kiss off," the world was not quite ready to tell Roberto the same thing. And soon those who remembered Duran's daring exploits through seventy-three fights plus seven rounds began beseeching Roberto to come back, to wipe the only stain off his now somewhat tarnished escutcheon.

The president of Panama sent Duran a telegram which read, "You made Panama. You're our idol. Come home." Many others were to echo the words of El Presidente.

For Roberto Duran was a hero to millions, a living legend. And he had to come back one "*más*" time so that the permanent picture we keep of him in our mind's eye is not the shameful picture of a man who waved his glove desultorily in the direction of his soon-to-be conqueror, Sugar Ray Leonard—and by extension, in the direction of everyone who had ever lived vicariously through Duran's seething machismo—but of the warrior he once was. The warrior who once gave flight and fancy to man's machismo everywhere. The man Roberto Duran was in previous movies. For this he had to come back. To be Roberto Duran Again.

Ring Magazine, 1980

Larry Holmes vs. Muhammad Ali
Caesars Palace, Las Vegas, Nevada
October 2, 1980

Sugar Ray Robinson sat paralyzed in his seat, tears welling up in his eyes. Scott LeDoux, head down, could only mumble, "I feel like they just shot my dog Spot." And thousands of others in the funereal surroundings of a parking lot outside Caesars Palace felt the same way. And worse. To them, it was as if both the Easter Bunny and Santa Claus had been destroyed. Muhammad Ali had lost.

In what was meant to be a religious revival for the Ali faithful, Muhammad Ali, who had already tied the Guinness Book of Records' mark for most miracles by a mortal—tying with Moses at two apiece—promised them yet another. And 24,790 made the pilgrimmage to see the self-proclaimed "Greatest" do it again. But there was to be no "again." The clock had struck twelve. And Muhammad Ali, once the fastest afoot, the quickest of hands, had turned out to be a mere mortal. And an old, washed-up mortal at that.

His bag of tricks came up empty. The magic show was over. It was Carl Ballantine and Art Matrano "faking" it. He could no more come back than Houdini could come back from the dead after having told his followers he would.

Sure, he conned us. But, then again, when hasn't he? And it wasn't his fault. We wouldn't have been conned if we didn't want to believe. And we wanted to believe. Desperately. We were in on the "sting" because we were part of it. And we made Ali a 6½–5½ underdog at the end. It should have been Ali +28 points.

The fight? There was no fight. It was a futile left jab that never jabbed. A cocked right that never uncocked. A mysterious battle plan that never went into battle. And a legend that died.

For outside of the foreplay immediately prior to the fight—the only time he looked like the Ali of old—the Muhammad Ali who showed up for "The Last Hurrah" was merely the ghost of Ali past. A younger, tougher and better Larry Holmes "whupped" him in every which way, even charitably holding back several times or "accidentally" missing so that he wouldn't hurt the spectre that once was Ali standing directly in front of him.

Ali knew it was all over "after the first round." Some of the more faithful took additional time to come to the same conclusion; and even then, reluctantly. But it was painfully evident that "The man with the plan" had nothing. Larry Johnston, who had come all the way from Newark, New Jersey, left the arena after the second round. He couldn't stand it any more. "Ali put me through college," said Johnston, referring to the scores he had made betting Ali. "I grew up with him. I don't want to see him like this."

But see him they did. A pitiful hulk of a man who once was. By the end of the ninth round, when it was obvious he was defenseless, the referee, Richard Green, went over to his corner to inquire into his well-being. Ali and his manager, Herbert Muhammad, pleaded for just "one more round." And so, as the bell rang for Round 10, a bone-weary Ali came to the center of the ring, his eyes staring down in abject depression, his arms lowered to his side, his glories seemingly a thousand years past.

The tenth was no different than any of the previous rounds as Holmes drove him to the ropes, battered his already sore body, raked his puffed eyes and prolonged the misery by holding back right-hand shots to a by-now thoroughly unprotected midsection. The crowd was silent, as if at a wake, which is exactly what it was. Three more minutes of pure agony for Ali. And his faithful. Then the bell.

Green now hurried over to Ali's corner, concerned about the three-time champ's inability to defend himself. This time Angelo Dundee—the man who had pushed the-then Cassius Clay off his stool fourteen years before in the sixth round of his fight with Sonny Liston when Clay had wanted to quit with a "This is your night"—wig-wagged his hands. This was *not* his night. But, suddenly, Bundini Brown, refusing to believe that the party was over, pushed at Dundee. While the push was coming to shove, the third man in the corner, Pat Patterson, looked down at Herbert Muhammad for confirmation. Having seen enough, Herbert gave the time-honored signal for "cutting," which Patterson communicated to Dundee and Dundee to Green. Muhammad Ali looked up at Angelo and, through swollen lips, muttered "Thank you."

And so the man who had won fifty-six of his fifty-nine fights, had added the pelts of two seeming invincibles, Sonny Liston and George Foreman, to his belt and had given us many memories over the past two decades gave us one more: A defeated warrior sitting forlornly on his stool, going out with less a bang than a whimper. There would be no tintype in our mind's eye of his finish as there was of Joe Louis being knocked through the ropes by Rocky Marciano or of Jim Jeffries being beaten to his knees by Jack Johnson. Just a picture of another man grown old, a legend who had become mortal, sitting on his stool.

For Ali, unlike Louis and Jeffries, did not even try to return to his glorious days of yesteryear. That was the shame of it. His entire effort seemed to be concentrated on melting off some forty pounds-plus change from his Pillsbury Doughboy shape and showing us some of the same faces that had once captivated us coming from the face of a youth. Outside of those two efforts, Muhammad Ali was a mere mortal in the ring last October 2nd. And that was his biggest sin. The hopes and dreams of all our years were taken from us that night.

And Larry Holmes? What can be said of a man who was in what he himself called a "no-win" situation? He conducted himself— both as a man and as a boxer—as a champion. Holmes eschewed going to the body when going to the body might mean perma- nently hurting the man he, along with everyone else, idolized. He refused to degrade the man he had beaten afterwards, offering up an olive branch to "my brother, a great man." Larry Holmes was the only real winner on that October evening in a parking lot in Vegas. A man who invests boxing with a dignity it sometimes doesn't deserve, he deserves better than he has received.

This man can do it all. He now has eight straight knockouts in defense of his crown, tying Tommy Burns' all-time record. ("I'm gonna make Tommy Burns famous," he was to say before the bout.) He has done all that has been asked of him. And more. And he has done it better. It is his misfortune to come after the man who won the hearts of boxing fans everywhere.

Ring Magazine, 1980

Sugar Ray Leonard vs. Thomas Hearns
Caesars Palace, Las Vegas, Nevada
September 16, 1981

That blockbuster mentality that makes every fight sound like the Second Coming—and has given us enough "Fights of the Century" to take us through the era of Buck Rogers, 2400 A.D., has now given us a lesser celestial happening called The Showdown. But a recent performance was lesser in name only; not in magnitude. No matter what they called the Leonard-Hearns to-do, it was one helluva fight staged in front of almost 24,000 recently-released mental patients who seemed collectively dedicated to the deafening of America. And, in the end, Sugar Ray Leonard acquitted the hype by soundly thrashing the supposedly invincible Thomas Hearns in a fight with more twists and turns than could be found in an early O. Henry potboiler. In so doing he laid claim to the undisputed welterweight championship of the world. As well as to a place among the all-time greats.

Leonard won more than just the fight. He won what Rodney Dangerfield, for lack of a more descriptive phrase, would call respect. Not only from his hard-hitting opponent but from hard-boiled sportswriters as well, many of whom had discounted Leonard's stock, belittling his accomplishments as part of a media buildup.

For ever since Leonard exploded on the media scene and on the national screen he has been regarded by many doubting Thomases, Jims, and Larrys as a media phenomenon. Maybe Howard Cosell, who had hitched his braggin' to a star, was the reason for the press downplaying Ray's abilities. But Howie knows a winner when he sees one, and Ray always had the makings of one. Nonetheless, "Forget it!" said the rest of the media, who continued to view Leonard merely as the greatest boxer ever to come out of Palmer Park, Maryland. Nothing more. It seemed that most of the boxing writers could never bring themselves to acknowledge that Leonard was as good as he was because that other, unspeakable medium, TV, found him first.

Or maybe it was the fact that Leonard was denied the ultimate satisfaction of destroying the man who had beaten him previously: Roberto Duran. Such triumphs, of course, had served as the anchor of so many other legends—Sugar Ray Robinson, who had turned the tables on Jake LaMotta, Randy Turpin, and Carmen Basilio; Muhammad Ali, who came back to "whup" Joe Frazier twice; Joe Louis, who destroyed Max Schmeling the second time around; Gene Tunney, who beat the only man who ever bettered him, Harry Greb; and Jack Dempsey, who almost came back to beat Tunney in the Battle of the Long Count. The centerpiece for each and every one of these ring worthies had been his comeback win over the man who had previously bedeviled him. All Leonard was remembered for was a desultory wave of a hand and the cry, *"No más, no más."* Of such things are legends unmade.

Moreover, according to many old-timers, for whom boxing goes in one era and out the other, there was only one "Sugar" and that accolade was reserved for one man and one man alone—Ray

Robinson. (In fact, Robinson himself had tried to preserve that title of respect for himself in the face of other Sugars. One time, so the story goes, when Robinson faced another of the pretenders to the Sugar crown, George "Sugar" Costner, he reputedly told Costner during the pre-fight instructions, "Now I'll show you who's the real Sugar," and proceeded to prove his point by laying out Costner in one round. Afterward, Robinson chided the artificial Sugar with, "Now go out and earn yourself the name.")

But it was not only the press and the old-timers who denied Ray Leonard his rightful place. He was thrice denied, this time by the betting fans, who made Hearns a 6½–5 favorite.

And so it was that Leonard, seeking to rid himself of so many dybbuks, came to an inferno called a ring that hot airless night in Vegas wearing a robe emblazoned with the solitary word, *Deliverance*. It was an eloquent message that should have tipped off those who were supposedly "in the know" that Leonard was driven to exorcise the many demons that possessed him.

Yet the task facing Leonard was monumental. As was his opponent, the 6'-going-on-6'1½" Hearns, a legitimate welterweight with a heavyweight wingspan of seventy-eight inches—at least four inches longer than that of Leonard and longer still than many heavyweight champions. It was that reach, or so the reasoning went, that would allow Hearns to hold Leonard at bay, much as he had Pipino Cuevas, while setting up his lethal right hand. Hearns, however, was disabused of any such notions as Leonard slapped away his tentacle-like left time and again during the first two rounds. But while one of Hearns's favorite ploys was being negated by Leonard, Hearns was also defusing one of Leonard's, the tactic he had employed so successfully in the New Orleans fiasco—freaking out Duran with his mugging act.

For the first two rounds, the gladiators, who had apparently studied each other's playbooks, played with one another. Hearns, who chose to be introduced by the nickname the "Motor City Cobra," in preference to his more familiar moniker of "The Hit

Man," acted more like a cobra than a hit man. Leonard's game plan was to circle the stationary cobra, first one way and then the other, in the manner of a mongoose, attempting to tire out the man who had gone more than four rounds only eight times in his entire career. And so it went, Leonard darting back and forth, his eyes transfixed in a fierce determination not to blink, almost as if held open by toothpicks, and Hearns resorting to long left jabs and an occasionally head-hunting right, most of which Ray avoided by pulling his head back Ali-style. The closest Hearns came to his tormentor was after the bell, when Leonard gave him a love-tap-cum-punch and Hearns clobbered him without turning the other cheek.

With Angelo Dundee's words, "Go out there and get him," ringing in his ears and a freshly-minted mouse beginning to erupt under his left eye, Leonard went out in the third to take the fight to Hearns. The first thing he took was a right to the jaw. And, surprise of surprises, he didn't even blink. Now he knew he could catch anything Hearns threw. The insight was heady as Leonard stood his ground and swapped shots with Hearns, who was fighting in one-punch combinations. For the first time, Leonard scored with his right and backed Hearns up; momentarily confused by Leonard's quick hand speed and agility, Hearns went on the retreat. At the bell, Leonard raised his hands in a victory salute. He now knew he would win, not merely that he could.

Rounds 4 and 5 mirrored the first two—sandwiched around Leonard's third—with Hearns pecking away at Leonard's angry-looking eye. But even in the face of Hearns's rapierlike left, Leonard was quietly moving inside with shots to the body. And, to the head, when he could reach the lanky WBA champion. Still, they were rounds for Hearns. Barely. But round 6 was to change the complexion of the fight.

For the first time, Leonard, having taken control of the fight despite Hearns's elongated left, was now crowding Hearns. Moving inside. And, what's more, beating Hearns to the punch. More correctly stated, he was beating him to many punches. First it was Leonard's right over Hearns's low left; then it was a left over

Hearns's equally low right. Suddenly, a wild left hook to the head caught Hearns's attention. And turned his head. As Ray's corner screamed, "Speed, Ray, speed," Ray obliged with a rat-a-tat-tat staccato. Suddenly the Hit Man was the Hittee Man, wobbling under a barrage of blows almost too numerous to count. But numbered among them was one punch in particular—a hard left hook to Hearns's unprotected rib cage—which caused the Cobra to grimace in pain. Its effects could not be appreciated then—it was one of a rapid-fire series of blows, as incapable of being severed from the rest as one pearl from a string—but one whose effects would be telling on Hearns. And, on the outcome of the fight.

Round 7 saw Leonard pick up right where he had left off, rattling more left hooks off Hearns's jaw than the Hit Man had experienced in his previous thirty-two fights. Over and over Leonard was to penetrate the would-be defenses of his spindly opponent, landing left hooks from in close as the crowd picked up the chant, "Leo-nard, Leo-nard. . . ." Hearns, unable to stave off the swarming Leonard and unable to tie him up inside, merely grappled to keep him away, pushing at his tormentor. And yet, as Hearns began to take on the appearance of a pinball, ricocheting from pillar to rope, he evinced that intangible known as courage, a rare commodity in any fighter and one that separates the greats from the near-greats. It worked to keep his unsteady pins under him.

At the end of the round Hearns staggered off in the vague direction of his corner, much the worse for wear. But Leonard also looked weary from his prolonged fungo practice, breathing heavily as he plopped on his stool. Later, Ray was to say, "I had him, but he didn't cooperate," which translated into, "I was arm-weary."

The eighth saw Leonard continue on the attack even as he wound down, with right leads and rights to the body in dutiful response to his corner's exhortations of "Body, Ray . . . Body, Ray . . ." Hearns, trying desperately to stem the seemingly inexorable tide that was all Leonard, attempted to catch Ray with a right. But, as the round came to a close with Leonard swarming in, he took off on his bicycle, throwing out his long left in a getaway manner. However, just as the fight had turned once, it was soon to turn again. Beginning with the bell for the ninth, Thomas Hearns reverted to the style that had seen him win 163 amateur fights, only eleven by knockout. Gone was the attempt to gain leverage by leaning in; gone was the low-held left and gone was the menacing Hit Man who instilled fear in the thirty-two opponents he had faced up to now. But gone, too, was the stationary target Ray had found so inviting. And, in its place, there suddenly appeared a masterful boxer, one who could finally take advantage of his seventy-eight-inch reach. It was the most startling role reversal since Edward G. Robinson played the leading man in *Woman in the Window*. The puncher had turned boxer and the boxer had turned puncher. And the puncher-boxer was clearly outpointing his supposedly faster opponent.

So it went through rounds 9, 10, and 11, with enough rights thrown to count on your right thumb. Hearns was clearly dominating the action—what little there was of it as the high-rolling parishioners began clapping and whistling for more. But he was always just one punch away from "Queer Street," the street he had come down before, the pavement barely beneath his feet. But Hearns's befogged condition was not apparent. Not apparent to anyone, that is, except trainer-manager Emanuel Steward, who spent his time between rounds doing anything and everything he could to snap Tommy out of his severe case of mal-de-ring—up to, and including, shouting at his charge, "If you're not goin' to fight, damn it, I'm goin' to stop it!"

Somehow, Steward's shock treatment worked and Hearns came back. Strong. So, too, did his followers, and by round 12 they had worked themselves up into a frenzy, with Hearns himself leading their vocal exhortations as their hopes took flight and form in roars of "Tommee, Tommee. . . ." No longer moving, Hearns came in on the one-eyed Cyclops who was stalking him, landing battering-ram lefts and rights to the body. It was Hearns's round. And his last hurrah, something even Hearns might have sensed had he been able to analyze his right-hand haymaker thrown at the half-blinded

WBC champion, who somehow, someway, pulled his head back at the last instant.

Round 13, incredibly, saw still another turn in the tide of battle. Up off his stool came Ray, first pushing Hearns to the canvas as their legs entwined, then punishing Hearns with a right over a left and three left hooks to the head. Hearns tried mightily to hold Leonard off; unsure of how to clinch, he tried to throw a right. But Leonard beat Hearns to the punch, catching him and jarring him off balance. Another left by Ray, still another and a third, and suddenly Hearns was careening about the ring, his head rolling like a rag doll's, his motions uncoordinated. Leonard was atop Hearns as Hearns first leaned, then fell, into the ropes from a series of punches fired off too rapidly to count. Suffice it to say it was "Enough," as writer Vic Ziegel noted.

Finally, after a fusillade of rights the lanky Hearns, in his best imitation of an accordion, gently folded through the ropes. Referee Davey Pearl, who had ignored an obvious knockdown in the Larry Holmes-Earnie Shavers fight, deemed Hearns's exit from the ring more a fall than a knockdown—although they looked as if they were part of the same cause and effect—and told Hearns to "get up." As Hearns slowly reclaimed his feet and recollected his mind, trainer Angelo Dundee was up on the ring apron screaming, "Bullshit." Pearl motioned him down to his corner and looked back to find Leonard raking Hearns with another volley of punches, seemingly fired in a desire to prove something to somebody. This time he proved to Pearl that the Thomas Hearns leaning against the ropes on his haunches was knocked down by the collective force of his punches.

Pearl took up the count while Hearns tried to haul himself up to his six-foot, one-inch height, no easy chore and one which had the appearance of a balloon slowly inflating. Finally, Prometheus was unbound and Hearns was up, albeit unsteadily, as the count reached nine, just at the bell.

There seemed to be no doubt of the outcome now. At least not to 23,615 fans seated in the makeshift arena atop the tennis courts behind Caesars Palace. But the three judges, who undoubtedly had been watching tennis instead of boxing, still had Hearns ahead. Leonard was to make sure that there would be no disputed verdict. He wanted the welterweight title and went out to do it himself. He leaped off his stool at the bell for the fourteenth round—the longest Thomas Hearns had ever gone in a fight—and went right at Hearns, throwing rights and lefts as Hearns tried to avert them by twisting his body back and forth from a right-handed stance to southpaw and back again.

It was all to no avail as Leonard kept coming, throwing lefts to the body that made the exhausted Hearns wince and lefts to the head that made him blink. Finally Leonard landed his Mary Ann, a straight right to the chops, and threw up his hands in his traditional victory signal. But, miracle of miracles, Hearns wouldn't, or couldn't, fall and pitched backward into the ropes. Leonard wouldn't let him off the hook now and—between waving furiously to referee Pearl to stop the fight—raked Hearns with right upper-cuts, left hooks, and hard rights. Still, Hearns wouldn't go down. But even if Hearns hadn't had enough, referee Pearl had. He pulled Leonard away as Hearns looked in his direction as if to quizzically ask, "Wha' happened?" and then reeled off in the direction of his corner, at 1:45 of the fourteenth round, the *former* WBA welterweight champion of the world.

At the press conference the next day, with both fighters sporting dark glasses and looking like Elwood and Jake Blues, Thomas Hearns was to show his respect for the "new champion, Sugar Ray Leonard. . . ." It was a long time acomin', but maybe, just maybe, Sugar Ray Leonard will get the respect he deserves. And, yes, Virginia—and Maryland, and all points north, west, and south—there is a new "Sugar Ray," on the boxing block.

Ring Magazine, 1981

Mike Tyson vs. Evander Holyfield
MGM Grand, Las Vegas, Nevada
June 28, 1997

The dog, to gain some private ends,
Went mad, and bit the man . . .
The man recovered of the bite
The dog it was that died
　　　An Elegy on the Death of a Mad Dog—Oliver Goldsmith

Just when you thought you had seen everything—and I mean *everything*—in that Theatre of the Bizarre known as boxing, something happens that defies explanation. That "something" in this case was "The Bite Heard 'Round the World." Mike Tyson's inexplicable gnawing on Evander Holyfield's ears in their championship rematch last June 28.

Tyson had been underwhelming against Holyfield in November last year, his primary weapon of intimidation of no use against Holyfield, who gave much better than he got and took out Tyson with 273 or so lucky punches.

But the fight crowd, a crowd so cynical they could walk into a room of roses and look around for the corpse, thought Holyfield's

245

one-sided ass-whuppin' was a "fluke," and when the rematch was announced, once again installed Tyson as a 7-2 favorite to reverse the drubbing he had received from Holyfield. To them, Evander Holyfield was anything but the "Real Deal." Tyson had merely underestimated him and since Holyfield had never put together two back-to-back great fights—or so the reasoning went—Tyson would assuredly recapture his pride and his title in the rematch.

The odds reflected an overblown assessment of Mike Tyson, who had lost the only two times he had ever been to the well—against Holyfield and Buster Douglas—and both times come back with an empty pail.

Moreover, his greatest win, the one which had earned him his reputation as an invincible warrior, a one-and-a-half minute dismantling of Michael Spinks, had been nine years before. Truth to tell, his prime was so far behind him, he couldn't find it in his rearview mirror.

The other side of the coin was the underestimation of Holyfield, still disparaged as being a "blown-up cruiserweight." He seemed destined to be forever in Tyson's shadow, though his win in their first match had validated his credentials as the best heavyweight since Larry Holmes.

As the days dwindled down to a precious few before the scheduled May 3 fight, Tyson pulled out after suffering a cut eye in training and "The Sound and the Fury" was rescheduled for June 28 at the MGM Grand.

The extra time was supposed to give Tyson more time to train, to perfect the errors he made in the first fight—no combinations, no in-fighting, no jab, no defense, etc., etc., etc.—and to get acquainted with new trainer Richie Giachetti. It also gave him more time to mull over his devastating defeat at the hands of Holyfield and find excuses to explain it away.

Holyfield, on the other glove, just went about his business, training for the rematch, confident in his mind's-eye he could duplicate his victory and prove the first fight was, in his own words, "no fluke."

Two days before "The Sound and the Fury," the only sound and fury was that coming from Team Tyson, which objected to the selection of Mitch Halpern as the third man in the ring, as he had been in the first fight. What they should have done was object to Holyfield, not Halpern.

Team Tyson won their appeal when Halpern excused himself from the goings-on and the Nevada Athletic Commission filled his position with Mills Lane. It was to be a classic case of "Be careful, you might get what you wished for," as Mills would play a major role in the "Ear-Rie" events soon to take place.

The bell for Round 1 was barely audible through the din as Tyson came out of his corner tentatively, a departure from his usual freight-train-out-of-control running starts from his corner. After two minutes of clinching and wrestling mid-ring, Holyfield connected with a combination to the body and then with a left and a big right, hurting Tyson and driving him to the ropes. As the MGM Grand Garden crowd cheered for Holyfield, he continued his assault up to the bell. The first round was Holyfield's, the first time Tyson had ever lost a first round—in fact, twenty times he had never heard the bell ending the round, having ended his opponents' nights in that opening round.

The second round began as the first had, with Tyson coming out of his corner cautiously, almost too cautiously and throwing a wild, here-it-comes-ready-or-not left that missed badly. There is some blood over Mike's right eyelid which he continually wipes at, almost as if startled to find his own blood on him. Tyson looks at his corner, a little disconcertedly, then begins complaining to Mills Lane about what he perceives as a head butt. But Lane pays him no-never-mind. In a clinch, Tyson's head comes up as Evander's comes in, causing a collision and a deep gash in Tyson's eyelid. He again complains, but Lane tells him, it was "accidental." Holyfield begins shoving the smaller Tyson off in clinches and is warned by Lane as Tyson appears infuriated by Lane's refusal to intervene. End of round, another for Holyfield.

Now comes Round 3, one of the most infamous rounds in the long, infamous history of the sport of boxing. Tyson comes out of his corner without his mouthpiece, which Evander sees and signals both to Lane and to Tyson's corner, which corrects the omission. Tyson connects with a good overhand right and then, with more aggression than he's shown in the previous six minutes, connects with two right-hand leads. Holyfield begins to hold on, trying to blunt Tyson's attack. With a minute left, Tyson throws a good left and a strong left-right combination. Holyfield ducks under a Tyson hook and the two clinch.

What happens at this magic moment is open to debate. Not as to the actual happening, but as to the motivation. For as the two clinch, Tyson spits out his mouthpiece and gnaws at Evander's right ear, biting off a piece and spitting it out, onto judge Duane Ford's scorecard. Evander steps back and starts jumping up and down like Rumplestiltskin, as much in pain as in anger at Tyson's action. As he jumps away and turns his back, Tyson rushes him and pushes, not punches, him. Lane steps in between the two and tells Tyson, "That's one, another one and that's it," and takes two points away from Tyson—one for his biting and another for shoving.

After a four-minute hiatus, in which ringside doctor Flip Homansky comes into the ring to examine the damaged ear and determines it is cosmetically damaged, but that Holyfield can continue, Tyson continues to pace in his corner, much like a caged animal. Holyfield, standing in his corner, instructs trainer Don Turner, to "put my mouthpiece back in, I'm going to knock this guy out," and charges out of his corner. After two angry swings, the two again clinch, and Tyson again spits out his mouthpiece and this time bites Evander's left ear, evening up the score and the ears as well. After another few seconds, the round ends and Lane walks over to Tyson's corner and tells Tyson's corner he is "disqualifying" him—which Giachetti misinterprets, thinking Lane is stopping the fight because of Holyfield's inability to go on. At first Tyson screams, then rages out, in search of Holyfield, swinging at everything in his path, including two Las Vegas policemen who now have entered the ring to try to keep the peace.

Tyson is rabid, trying to get at everyone and anyone—especially Holyfield. But Holyfield and his entourage slip out of the ring. As a finally subdued Tyson is taken out of the ring, he jumps over seats trying to get at fans who are throwing things in his direction and taunting him, while the rest of the house stands in stunned disbelief.

Without pretending to be a psychiatrist without a license, Tyson's actions at making Evander "The Real Meal" can only be explained as his trying to get what he would later call "retribution" against Holyfield for his perceived head butting. And, having tried to invoke the help of Lane and finding he had no ally in the man his spokespeople had brought in to replace Halpern, decided to take things in his own hands. And teeth. Another explanation, put forward by Holyfield, was that Tyson, knowing he was losing both the fight and the battle of wills that went with it, had taken the easy way out. And still another had it that Tyson's bullying background and street style had him reverting to form.

Whatever, Tyson remained a man who had proven his bite was worse than his bark and will forever be known in boxing history not for his dominance of the division for almost a decade, but for having tried to make Holyfield into E-Van Gogh Holyfield.

Tyson, a man who has always been on the edge of falling into his own volcano, will forever be labeled. And although, in his dressing room, he continued to say, over and over again, "I'm through . . . I'm through . . . I'm through . . . ," he may not be through. Maybe Don King can get him a match with Hannibal Lecter.

S.A. Sports Illustrated, 1997

IV
History

The Way Out

I

To understand boxing one must understand its roots. From its beginnings, the sport has resonated with urban ethnicity, drawing its recruits from the tenements, the ghettos, the projects, the barrios, the "nabes," places that offered little presence and even less of a future. Many a troubled and troublesome youngster has embraced "The Sweet Science" as a way out, a social staircase out of the mean streets that formed his limited world, fighting his way, bloody hand-over-bloody hand, up the ladder of acceptance the only way he knows: with his fists.

It has always been thus. The trail began in the back streets of London slums and led to the teeming tenements of a young America where a new species of ruffian was first admitted to full fellowship in street battles and then turned its hands to boxing.

Ring archaeologists trace America's boxing roots back to the late 1840s when American politics and pugilism formed an unholy alliance of skull breaking and skullduggery. By the end of the decade, millions of Irish immigrants had fled their native land in the wake of the Great Potato Famine and arrived in America carrying only a valise of hope. That hope was soon thwarted in a world run by the hated White Protestant Establishment. Everywhere they encountered signs reading "NINA," meaning "No Irish Need Apply." They turned to the only world left open to them, the world of politics. The result was the most powerful and corrupt political machine ever known: New York's Tammany Hall. Tammany—which had built its political structure on the dual cornerstones of bullying and bribery—took to hiring thugs, all handy with their dukes, as "immigrant runners," so-called "gentlemen" who welcomed newcomers right off the boat and guided them to secluded spots where they would either be swindled or induced to vote the straight Tammany ticket. In the opposite corner, so to speak, were the "toughs" employed by the Native American Party, equally adept at using their fists. Dubbed the "Know Nothings" because of their practice of answering any and all questions with "I know nothing," this anti-Catholic party was formed to counter what they viewed as alarming waves of immigrants flocking into America, particularly from Ireland. Dedicated to keeping the despised "Harps" "in their place," the Know Nothings frequently resorted to force.

It was inevitable that there would be wars between the camps. Not so inevitably—and yet natural still—the antagonists would become America's first pugilists. Among those with Tammany stripes were such thugs-cum-fighters as John Morrissey, Lew Baker, James Turner, and "Yankee" Sullivan, while the Know Nothings could call on the likes of Tom Hyer and Bill Poole. Prizefighting was then regarded as nothing more than an unlawful activity engaged in by outcasts, a furtive trade carried out in secluded spots, often taking place in the back rooms of saloons or on river barges or in rings pitched in the pine, usually one step ahead of the local constabulary.

Challenges and fists began to fly in equal proportions as Tammany and Know Nothing toughs faced off in continual brawls. When the dust had cleared, one man, John Morrissey, stood as the best of the motley lot. After meeting every *defi* hurled in his direction, Morrissey retired from combat and, slipping white gloves over his grotesquely misshapen fists, turned to the world of politics, becoming a prominent figure in Tammany and twice winning a seat in Congress. He became a very wealthy man, establishing lucrative gambling houses in New York City and at Saratoga Springs where he built the famous racetrack that still stands, monuments to his successful escape from his ignoble roots.

In the two decades after Morrissey retired, other Irish fighters—many, like Morrissey, from the Auld Sod—began to fight their way up the fistic ladder. It would remain for one fighter, however, to embody the Irish spirit and their battle to kick over the traces of their second-class status: John Lawrence Sullivan.

By the 1880s, cocksure and confident of its future, America was casting about in search of national heroes to tie its patriotic kite tail to. In those politically incorrect days when men were men and women were damned glad of it, the man most men wanted to be was this swaggering, boastful bully boy called everything from "The Boston Strongboy" to "His Fistic Highness" to "The Prizefighting Caesar" to "The Great John L." to just plain ol' "Sully."

This American tintype was tailor-made for the lusty era in which he fought. Meeting President Grover Cleveland, Sullivan challenged established protocol by extending his burly paw in the direction of the president and booming, "How are ya, Boss? Sure glad to shake your hand." Cleveland loved it. So too did Sullivan's legion of fans, many of whom made shaking the hand of John L. the highlight of their lives. Untold thousands extended theirs proudly to others proclaiming the catchphrase of the era: "Shake the hand that shook the hand of the Great John L."

In a day when the world got all its news via two channels, the while-you-get-your-hair-cut weeklies and word of mouth, John L.'s exploits monopolized both, his legend continually increasing in range and breadth with every telling and retelling. And the stories, all propped up with reverential anecdotes—his "I-can-beat-any-sonuvabitch-in-the-house" chest-thumping challenge to one and all, his week-long benders, his romances with the Bloomer Girl of the Month, and, of course, his many triumphs in the ring—didn't end at the twelve-mile limit. His supporters, many of whom were Irish and for whom he had become the symbol of their own struggle, swept blarney off its feet.

Sullivan continued to write legend with his fists, devouring opponents as easily as he did food and drink. One opponent remembered nothing of his battle with John L. other than that Sullivan's awesome right "felt like a telephone pole shoved against me endways." Another said, "It felt like the kick of a mule." Wins over Paddy Ryan and Jake Kilrain—in the last championship bareknuckle fight in boxing history—earned him the title "Heavyweight Champion of the World" in the eyes of the boxing community and "The Strongest Man in the World" in the minds of his fans. But John L. turned his back on the ring and his attention to the stage, choosing instead to tour the country in a vehicle tailor-made for his own meager talents entitled, "Honest Hearts and Willing Hands."

Catcalls rained from the balcony while calls for Sullivan's return to the ring poured in from everywhere else. In indignation, Sullivan took pen in hand to issue a written proclamation. It read, in part: "I hereby challenge any and all bluffers to fight me for a purse of $25,000 and a bet of $10,000. The winner of the fight to take the entire purse. First come, first served." Ignoring the black man Peter Jackson, perhaps the one most deserving of a shot at the title, he invoked his own version of a "Color Line," listing three potential challengers whom he labeled "bluffers." The third of these was James J. Corbett, who had, Sully proclaimed, "uttered his share of bombast." He added that "the Marquis of Queensberry must govern this contest, as I want fighting, not footracing." He signed the letter, "Yours truly, John L. Sullivan, CHAMPION OF THE WORLD," in capital letters, befitting its author.

The Way Out

The first to come forward and post good-faith money was the third of the aforementioned "bluffers," James J. Corbett, practitioner of something he called "Scientific Boxing." Despite Sullivan's prolonged layoff and bloated condition—John L. had not fought in thirty-three months and weighed some thirty-five pounds above his normal fighting weight—he was still installed as a 4–1 favorite by the "sports" to beat his challenger.

The fight was held on September 7, 1892 at the Olympic Club in New Orleans. It was really no fight at all. For twenty rounds Corbett gave an exhibition of his "Scientific Boxing." Moving briskly but never urgently, Corbett would give the champion a come-hither look, but never be at home when Sullivan came calling, remaining safely out of range of Sullivan's wild right-hand swings, leaving the champion growling and thrashing about the ring like a wounded bear. Finally, in the twenty-first, by now as weak as day-old ginger ale and winded by his vain pursuit, Sullivan stopped stock still in the middle of the ring and demanded that his opponent come and fight. Corbett obliged him, answering the taunt with his own right hand, driving Sullivan to the canvas face first. As he lay there being counted out, his fans in the gallery quickly began to rid themselves of their Sullivan colors, throwing down their green banners upon the stricken gladiator until they covered the ex-champ like a shroud.

When he finally groped his way out from under his colors, Sullivan turned to his second, lightweight champ Jack McAuliffe, and asked, "What happened?" With tears in his eyes, McAuliffe told Sully the awful truth: he had been knocked out. Grasping the significance of having fought into the Indian Summer of his career, the unsteady Sullivan, helped to the ropes, firmly grasped the top rope and spoke to the assemblage: "The old man went up against it just once too often. He was beaten . . . but by an American." And then he ended with his usual flourish, "Yours truly, John L. Sullivan."

The torch had passed, not only to an American, as Sullivan had proclaimed, but to an Irish-American. And yet Sullivan's legion of fans were not about to pass on their adulation to the man who had humiliated their hero. In a case of illogical free association that could only be explained by Professor Rorschach toppling over his inkwell, Sullivan's Irish-American fans scorned their hero's conqueror, calling him derisively, "Pompadour Jim," and "Gentleman Jim," in obvious reference to his effete and foppish style of dress. In several cities, gangs of Irish toughs took out their frustration by waylaying anyone rash enough to admit they had bet on or even rooted for Corbett, Irish-American or no.

To them, and to Irish-Americans everywhere, John L. Sullivan was the holder of the original copyright as the first great Irish-American hero. No imitators need apply, thank you. Just as he had battled his way up the ladder of success, his non-boxing brethren were battling their own way up. In the process they would become policemen, politicians, and part of the middle class. In a real sense, they were fulfilling their hero's legacy by exiting their enforced positions as second-class citizens in a society that promised that all men were equal.

More Irish-American fighters would follow Sullivan's lead, with Irish-Americans enthusiastically embracing them. One old story, told by cauliflower tongues of the time, tells of the fight between Peter Maher and Tom Sharkey at the Lenox Club in New York back in 1897. It seems that feelings were running high between the rival camps backing the combatants. One old fellow, a townsman of Maher back in Galway, sat in the balcony overlooking the ring waving an Irish flag and proclaiming to everyone within earshot what his boy would do to Sharkey, offering to bet all kinds of money that Maher would "knock Sharkey kicking" with a single punch. When the men had taken their places in the ring, Charley Harvey, the announcer, advanced to the center of the ring and began the usual pre-fight ritual: "In this corner," he roared, without benefit of megaphone, "we have Peter Maher of Galway, Ireland!!!" At that the old Irishman began cheering wildly, waving the banner bearing the proud harp of his homeland and slapping everyone in the vicinity on any part of the anatomy available to him. "And," continued Harvey, "in that corner is Tom Sharkey of Dundalk, Ireland." The old Irishman now sat quietly in his seat. After a few seconds, he turned to his neighbor and said, "So Sharkey comes from Ireland, too, does he? Sure 'n I thought he came from Australia. . . . Well, if that's the case, I don't give a damn who wins!"

Much as the old Irishman was confused by the entry of a new "player," so, too, were thousands of other Irish fans who cheered for their "own." Or fighters they *thought* were their own. So powerful was the Irish hold on boxing that it now became fashionable for fighters to adopt Irish names in the belief that it was the only way to make their "name" in the sport, even if it wasn't their own name. And so it was that boxers whose surnames were Piaga, Goldberg, Carrora, Anchowitz, and Giordano hid behind names like Young Kid McCoy, Kid McGowan, Johnny Dundee, Charlie White, and Young Corbett III, and on and on. It began to look like, as the old Irish saying made popular by Rudyard Kipling put it, "The colonel's lady and Judy O'Grady [were] sisters under the skin."

Until this time, the Irish had had an all-but-exclusive hold on boxing. Now others began to make inroads. They came from the same background as their predecessors, the ripe fruit of tenement-house growth, particularly those warrens on the Lower East Side of New York where, according to journalist and social reformer Jacob Riis, "12,220 of the 32,390 buildings classified as tenements" could be found. And most of those battling their way out of the tenements were Jewish, sons of the second great wave of immigrants.

The first great fighter to come out of the Lower East Side was Leach Cross who was, in reality, a dentist whose given name was Louis Wallach. Like so many others of the time, he adopted a *nom*

de guerre, and an Irish-sounding one at that. Wallach-Cross was a
lightweight who began fighting in 1906 and was soon taking on the
cream of his division: Jem Driscoll, Packey McFarland, Tommy
Murphy, and Dick Hyland among others. Leach Cross was something else as well: the first real Jewish sports hero, important enough
to be the first athlete ever to appear on the "front page" of *The Jewish Forward*. (As sportswriter Barney Nagler once pointed out, the
Forward was the only paper you read backward; reporters would
run in with late-breaking news hollering, "Hold the back page.")

In becoming the first *real* Jewish sports hero at the end of the
first decade of the twentieth century, Cross supplanted another
"Jewish" hero, baseball pitcher Christy Mathewson. Although
non-Hebraic, Mathewson inspired thousands of Jewish mothers,
unable to keep their first-generation American sons from playing
America's Pastime, to hold him up as a *beau idol*. They were hoping
against hope that their sons would at least pattern themselves after
the great New York Giant superstar who, not incidentally, had gone
to college and played chess.

"Leachie," as his fanatic followers called him, popularized boxing among the many Jewish fans who would never have followed
the sport were it not for him. And his success not only blazed a trail
for other ghetto gladiators, but gained respectability for the Jewish
community, much as the Whitechapel district of London had been
the beneficiary of the ring success of the great eighteenth-century
bareknuckle champion Daniel Mendoza. Known as "Mendoza the
Jew," he had single-fistedly raised the community's social influ-
ence by being accepted by royalty and the social elite.

One "Son of Mendoza" who crossed through the ropes after
Leach was Benny Leonard, known to his fans as "The Great
Benny Leonard." Famed novelist Budd Schulberg remembers
hearing his father, movie pioneer B. P. Schulberg, saying of their
hero: "There was 'The Great Houdini.' 'The Great Caruso.' And
'The Great Benny Leonard.' That's how he was always referred to

in our household," Schulberg wrote. But "The Great Benny Leonard" was neither "Great" nor "Leonard" in his youth. Truth to tell, his real name was Benjamin Leiner, and he grew up on New York's Lower East Side in a world where almost daily he was called upon to defend his Jewishness with his fists.

It was a world of hyphenated Americanism where street gangs were a way of life and youngsters of all persuasions not only staked out their so-called "territory," but fought to preserve it against out-siders. If it happened that some unlucky member of one gang strayed into another ethnic group's "territory," woe be to him as he had no choice but to fight his way out. Epithets like "Mick," "Kike," and "Wop" would fly as fast as sticks, stones, and fists, es-pecially in the area which lay just beyond the street where Leiner lived, an area designated by the city fathers as Eighth Street and Avenue C, but known locally as "No Man's Land."

Many of the free-for-all street skirmishes that were fought for supremacy and territory were ultimately decided by chosen repre-sentatives from each gang taking on each other in one-on-one set-tos. Although a scrawny lad of only 128 pounds, dripping wet, Leiner was almost always chosen as his gang's "designated hitter." And almost always he acquitted himself well in these head-on matches. One particularly grueling match took place against an Irish youngster named Joey Fogarty, a tough whose fists had be-come a permanent part of almost every Jewish kid's face in the neighborhood. Benny won the match and received the winner's share of sixty cents from the "gate" of one-cent admissions charged to members of both gangs. The 15-year-old Leiner soon decided to turn his talents into more, and larger, coin of the realm.

Adopting the name "Leonard"—after the famed minstrel per-former of the time, Eddie Leonard, in the hope that Mama Leiner would not discover his new pursuit—Benny turned professional scant months after his brawl with Fogarty. His first fight was against one Mickey Finnegan for the princely sum of five dollars.

Stopped in three rounds, Benny went home that night with nothing more than a bloody nose and the five dollars to show for his efforts. He was met at the door by his mother, who asked, in that disquieting way of mothers everywhere, "Where did you get this money?" Benny quietly answered, "By fighting, Mama." While his mother continued nattering on about how no son of hers would ever be a fighter, Benny's father sat staring at the five gold coins in his son's hand. Finally, Papa Leiner broke through the harangue to ask, "Benny, when will you fight again?"

And fight again Benny did, more than two hundred times over the next two decades. And in all but five of those fights—all five losses to Irishmen—Benny would rush to a telephone after the fight to call his beloved mother and tell her, "Hello, Ma. I won and I'm not hurt a bit." The busted beak fraternity took to calling him "Mama's Boy." But his devoted fans knew the man who ruled the lightweight division for seven long years as "The Great Benny Leonard."

Benny Leonard was but the first stone to hit the water, creating, in ever-widening circles, wave after wave of fighters from the ghettos of New York and elsewhere. In his wake came Maxie Rosenbloom, Al Singer, and Sid Terris from New York. Chicago spawned King Levinsky, Barney Ross, and Charlie White (born Charles Anchowitz), whose talents inspired Ernest Hemingway to pen the priceless line: "Life is the best left hooker I ever saw, although some say it was Charlie White of Chicago." There were Battling Levinsky, Lew Tendler, and Benny Bass from Philadelphia, and Jackie Fields (Jacob Finkelstein) from Los Angeles. And hundreds of ghetto battlers were also surfacing on the other side of the Big Pond, with first Ted "Kid" Lewis (Gershon Mendeloff) and then Jackie "Kid" Berg (Judah Bergman) carrying the banner for their adoring Jewish fans in London's Whitechapel. Berg would drive his followers literally "bonkers," as they say in Blighty, by climbing into the ring waving his *tzitzis*, or holy cloth, which he would proceed to hang on the ringpost as his battle flag.

Jewish fighters became so prevalent that Jewish fans would identify with anyone they thought was Jewish, much as their Irish brethren had decades before, cheering wildly for Max Baer, who wore a Star of David on his trunks but was not Jewish. (Not at least, according to long-time trainer Ray Arcel, who was asked to verify Baer's ethnic heritage. The old handler replied with relish, "He wasn't [Jewish]. I saw him in the shower.") And there was Sammy Mandell, who, in a manner similar to the fighters of a by-gone era who had changed their names to appeal to Irish fans, shortened his name from Mandella to appeal to Jewish boxing fans in and around Chicago.

By the beginning of the thirties, the descendants of "Mendoza the Jew" so dominated the sport that boxing authority Joe Humphreys wrote: "The United States today is the greatest fistic nation in the world and a close examination of its four thousand or more fighters of note shows that the cream of the talent is Jewish."

By the 1930s the ring had become an extension of the street. And the street wars that had once been part and parcel of every inner city had now moved into the freelance world of the ring where matchmakers began to practice an early brand of "target market-ing" long before Proctor & Gamble made it a standard practice. They structured their offerings to pit representatives of one ethnic group against those of another. Only now they were not fighting over turf, but for ethnic pride—and for the bragging rights that went with a win.

From these race war conditions three men emerged as emis-saries of their respective ethnic groups, providing their fans with identification and rooting interest: Jimmy McLarnin, an Irishman; Barney Ross, a Jew; and Tony Canzoneri, an Italian.

Canzoneri—or "Canzi," the diminutive nickname adopted by adoring fans of the equally diminutive five-foot, four-inch boxer—was but the latest in a long line of great Italian fighters. Almost all before Canzoneri, however, had changed their surnames in order to enter boxing's mainstream. Thus a Peter Gulotta fought under the name Pete Herman, a Rocco Tozze as Rocky Kansas, a Rafelle Capablanca Giordano as Young Corbett III, and a Giuseppe Carrora as Johnny Dundee.

The story behind Johnny Dundee's name was one of the great boxing stories of the time. It seems that Dundee's manager, Scotty Monteith, liked everything about his fighter except his name. "Carrora," Monteith would tell everyone who would listen, "sounded like carrots. Which made sense because his father used to run a market. I told him, 'If you fight with that name, they'll start throwing vegetables at you. You should take the name of my hometown in Scotland, Dundee.'" And so "Dundee" he became, the beloved "Scotch Wop." The name tripped easily over the tongue and was soon echoing through fight clubs large and small across the land, as his fans shouted for "Dun-dee . . . Dun-dee!" It also inspired other Italian fighters—Joe, Chris, and Angelo—to take the name of the Scottish town that Johnny had adopted.

Unlike those who had come before, Canzoneri came wrapped in the red, white, and green colors of his heritage, proudly bearing his family name. And he would bear the colors of his Italian fans proudly. But not immediately. With the build of a fireplug and the style of a house afire, Canzi built his career and his credentials by meeting and beating many of the day's top fighters in the lower weight divisions. Only nineteen when he won the featherweight crown from Benny Bass, Canzoneri knocked out Al Singer in the first round to win the lightweight championship in 1931, and Jackie "Kid" Berg in the third to claim the junior welterweight title the following year.

But, if popularity is glory's small change, even while Canzoneri was winning the glory, popularity eluded him. As it did in 1927 when he demolished the aging idol, Johnny Dundee. The cheers in Madison Square Garden that night were reserved for the fallen hero of Italian fight fans, Dundee, whose name it was that re-sounded from the rafters for almost an hour after the fight.

Four years later Canzoneri beat the dashing Cuban Kid Choco-late, but found himself again the target of small change, together with catcalls, jeers, cigar butts, and other miscellaneous flybys launched from the galleries of that psycho ward that was the old Garden. At a loss to explain his unpopularity, Canzoneri, choking back tears, could only say, "I don't know why they did that to me. I tried to make the fight and I won. . . . Some nights you just can't please 'em. . . ."

But it's a bad bargain that doesn't run two ways. And two years later Canzoneri was able to "please 'em," knocking the Cuban Bon Bon kicking in two rounds. For a full five minutes the gallery gods on the Forty-Ninth Street side of the Garden responded with an ear-splitting roar, stamping and calling for their new hero, Can-zoneri. "Canzi" stood in mid-ring soaking up his newly-won adula-tion, saying over and over again, "I made them like me. . . . I made them like me. . . ."

After only eight years, Canzoneri was an instant success. And, in his newfound status as an authentic Italian hero, a real *paisan*, he fathered a new generation of Italian fighters, all born of the same hardscrabble homes and harder streets that earlier had bred Irish and Jewish fighters.

One of the most notable of the Italian stallions to follow Can-zoneri's lead was Rocco Barbella, better known as Rocky Graziano. A favorite of the fight crowd from Sunnyside, Queens, all the way to Madison Square Garden, Graziano never lost the special rhythms and sounds of the New York streets. Time after time, in interviews peppered with "dese" and "dose," he said of his less than exem-plary "yoot," "I never stole nuttin' unless it began with a 'A' . . . 'A truck' . . . 'A car' . . . 'A payroll.'" And, in a telling indication of just what the sport had meant to him, he would add, "If it wasn't for boxing, I woulda wounded up electrocuted at Sing Sing."

As Italian fighters took their place at the boxing table, the battles once fought on street corners for territorial rights now took place in the ring, ethnic undertones underlining almost every fight. Thus it was the Auld Sod versus the old tenement when a McLarnin took on a Leonard or an Al Singer or a Ruby Goldstein; or the old neighborhood versus the old ghetto when a Canzoneri met a Barney Ross or a Benny Bass or a Jackie "Kid" Berg. And each one of these mini-race wars lit up boxing's skies in an era before society was forced to conform to the latest fashion in political correctness.

But even as the sons of Erin, the sons of Mendoza, and the sons of Italy were fighting their way up the fistic ladder, there was something missing: the presence of black fighters, most of whom were toiling in relative obscurity or total invisibility, their fight for recognition thwarted by racial prejudice.

Such had not always been the case. Throughout boxing history, black fighters had been a part of the boxing scene. Their participation had begun early in the 1800s when ex-slaves Bill Richmond and Tom Molineaux left America to take on the reigning bareknuckle champions of Britain. Black participation continued throughout the nineteenth century and the first decade of the twentieth with the ascension of such great black fighters as Barbados Joe Walcott, George Dixon, and Joe Gans to world championships. But their titles were all in the lower weight classes, not in the heavyweight division, that being the special province of what white society called "The Strongest Man in the World." And specifically reserved for whites only.

The lone black heavyweight of note in the early days was the West Indian-born Peter Jackson. Unable to find opponents in his adopted land of Australia—he even offered to fight with his right hand "barred"—Jackson decided to try his luck in boxing's land o' plenty, America. His challenge was accepted by the outstanding contender for John L. Sullivan's title, James J. Corbett, with the assumption being that the winner would meet Sullivan for the championship. Although Corbett was a favorite of the California fight crowd, Jackson was the favorite among the "sports" who made him a 100–60 favorite to win. The bout took place on May 21, 1891, at San Francisco's California Club, the first in America ever conducted under the Marquess of Queensberry Rules, with gloves and three-minute rounds. It was one of boxing's all-time classics. Corbett would remember, "I soon discovered he was shifty and fast. And I thought I was fast!" After sixty-one evenly contested rounds, the referee approached both fighters and proposed that they call it "No Contest." Weary of the battle, both accepted.

Of course, Sullivan's impenetrable "Color Line" barred all men of color, so the title shot went instead to Corbett, who was pleased that he "would never have to face another sixty-one-rounder with Jackson again." The latter, according to his biographer David Wiggins, "developed a sadness and intimacy with misery" and partook of the camaraderie of newfound friends who lionized him in song and wined him in drink. This dual dissipation made a physical wreck of the once-great form that had been Peter Jackson. And although he was to fight a few more times, he was living on borrowed time. That time finally ran out on July 13, 1901, when he passed into, as it was then called, "the great majority." The official cause of death was listed as tuberculosis, although many believed that a broken heart contributed mightily to his demise. His epitaph sums up the man they called "The Black Prince" in just four words: "This was a man."

One man would prevail over boxing's caste system and that ineluctable verity which held that no black man could ever become the heavyweight champion of the world. That man was John Arthur Johnson. Known as "Li'l Artha," he was initially denied a chance to sink his roots in big-time boxing and forced to hone his skills against other black men on the so-called Chitlin' Circuit. With a victory over Sam Langford, his superior skills could no longer be denied and he began to menace white heavyweights much as

Attila the Scourge of God had threatened the Romans. Dubbed "The Galveston Giant" by the press, he began taking on and quickly dispatching the likes of Joe Jeanette, Bob Fitzsimmons, and Jim Flynn. All that remained was the current champion, Tommy Burns, who chose to remain elusive. But Jack Johnson was inevitability personified. He followed the champion to faraway Sydney, Australia where, after much pleading and even more wheeling and dealing, he got his long-awaited opportunity.

Fighting with an assurance that bespoke effrontery, Johnson soundly drubbed the champion on the day after Christmas, 1908. The victory unleashed a dammed-up wall of white hatred. But Johnson, whose natural ability was only rivaled by his contempt for the mores of white society, paid it no never mind. And, instead of practicing the obsequies and servilities expected of him, he marched across America disposing of brave plowboys, willing white women, and tall glasses of rum, all the while flaunting his color in the white man's face. The white man's "burden" had become its master.

Faced with this shocking, almost indigestible, challenge to Anglo-Saxon pride, writers like Jack London called for someone, anyone, to come forward to "remove that smile from Johnson's face" and avenge the defiling of the white Desdemona by this black Othello. A crusade was mounted to put the intruder in their midst back in his place, to remove this charge upon their honor.

Initially the crusade took the bloated form of former heavyweight champion Jim Jeffries, who was brought back to do battle with Johnson; a battle in the popular perception between the forces of good and evil. But the black man prevailed and the crusade failed. Momentarily. Next, a call went out for a "Great White Hope" to wrest the heavyweight crown from the infidel's hands and was answered by a ragtag lot of miners, cowpokes, gandy-dancers, and lumberjacks. In 1915, a 265-pound former cowboy named Jess Willard came riding out of the West and, in twenty-six rounds under a hot Havana sun, removed that "smile" from Johnson's face and with it the threat to the Caucasian race.

(Johnson would make headlines one last time when, driving to New York to witness the second Joe Louis-Billy Conn fight in June of 1946, he lost control of his roadster near Raleigh, North Carolina, and died in the resulting crash. In one of sportswriting's immortal lines, John Lardner described it thusly: "Jack Johnson died crossing the white line for the last time.")

Dating from that day in 1915 when Johnson got his "due" until the early 1930s, the boxing establishment exacted revenge for the real and imagined slights of Johnson by turning its back on black fighters. In many cases promoters simply wouldn't promote a mixed bout, either due to prejudice or because a black fighter was not commercially saleable to the fight crowd, as it was then constituted. In others, many white fighters, invoking John L. Sullivan's sacred "Color Line," refused to fight blacks. And, in still others, some states outlawed fights between whites and blacks, not that the white fighter couldn't, or wouldn't—often by prearrangement—beat the black fighter, but the mere fact that a black man standing in the same ring with a white man conferred instant equality on the black man and white society couldn't have that. Whatever the method, the result was the same: the black boxer was relegated to the back of boxing's bus.

It was an era in which the heavyweight division was dominated by the commanding figure of Jack Dempsey, who wrested the title from Willard in 1919, knocking him down seven times in the first round. Dempsey was the perfect picture of the ring warrior. Approaching an opponent in his peculiar metronomic sway, teeth bared, black eyes flashing, and blue-black hair flying, the man the press called "The Man-Tiger" bore the look of an avenging angel. And any Dempsey opponent who could walk away from a fight considered it a success: some sixty foes, including those he met in exhibitions, failed to walk away from the first round. But Dempsey's place in boxing history cannot be measured by statistics alone. What Dempsey possessed, perhaps more than anyone ever on the landscape of American sport, was his ability to capture the imagination. Alone, he spawned what Paul Gallico called "The Golden Age of Sports" and was enshrined in the pantheon of 1920s greats long before Babe Ruth, Red Grange, Bill Tilden, or Bobby Jones. He was the greatest gate attraction of all time, without exception. The press coined the term "Million-Dollar Gate" solely to describe his many title defenses.

None of those title defenses, however, came against a black fighter. The "Color Line," dating back to John L. Sullivan, was invoked to prevent Dempsey from defending his title against a black contender. When the great Sam Langford, by then a half-blind old warrior in his third decade of boxing, came to Dempsey's manager, "Doc" Kearns, to beg for a chance to fight for the title, Kearns told him, "I'm sorry, Sam, we're looking for someone easier." And when Harry Wills, the universally accepted number one contender signed to fight Dempsey, Tex Rickard, then the leading promoter, refused to stage the bout, citing the riots which had ensued after the last mixed match he had staged between Johnson and Jeffries. Furthermore, the New York State Athletic Commission and Governor Al Smith were opposed to mixed matches. And so Dempsey, feigning a headache or a similar infirmity, forfeited the $50,000 called for in the contract rather than face the man known as "The Brown Panther."

Al Reach, the publisher of *The Sporting News*, described the tenor of the times best when he chronicled the difficulties facing "Panama Joe" Gans, known as "The Black Secret." Reach wrote, "Jack Britton, the world's welterweight champion, was offered $20,000 to box Gans at Madison Square Garden; $25,000 was offered to Johnny Wilson, the present middleweight champion, but both champions decided to stay on the sunny side of the street and let this dark cloud roll by."

And so, with rare exceptions, black boxers were forced to sit on the curb as the parade passed them by. Some, like Tiger Flowers and the aforementioned Kid Chocolate, managed to break through the Caucasian curtain, but most were consigned to second-class citizenship, reduced to fighting each other, as Wills and Langford did a record twenty-two times. So good were many of them that one long-time observer called them "Black Murderers' Row." But regardless of their quality there still was no equality, no room at the boxing inn for them. Until 1934.

Nineteen thirty-three had seen the nation in the depths of the worst depression in its history. Not incidentally, it was also the worst of all years for the sport of boxing. Attendance and gate receipts hit an all-time low and the heavyweight champion, Primo Carnera, was a clown and a joke. If boxing had been a wake, it would have been an insult to the deceased. There was nowhere to go but up. In this darkest of times a white knight came to the rescue.

The white knight was, in reality, a black fighter out of Detroit. Christened Joseph Louis Barrow, his name had quickly been clipped by economy-minded ring announcers. National AAU light heavyweight champion in 1934, Louis had turned pro in July of that year with a one-round knockout of an anonymity by the name of Jack Kracken. Louis registered eleven more wins that year, nine by KO, leaving his opponents with little physical capability save respiration. Word soon reached New York of Louis's exploits. Promoter Mike Jacobs negotiated a contract for exclusive rights to all of Louis' future bouts and put together a press party of twenty-five newsmen to see Louis fight in March of 1935, in Detroit. After an easy win over Natie Brown, their glowing reports about this unbeatable newcomer who had now won seventeen in a row, thirteen by KO, created a public demand for a look-see at the new heavyweight hope. That look-see came on June 25, 1935 in Yankee Stadium against the by-now ex-heavyweight champion Primo Carnera.

For twenty long years, from Jack Johnson to Joe Louis, no black fighter had ever stood on boxing's center stage. His victory was one for blacks everywhere. In her novel, *I Know Why the Caged Bird Sings*, Maya Angelou remembers what that evening of June 25, 1935 meant: "'[Carnera's] got Louis against the ropes,' said the announcer. . . . 'And it looks like Louis is going down.' My people groaned. It was our people falling. It was another lynching, yet another black man hanging on a tree. . . . It was hounds on the trail of a man running through slimy swamps. . . . It was a white woman slapping her maid for being forgetful. . . . We didn't breathe; we didn't hope; we waited. 'He's off the ropes, Ladies and Gentlemen!' shouted the announcer. . . 'Carnera is on the canvas. . . .' A black boy. Some black mother's son. He was the strongest man in the world."

Even while Louis ascended to the top of the heavyweight mountain, one he would ultimately scale by knocking out Jimmy Braddock for the title in 1937, another black fighter named Henry Armstrong was making a name for himself on the West Coast. Armstrong had been a struggling featherweight, fighting in and around Los Angeles with mixed results against opponents as unknown as the soldier buried in Arlington National Cemetery. With Louis claiming more and more of the public attention, Armstrong felt he had to make a move. As he saw it, Louis was about "to take all the popularity, everything, away from me, away from all the fighters, because everyone was saving their money to see Joe Louis fight." Something had to be done before Armstrong—indeed all fighters, especially the black ones—were relegated to small Depression purses and even smaller agate newspaper type. Armstrong's Hollywood brain trust, Al Jolson and George Raft, came up with the "Big Idea": Armstrong would make ring history by going after three of boxing's eight divisional titles.

By the end of 1938, this perpetual motion machine had pulled off boxing's version of the "hat trick," winning the featherweight, lightweight, and welterweight titles—and holding them all simultaneously. Together, Louis and Armstrong became twin lighthouses, illuminating the path for other black fighters.

Still, it was Louis who was the main beacon. For no man was so admired and revered as this son of an Alabama sharecropper who carried his crown and himself with dignity and honesty. Using his words with the same commendable economy as he used his punches, Louis said a surprising number of things and said them in a way every American wished they had. There was his evaluation of his country's chances against the Axis powers in World War II: "We'll win 'cause we're on God's side." Dignity. And his enunciation of his opponent's chances in the second Billy Conn fight: "He can run, but he can't hide." Honesty. And with an obvious disinclination to repeat the mistakes of Jack Johnson in flaunting white society, Louis's manager, John Roxborough, laid down a harsh set of guidelines to regulate his conduct away from the ring:

1. He was never to have his picture taken alongside a white woman.
2. He was never to go into a nightclub alone.
3. There would be no soft fights.
4. There would be no fixed fights.
5. He was never to gloat over a fallen opponent.
6. He was to keep a "dead pan" in front of the cameras.
7. He was to live and fight clean.

Louis even eschewed being photographed eating one of his favorite treats, watermelon, lest it provide white society with ammunition to further stigmatize blacks.

When it was announced that Louis would defend his title against the German Max Schmeling in 1938, the event quickly became more than just a fight for boxing supremacy; it became a battle for supremacy between two warring ideologies. Inviting Louis to the White House, President Franklin Roosevelt tapped the champion on his massive, smithy-like arms and exhorted him to carry the standard for all Americans in democracy's war against totalitarianism, saying, "Joe, we're depending on those muscles for America."

Now the credentialed emissary of democracy, Louis already bore more than the twin burdens of heroism and patriotism on his shoulders as he climbed into the Yankee Stadium ring that night of June 22, 1938: the man in the other corner was the only one ever to have beaten him. But this time it wasn't much of a fight, more like a mugging belonging on page three rather than the sports page. Louis' murderous body punches bent Schmeling double and ferocious head shots reduced the representative of the so-called "Master Race" to resin. It took just two minutes and four seconds.

Joe Louis was a national hero. In the words of sportswriter Jimmy Cannon he was, "A credit to his race . . . the human race." And millions of Americans, black and white, now felt that way about the man most responsible—nine years before Jackie Robinson—for the democratization of American sports.

It would be nice to say that the process now repeated itself as thousands of black fighters followed the trail Louis—and to a lesser degree, Armstrong—had blazed, like their Irish, Jewish, and Italian predecessors. Nice, but untrue. For even though Louis and Armstrong had entered the white arena, the catalogue of black constituents still numbered just two. The rest of the black boxers were still being dealt to from the bottom of the deck, when they were dealt to at all. One who witnessed this discrimination first hand was trainer Ray Arcel, who told interviewer Ronald Fried, with a sense of moral outrage, "The blacks of the '30s were the best fighters. There were no better fighters who ever lived than these fighters. They could do everything. They were in the gym waiting to substitute. But they never got work."

Most were resigned to their fate. But some, like "Tiger" Jack Fox, "Jersey" Joe Walcott, Elmer "Violent" Ray, "Snooks" Lacey, and "King Kong" Mathews, did find work, mostly at black fight clubs, like the Rockland Palace, Harlem's answer to Madison Square Garden. Still, according to fight publicist Irving Rudd, who worked The Palace: "There were two sets of unwritten rules, one for the fights between blacks and blacks and the other for fights between blacks and whites. It's not hard to figure . . . when a black guy goes up against 'one of his own kind,' the fight is a regular one, no deviations. But if a white guy is going against a black, the black fighter has to wear 'handcuffs' [take it easy], or do a tank job."

Even when black fighters did get work, they were still subjected to the indignities visited upon blacks in general by the white society of the time. Again, trainer Ray Arcel, who had a good heavyweight named Jimmy Bivins in Washington, D.C. for a fight in the early '40s: "The room they got him in a black hotel was a steambath," Arcel remembered. And so Arcel quickly approached a friend who managed a whites-only hotel where the trainer was staying. "I'm gonna ask you a favor," Arcel said to the manager. "I brought my valet with me." (The valet was, of course, Bivins.) "I got a room up there with two beds. Let him sleep up there, let him stay there." The manager answered, "Now listen to what I'm telling you. I'm gonna let you do it. But when you order his meals, you order for yourself. Don't let anybody see him. When they come up to take the dishes out, put him in the bathroom. No hanging out in the lobby. When he goes down that elevator . . . out, out the hotel. 'He made a delivery.' Know what I mean?" Arcel added, "And this was Washington, D.C., the capital of the United States!"

Even while black boxers were denied entry into the mainstream during the early '40s—their accomplishments standing out like labels on oceangoing steamer trunks—a seachange began taking place. Madison Square Garden, then the Mecca of Boxing, seeking to refresh its pool of boxers, began bringing talented black fighters into the Garden for its regularly scheduled Friday night fights, fighters like Bob Montgomery, Ike Williams, Beau Jack, and the most exciting fighter yet, Sugar Ray Robinson.

These fighters, however, were in the lighter weight classes. The "big" breakthrough did not occur until December 5, 1947. "Jersey" Joe Walcott, who had been plying his trade in the backyards of boxing for almost two decades, was brought in to face heavyweight champion Joe Louis. Although Louis had defended his title twenty-three times before, Walcott was only his second black challenger. Surprisingly, the fight proved to be close, with the crowd-pleasing Walcott losing a controversial fifteen-round decision. Despite the loss, he won something less tangible but far more important: he opened doors to black boxers that had been closed to them since the time of Jack Johnson.

No longer treated like lepers, black fighters soon rose to the top in nearly every weight class: Archie Moore in the light heavyweights, Sugar Ray Robinson in the welterweights, Ike Williams in the lightweight division, and Sandy Saddler in the featherweight division, just to name a few, all using their fists to escape the lower rungs of society. In generations to come, the legacy of Louis would be carried on by others: Muhammad Ali, who would transcend the sport to become the symbol of his age, the turbulent '60s, much as John L. Sullivan and Jack Dempsey had reflected theirs; Marvelous Marvin Hagler, who refused to surrender to the streets and, through his fists, was able to retire with dignity and million-dollar trust funds for his children; and Mike Tyson, who was able to break the vicious grip of dependency, his children "being the first of my family members not on welfare." These African-American boxers, and many, many more, redeemed the down payment made by Louis sixty years before as boxing, to cop a time-worn phrase, finally, "regardless of race, creed or color," became "The Sport of Hope" for all.

Well, not *all*. Not yet, anyway. For there remained one group missing from boxing's group picture: the Hispanic or Latino fighter.

The first great American-born Latino fighter had been Manuel Ortiz, who ruled the bantamweight roost from 1943 to 1949, with one short two-month hiatus. But the list of other Latino fighters could be written on a postcard with a description of their neighborhoods on the other side and more than enough room left over for a return address, one that usually read "From Mexico" or "From Puerto Rico"—addresses early-day Latino boxing stars like Baby Arizmendi and Sixto Escobar called home.

The first trickle of American-born Latino fighters came in the 1950s as Art Aragon and Lulu Perez, among others, began to climb the fistic ladder. But it remained a trickle. One ascending the ladder was José Torres. A native of Ponce, Puerto Rico, Torres was a proud warrior and equally proud of his heritage. Before an early fight in the Bronx he grabbed the microphone and urged a noisy crowd of his compatriots to show pride. He asked them, "Did you know that Spanish was the first European language spoken in the western world? And that the first university in the new world was San Tomas Aquinas in Santo Domingo, the second San Marcos in Peru, and that ninety-nine years later the third was Harvard?" It was this kind of pride that fanned the sparks of self-esteem amongst Latino boxing fans.

Still, Latino fighters were as overlooked as Whistler's father. At least they were until the night of June 28, 1972. That night a quintessential warrior who gave new meaning to the Spanish word "machismo" burst upon the scene: Roberto Duran. That night he practically gelded Ken Buchanan to take the lightweight championship of the world. His victory heralded the advance of an army of Latino fighters who came tumbling out of the barrio to follow the banner of the man they called "The Hands of Stone."

It mattered little that Duran was a Panamanian, for this macho man gave heart to his American-born *hermanos* a heightened sense of themselves. There was a sense of poetic justice to this, almost a reversal of Christopher Columbus pointing across the ocean and declaring, "There's a new world over there." Youngsters in the barrios who had had to scrap for everything now developed a strong appreciation of their Latino identity and marched—with a salsa or merengue beat—to the gyms.

The trickle rapidly swelled to a torrent as the likes of Bobby Chacon and Danny Lopez emerged. Soon it became a Niagara as

Michael Carbajal, Johnny Tapia, Oscar De La Hoya, and hundreds of others stepped into the ring, all proudly bearing the mellifluous surnames that readily identified their Hispanic roots.

It was yet another variation on the time-honored theme: those on the lowest rung of society finding hope of a way out, a way out of a place where hope had always been a foreign language. With the emergence of the Latino fighters, boxing was truly an all-American sport, one which rang with the multicultural diversity of all of its ethnic groups.

II

Most of those from the tenements, the ghettos, the projects, and the barrios would never have succeeded in the ring, however, were it not for the trainer. No matter his background, the boxer was only one-half the equation, only one part of the story. The other was the trainer, whose emergence on the scene mirrored the pattern of the boxer, albeit a stutter-step behind.

In the early days, the trainer was little more than a "second," an aide whose function derived from dueling, the practice on which James Figg patterned boxing. As such, the trainer-second assisted the fighter in his preparation for the bout and acted as an intermediary in deciding the terms of the contest.

In time, one of the trainer's most essential functions emerged as he assumed the role of physical culturist. In one of the earliest tracts on the sport, *Fistiana*, Pierce Egan described the violent conditioning methods of the late eighteenth century:

> The skillful trainer attends to the state of the bowels, the lungs, and the skin; and he uses such means as will reduce the fat, and, at the same time, invigorate the muscular fibres. The patient is purged by drastic medicines; he is sweated by walking under a load of clothes, and by living between feather-beds. His limbs are roughly rubbed. His diet is beef or mutton; his drink, strong ale; and he is gradually inured to exercise. . . . Beside his usual or regu-

lar exercise, a person under training ought to employ himself in the intervals in every kind of exertion, which tends to activity, such as cricket, bowling, throwing quoits, &c., so that, during the whole day, both body and mind may be constantly occupied.

Over the next century this regimen would change little. Once again we must invoke the name of John L. Sullivan to provide a case in point. Having signed to defend his bareknuckle championship against Jake Kilrain, Sullivan immediately repaired to his favorite training grounds, the local saloons, there to spar more with bottles and broads than with barbells and bags. As the weeks leading up to the fight dwindled down to a precious few, and Sullivan began to resemble less the picture of a heavyweight champion than that of the dissolute wastrel, his frenzied manager, Billy Madden, prevailed upon the high priest of physical culture of the time, one William Muldoon, to take their battler in hand and end his slide into decadence.

Muldoon found Sullivan at one of his favorite watering holes doing battle with a stein of straight liquor. Called by his followers "The Noblest Roman of Them All," Muldoon was himself an awesome presence. He confronted the Heavyweight Champion of the World and, dashing his stein to the floor with one blow, physically dragged him out of the saloon and off to his health farm in western New York.

A firm believer that the extremes of the moment dictate their own rules, Muldoon instituted a carefully supervised program to reverse the effects of dissipation. As the first order of business, he banned all tobacco and alcohol. He substituted a regular dose of what he called "a first-rate purgative," a vile concoction made up of equal parts calcified magnesia, powdered rhubarb, and pulverized ginger.

Next, he dealt with the champion's bloated condition. In a staggering example of understatement, he referred to his charge as "a man who made flesh rapidly." Muldoon set out a clearly defined routine for the champion to turn that fat into muscle. At first, he put Sullivan to work alongside his farm hands, chopping down trees, plowing fields, even milking cows. A grumbling John L. would work with them, sweat with them, keep their hours, eat with them, and then gratefully collapse into bed at the same hour and in the same bunkhouse they did. Then gradually, as Sullivan's muscles began to harden and his wind improve, Muldoon moved him into working with the punching bags and a twelve-pound medicine ball. Soon the champion, who had been unable to manage even a few dozen rope skips, was doing eight hundred to nine hundred repetitions at a time. In less than eight weeks, Muldoon had performed miracles to rival those of Lourdes, transforming the tottering 240-pound hulk he had rescued from a saloon into a toddling 209-pound bear of a man, one who would reduce Jake Kilrain to plowshares in seventy-five hard-fought rounds.

Before this would happen, however, Muldoon had departed the scene. The miracle worker had had the inevitable falling out with his charge and was quickly replaced by the traditional "seconds" of the time, a ragtag band of hangers-on, water bucket carriers, and ex-fighters. Together they comprised a group of "trainers" assembled more to help the champion while away his time in camp than to aid in training. The champion was surrounded by the likes of manager Billy Madden, former heavyweight contender Joe Goss, buddies Pete McCoy and Bob Farrell, and his brother Mike, like Muldoon, Irishmen all.

The emergence of the modern-day trainer would have to await a new breed of boxer. And when that day dawned it would prove to be—as it had in Sullivan's day—a case of "like unto like," for the sport's new shining lights would be Jewish, as would their handlers.

Because history is, at best, imprecise, it is well-nigh impossible to identify the first Jewish trainer. Depending upon which yellowing newsclip one reads, it may well have been either Manny Seamon or Charley Goldman.

Goldman found his way into the corner through what would become the Ellis Island of all trainers: that of once having been a boxer. As a youth in the tough Red Hook district of Brooklyn, Goldman's start was the standard story, size seven. As he told author Ken Blady, "Little kids called you a 'Jew bastard,' so you punched them in the nose. I got to love it. Every time somebody called me a name, it meant I could have a fight without picking one."

Soon the young Goldman was hanging around with another neighborhood tough, Terry McGovern. But while "Terrible Terry" would go on to win the bantamweight and featherweight championships of the world, Goldman's career was far less illustrious, consisting of 137 documented fights, although Goldman put the number closer to three hundred. Often he fought for as little as five dollars in a private club or the back room of a saloon. The closest he ever came to matching McGovern came when he fought Johnny Coulon for the bantamweight championship in 1912, and when he adopted the signature derby hat of the great McGovern, an affectation that endured for the rest of his life.

By 1914, now a finished fighter in every sense of the word, the 26-year-old Goldman became a trainer. His first charge was Al McCoy. Born Alex Rudolph, McCoy, like so many other fighters of the time, adopted an Irish ring name to hide his profession from his Orthodox Jewish parents. McCoy was an obscure fighter who got a shot at the middleweight title through what can only be described as a "fluke." He had signed to fight Joe Chip. But when Chip fell ill on the eve of the fight, his brother, George—not incidentally, the middleweight champion—was brought in as a replacement to save the payday. In those days of "no decision" fights, the title could only change hands by a knockout, and the out-of-shape middleweight champion, the victim of a knockout just once in seventy-five fights, took the light-hitting McCoy lightly.

Too lightly, it turned out. Goldman told his charge to "go in with a right-hand lead as soon as it starts and, when his guard comes up, hit him in the belly with everything you've got!"

McCoy did. And did. And the champion went down like a balloon with the string removed, air escaping, in just one minute and fifty-five seconds of the first round.

Goldman's gnarled hands would work many other corners, including those of champions Lou Ambers, Marty Servo, and Joey Archibald. The cornerstone of his fame, however, rested on his molding Rocky Marciano into one of the all-time greats.

The first time Goldman laid eyes on Marciano, then just Rocco Marchegiano, he had hitched a ride on the back of a vegetable truck from his Brockton, Massachusetts home to see the trainer. As Marciano disembarked, Goldman, so the story goes, took one look at the green goods and said, "You look worse than the cabbages." Goldman took Marciano in hand, studying his style—or lack thereof—the way a biologist does a specimen. What he observed was one of boxing's irregularities. As he told it, "Marciano was so awkward we just stood there and laughed. He didn't stand right, he didn't throw a punch right . . . he threw them from his behind. He didn't do anything!" And so the master alchemist went to work, teaching his charge the rudiments of boxing: the jab, the hook, footwork, the barest bones of the sport. The one thing Goldman wouldn't touch was Marciano's powerful right hand, which he dubbed the "Suzie Q." It was boxing's version of Pygmalion and Galatea as Goldman turned the piece of rock into a polished fighter named Rocky Marciano.

But even though Goldman could lay claim to having been one of the great trainers of all time, his claim to having been the first Jewish trainer is subject to dispute. The other candidate for that honor is Manny Seamon, who, at the tender age of 16, his face still a stranger to the razor, began his career "rubbing Leach," referring to the celebrated Jewish fighter Leach Cross. In another case of like-unto-like, Seamon also trained Benny Leonard and Ted "Kid" Lewis, two more Jewish greats. The crowning moment of his career, however, came when he took over as trainer for Joe Louis after Jack Blackburn's death in 1942.

Goldman and Seamon were but the first ripples in the stream. They were followed by wave upon wave of other Jewish trainers. And by the beginning of the thirties, just as the Jewish fighter had risen to the top, so too had the Jewish trainer. Two prominent examples were Ray Arcel and Whitey Bimstein, a duo fittingly called "The Siamese Training Twins." The 1930 Everlast Boxing Record Book wrote of the two:

> Trainers capable of acting as most capable seconds to a fighter in actual combat are as rare as an eclipse of the sun. Two young men, regarded as the leading exponents of the training and seconding are men who are giving their older conferees a close contest for honors, Ray Arcel and Whitey Bimstein, the Siamese Twins. The responsibility boils itself down to Arcel and Bimstein, who are given complete control of the boxer. Most managers, in fact, leave the seconding of their battler entirely in the hands of this duet, their methods having been successful.

Arcel would "train and second" such fighters as Charley Phil Rosenberg, Benny Leonard, Jackie "Kid" Berg, James J. Braddock, Ezzard Charles, and almost all of Joe Louis' opponents—so many, in fact, that he was known as "The Meat Wagon." One of his duties as handler of the Louis challengers included carting away their remains after they had been decimated by "The Brown Bomber."

Bimstein, who broke in seconding the great Harry Greb, was known as "The Surgeon" and is best remembered in the broken-beak biz for his surgical work in Rocky Graziano's corner during "Da Rock's" second fight with Tony Zale, "The Man of Steel." The fight, more savage than scientific, had been a seesaw battle. But, by the end of the third round, Graziano was by far the worse for wear, his right eye bleeding and swollen, stumbling around the ring blindly. As Graziano returned after the third round he screamed, "Get my eye open!" Bimstein spent the entire sixty-second intermission between the third and fourth rounds working on the damaged eye and arguing with the referee, who wanted to stop the fight. While applying pressure to the eye with a silver dollar in an effort to restore vision, Bimstein pleaded, "Give Rocky one more round!" According to Graziano, referee Johnny Behr responded, "If this wasn't a championship fight, I would never have let him last out the third round. One more, and if he don't come out of it, I got to stop it. . . . They give you the chair for murder in this state." With sight restored in the damaged eye, Graziano turned the fight around, knocking his opponent out in the sixth to win the middleweight championship. After the fight, in an ending tailor-made for Hollywood, a battered and beaten Graziano took the microphone and screamed at the crowd, "Ma, I told ya. . . . Your bad boy done it. . . . Somebody up there likes me!"

And then, just as Jewish trainers had followed Jewish boxers, Italian trainers now followed their Jewish counterparts into the corners.

The first of the famous Italian trainers was Al Silvani, who had been initiated into the brotherhood of trainers by Whitey Bimstein in 1936. Later he had worked with Ray Arcel after the two "Siamese Twins" had separated. In another like-unto-like scenario, Silvani then went off on his own to train heavyweight contender Tami Mauriello and later teamed with Bimstein to train Rocky Graziano.

However, Silvani's favorite story had nothing to do with Mauriello—whom he navigated into a title fight against Joe Louis—or Graziano. It involved a skinny Italian boy, then 119 pounds dripping wet, who once asked Silvani to train him in the finer points of "The Sweet Science." It was Frank Sinatra. As a favor, Silvani approached the Garden's powers-that-be and asked if they would let Sinatra sing the National Anthem before Mauriello's fight against Jimmy Bivins in March of 1943. Their initial response was, "This fight is going on coast-to-coast radio and we can't have an unknown singing the Star Spangled Banner." They later relented and Sinatra got his first national exposure. Unfortunately, he did better than Silvani's other protege, Mauriello, who lost a ten-rounder to Bivins.

Soon, other Italian trainers followed the path blazed by Silvani into boxing's corners. There were the Florio Brothers, Nick and Dan. And Chickie Ferrara. And the man Ferrara handed his arcane knowledge down to, like a family heirloom, Angelo Dundee. The latter had changed his family name, Mirena, to that traditional Italian fight name Dundee. And, in keeping with another boxing tradition—that of "like unto like"—his first champion would be a fellow *paisan*, Carmen Basilio. And then there was boxing's master psychologist, Cus D'Amato. And Lou Duva and Joey Fariello. And hundreds of others, all leaving their mark on boxing's long and rich history.

Conspicuously absent were black faces. Their presence in corners had mainly been a rumor, unreported in "the white man's papers" except as "bottle washers." One small mention appeared in a London newspaper of 1810 of a black "second" in the corner of Tom Molineaux, the ex-slave who had come to England to challenge Tom Cribb for the heavyweight crown. That "second" was Bill Richmond, known as "The Black Terror" during his fighting days. According to the account, Richmond, the son of a Georgia slave, had "raised his mauleys" to challenge the same Cribb five years earlier.

It would be another century-plus before Jack Blackburn followed Richmond as a trainer in a big fight. Blackburn was a lightweight who had taken on all comers during the first two decades of the twentieth century, including the great Sam Langford. Many times Joe Louis would say, "They fought more draws than a man draws breath." After hanging up his gloves, Blackburn turned his considerable boxing "smarts" to the training of fighters—mostly white fighters.

One day in 1934, Blackburn was in a Chicago gym when he was approached by John Roxborough, a Detroit numbers operator. Roxborough wanted him to handle his new heavyweight. When Blackburn told Roxborough to bring around his "white boy and I'll look him over," he was informed that his "boy was black." Skeptical of the opportunities available to a black heavyweight, Black-

burn shook his head and said, "I'll have no truck with a colored boy
... colored boys ain't got much chance fighting nowadays unless
they happen to be world-beaters." Roxborough laughed and said
that's exactly what he had. And what he had was Joe Louis.

But Blackburn was singularly unimpressed by his first look at
Louis. In a 1937 interview in *The Ring Magazine* Blackburn said:

> When Roxborough brought Louis to me, he was just a
> big, easy-going Negro boy with high water pants and too
> much arms for his coat sleeves. "So you think you can go
> somewhere in this fighting game?" I said to him, "Well,
> let me tell you something right off. . . . It's next to impos-
> sible for a Negro heavyweight to get anywhere. He's got
> to be very good outside the ring and very bad inside the
> ring. Mr. Roxborough, who has known you quite a while,
> is convinced you can be depended on to behave yourself.
> But you've got to be a killer, otherwise I'm too old to
> waste any time on you."

To which Louis replied, "I ain't gonna waste any of your time."
Louis wouldn't. A willing student, he quickly absorbed everything
Blackburn tried to impart to make him a complete fighter: balance,
how to deliver a good left jab, and how to step in while throwing a
punch. In short time Louis was disposing of his opponents with a
dismal monotony and startling variety. And the firm of Louis &
Blackburn began to assume epic proportions.

Inspired by Blackburn's success, the Fates, trying to balance
the ledger, shifted their attention to black trainers, somewhat in arrearages. Soon they were filling corners and speaking "soul to soul"
with their black charges, trainers like Eddie Futch, Georgie Ben-
ton, Manny Steward, and hundreds of others.

It was the same with Latino trainers as the Victor Vallees and
Edwin Viruets soon crouched in the corners of Latino fighters,
speaking to them the language of the ring in their native tongue.

And by the final decade of the twentieth century, the trainer had become more than merely a part of the second part; he had by now become part of the whole. Part of the equation.

The pairing of a youngster with a caring trainer is all important, for the trainer becomes a surrogate father, a father confessor, a mentor to a young man who may never have known his father.

How does a fighter choose a trainer? One London trainer, Harry Giver, once said, "I've lost count of the number of boys who have been referred to me by the local probation officers. I persuaded them that it was better to see their names in the sports pages of the local newspaper than the court reports, and in return I got absolute loyalty from them."

Most trainers "adopt" their charges not because, as Charley Goldman, Rocky Marciano's trainer, put it, "Training promising kids is like putting a quarter in one pocket and taking a dollar out of another." They do it because they care for them and it often becomes a mutual relationship. Despite his seemingly callous remark, Charley Goldman is said to have died of a heart attack in his room in training camp covered with one of Rocky's old robes.

The tales of a trainer's caring nature surface time and again. As former fighter Danny Kapilow told interviewer Ronald Fried, "Ray Arcel's greatest asset was his care . . . caring for you as an individual, as a person, beyond the fact that you might earn some money for him." That "care" manifested itself in many ways. "Pop" Foster trained and managed Jimmy McLarnin for his entire career and, when he passed away, he left his entire estate to his foster son, McLarmin, including a handsome parcel of real estate in downtown Los Angeles. When Joe Frazier got up off his stool for the fifteenth round of "The Thrilla in Manilla," his trainer, compassionate Eddie Futch, told him, "Sit down, son. It's all over. No one will ever forget what you did here today."

As Angelo Dundee, the trainer of Muhammad Ali and Sugar Ray Leonard, puts it, for the combination of fighter and trainer to be successful, "You got to blend yourself to the fighter." That blending consists of equal parts of being physician, baby-sitter, and psychologist, garnished with more than a healthy dose of caring.

Jack Blackburn was part psychologist when he told Joe Louis, before his fight with Buddy Baer, "Don't let this last too long because there's a good show up at the Apollo Theater later. Let's get up there." Then there was Whitey Bimstein. Described by journalist Hal Conrad as looking "like a clown without make-up," Whitey was never pictured in a fighter's corner without a Q-tip tucked behind his ear. One of his fighters, Vinnie Ferguson, characterized him as "one of the best psychologists in the world. He would light a fire under you. . . . He'd maybe tell you that the other guy insulted you. . . . He'd say, 'This guy can't carry your jockstrap' or 'This guy is a baby compared to you. . . .'"

One of the best stories about Bimstein as an amateur shrink comes from Fred Apostoli's 1940 match with Melio Bettina. Apostoli returned to his corner after taking a beating and asked, "What's the matter with me? I can't fight!" The trainer didn't say a thing, he just hauled off and hit his fighter in the face and hollered, "Now get out there and do your stuff." Apostoli went out in the next round and beat the bejabbers out of Bettina. When he returned to his corner he said to Bimstein, "That's what I needed. Sock me again, but hard! Get me mad!"

Most fighters are, like Apostoli, grateful recipients of the trainer's contributions to their success. Muhammad Ali said of Angelo Dundee, "After Frazier beat me, after Spinks beat me, he made me believe again. Angelo really had more confidence in me than I did."

As Ali, Louis, Marciano, and every other fighter who ever laced up his gloves knows, the trainer is the one element essential to ultimate success. And the care extended by their trainers is reciprocated by almost all who credit their managers with having taught them the proverbial "ropes"—in boxing and in life.

Ultimately though, every boxer is alone in the ring, naked but for his silk trunks, armed only with his fists and his wits, seeking to outbox, outwit, outlast his opponent. As Buster Mathis Sr. once said of his manager and trainer when they had used the pluralistic "we" once too often, "Where do they get that 'we' shit? When the bell rings, they go down the steps and I go out in the ring alone." It is a hard way of life. But boxing has never sought its enlistees from the debutante line at the local country club. Instead, it recruits them from the crucible of the streets, boy-men who have fought their way out of the slums, the ghettos, the projects, the barrios, the "nabes," expressing themselves the only way they could . . . with their fists in "The Sport of Hope."

Boxing, 1997